GRANT MORRISON has been working with DC Comics for more than twenty years, beginning with his legendary runs on the revolutionary titles ANIMAL MAN and DOOM PATROL. Since then he has written numerous best-sellers — including JLA, BATMAN and *New X-Men*—as well as the critically acclaimed creator-owned series THE INVISIBLES, SEAGUY, THE FILTH, WE3 and JOE THE BARBARIAN. Morrison has also expanded the borders of the DC Universe in the award-winning pages of SEVEN SOLDIERS, ALL-STAR SUPERMAN, FINAL CRISIS, BATMAN, INC., ACTION COMICS and THE MULTIVERSITY. Currently, he is writing the epic space adventures of Hal Jordan in THE GREEN LANTERN.

He is the co-creator of the 2017 hit SYFY television series *HAPPY!* based on his comic book, with season two shooting this summer in New York. Concurrently he is co-creator on a TV adaptation of Aldous Huxley's *BRAVE NEW WORLD*, in development for SYFY/USA.

In his secret identity, Morrison is a "counterculture" spokesperson, a musician, an award-winning playwright and a chaos magician. He is also the author of the *New York Times* best-seller *Supergods*, a groundbreaking psycho-historic mapping of the superhero as a cultural organism. He divides his time between his homes in Los Angeles and Scotland.

YANICK PAQUETTE is a Shuster Award-winning Canadian artist who has been drawing comics since the late '90s. He illustrated many comics for both Marvel and DC, including various X-Men titles, two TERRA OBSCURA miniseries with Alan Moore and SEVEN SOLDIERS: THE BULLETEER, BATMAN INCORPORATED and WONDER WOMAN EARTH ONE with Grant Morrison. An avid insect collector and naturalist from childhood, Paquette's tenure on Swamp Thing allowed him a rare occasion to conjugate his passion for biology and lush comics.

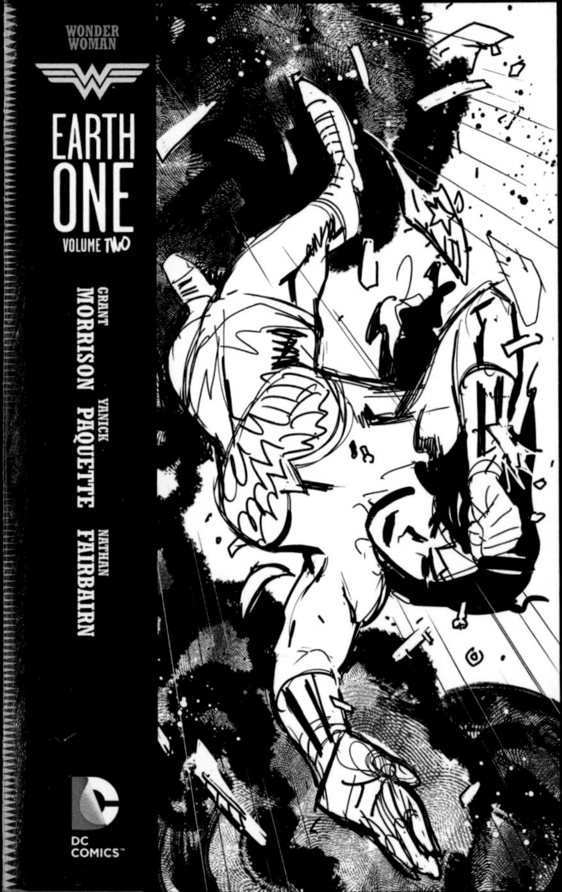
WONDER WOMAN
EARTH ONE
VOLUME TWO
GRANT MORRISON
YANICK PAQUETTE
NATHAN FAIRBAIRN
DC COMICS

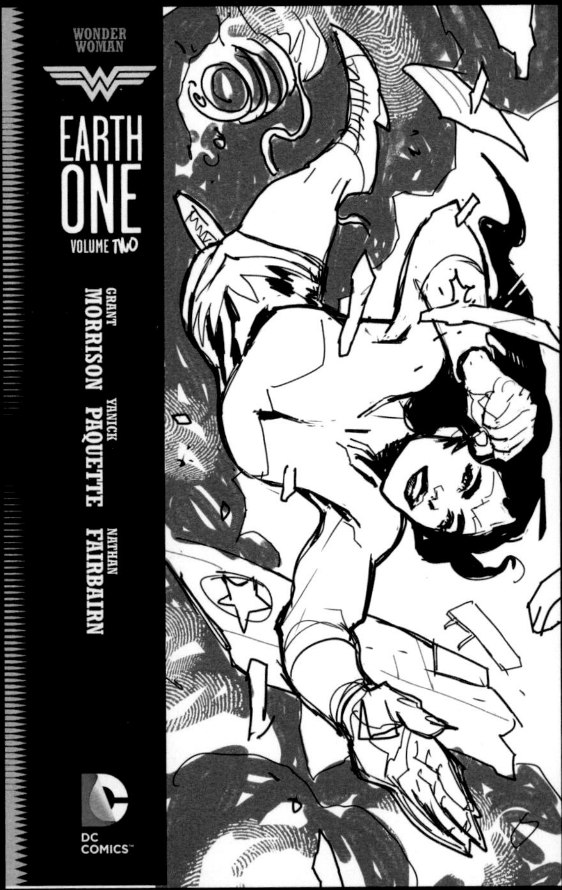
WONDER WOMAN
EARTH ONE
VOLUME TWO
GRANT MORRISON
YANICK PAQUETTE
NATHAN FAIRBAIRN
DC COMICS

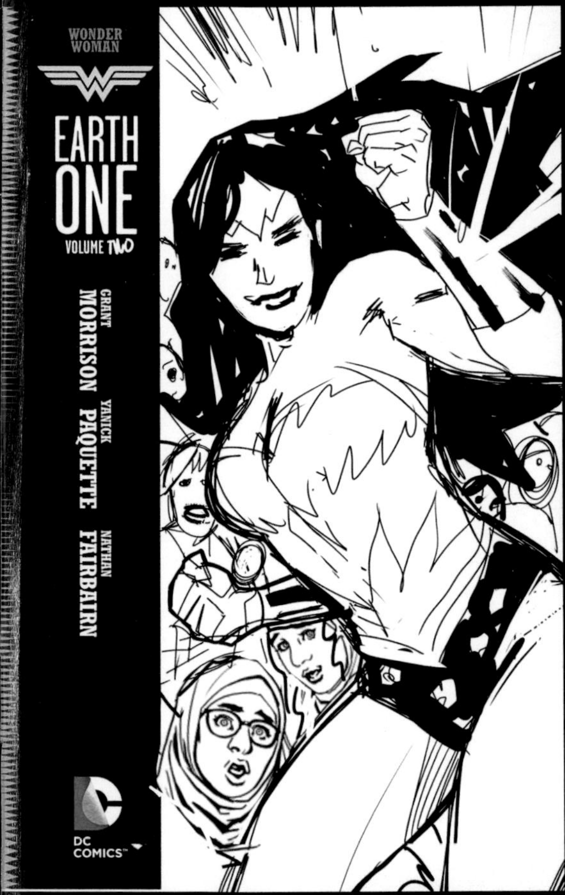
WONDER WOMAN
EARTH ONE
VOLUME TWO
GRANT MORRISON
YANICK PAQUETTE
NATHAN FAIRBAIRN
DC COMICS

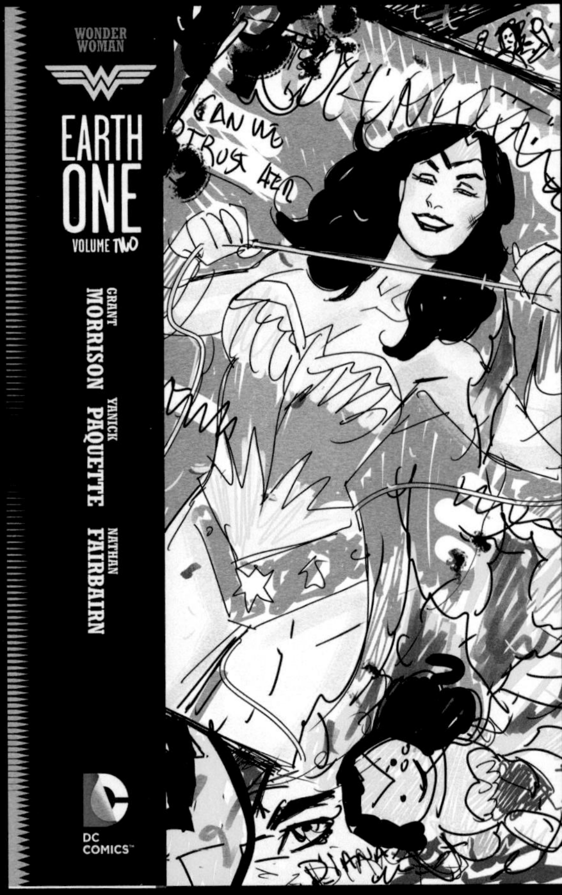
WONDER WOMAN
EARTH ONE
VOLUME TWO
GRANT MORRISON
YANICK PAQUETTE
NATHAN FAIRBAIRN
DC COMICS

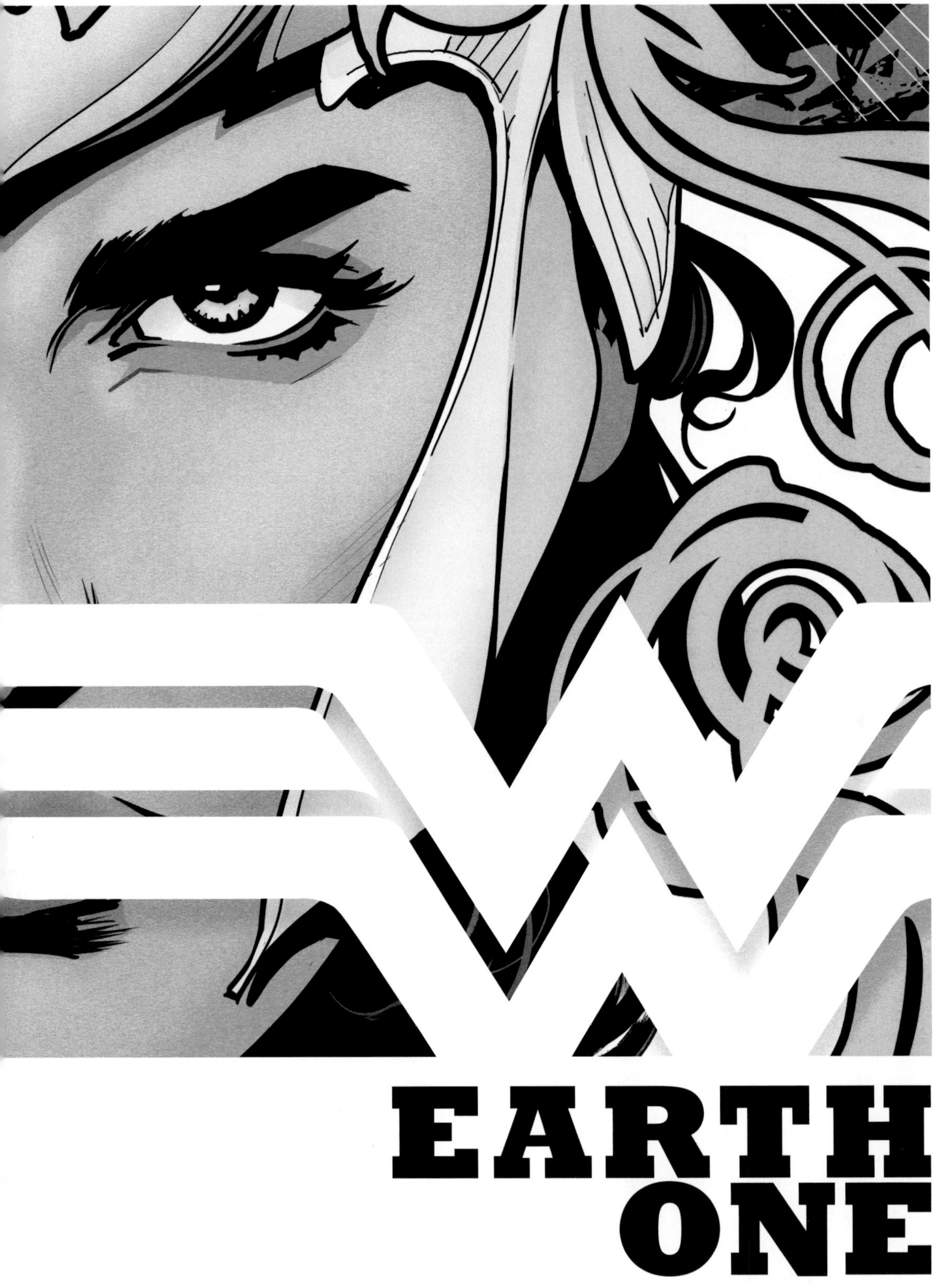

EARTH ONE

Written by Grant Morrison

Art and Cover by Yanick Paquette

Colors by Nathan Fairbairn

Letters by Todd Klein

Wonder Woman created by William Moulton Marston

Eddie Berganza and **Andrew Marino** Editors
Steve Cook Design Director – Books
Lou Prandi Publication Design

Bob Harras Senior VP – Editor-in-Chief, DC Comics
Pat McCallum Executive Editor, DC Comics

Dan DiDio Publisher
Jim Lee Publisher & Chief Creative Officer
Amit Desai Executive VP – Business & Marketing Strategy,
Direct to Consumer & Global Franchise Management
Bobbie Chase VP & Executive Editor, Young Reader & Talent Development
Mark Chiarello Senior VP – Art, Design & Collected Editions
John Cunningham Senior VP – Sales & Trade Marketing
Briar Darden VP – Business Affairs
Anne DePies Senior VP – Business Strategy, Finance & Administration
Don Falletti VP – Manufacturing Operations
Lawrence Ganem VP – Editorial Administration & Talent Relations
Alison Gill Senior VP – Manufacturing & Operations
Jason Greenberg VP – Business Strategy & Finance
Hank Kanalz Senior VP – Editorial Strategy & Administration
Jay Kogan Senior VP – Legal Affairs
Nick J. Napolitano VP – Manufacturing Administration
Lisette Osterloh VP – Digital Marketing & Events
Eddie Scannell VP – Consumer Marketing
Courtney Simmons Senior VP – Publicity & Communications
Jim (Ski) Sokolowski VP – Comic Book Specialty Sales & Trade Marketing
Nancy Spears VP – Mass, Book, Digital Sales & Trade Marketing
Michele R. Wells VP – Content Strategy

Special thanks to Arden Leigh

 WONDER WOMAN: EARTH ONE VOLUME TWO

Published by DC Comics. Copyright © 2018 DC Comics. All Rights
Reserved. All characters, their distinctive likenesses and related elements
featured in this publication are trademarks of DC Comics. The stories,
characters and incidents featured in this publication are entirely fictional.
DC Comics does not read or accept unsolicited submissions of ideas,
stories or artwork.

DC Comics, 2900 West Alameda Ave., Burbank, CA 91505
Printed by LSC Communications, Kendallville, IN, USA. 9/25/2018.
First Printing.
ISBN: 978-1-4012-8117-5

Library of Congress Cataloging-in-Publication Data is available.

PEFC Certified
This product is from
sustainably managed
forests and controlled
sources
PEFC/29-31-337
www.pefc.org

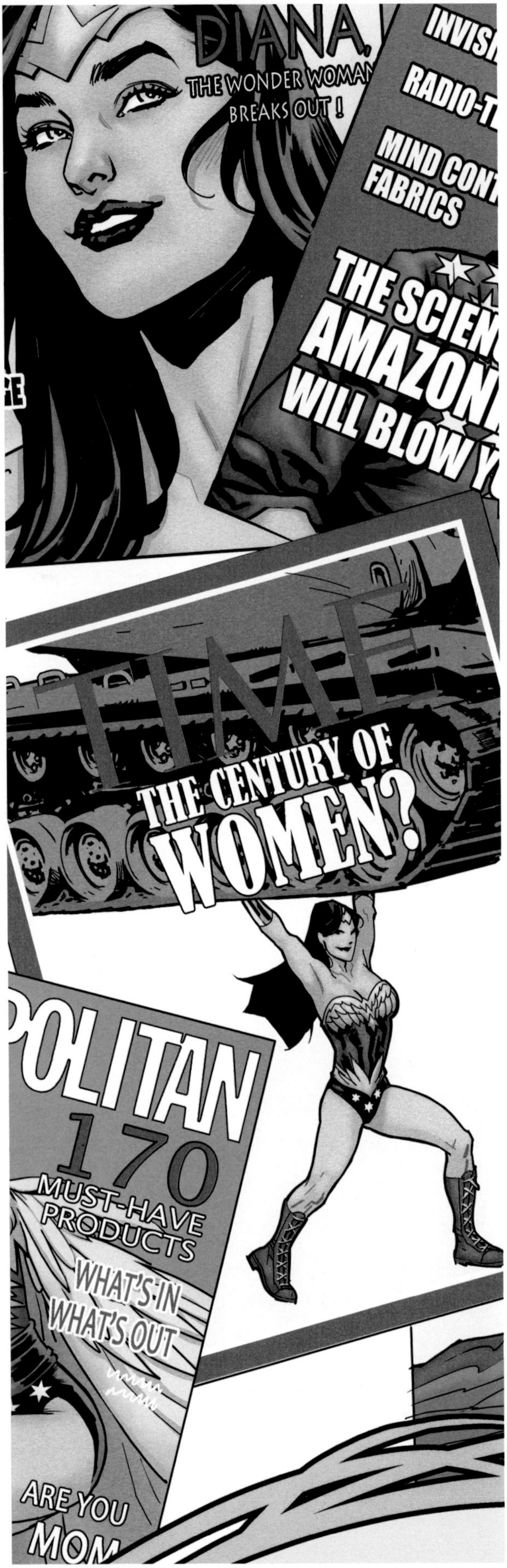
DIANA,
THE WONDER WOMAN BREAKS OUT!
RADIO-T
MIND CONT
FABRICS
THE SCIEN
AMAZON
WILL BLOW Y
TIME
THE CENTURY OF WOMEN?
POLITAN
170
MUST-HAVE PRODUCTS
WHAT'S IN
WHAT'S OUT
ARE YOU
MOM

DEDICATIONS

"To Kristan, with love."
Grant Morrison

"To My Soulmate, Marie-Pier.
With loving submission."
Yanick Paquette

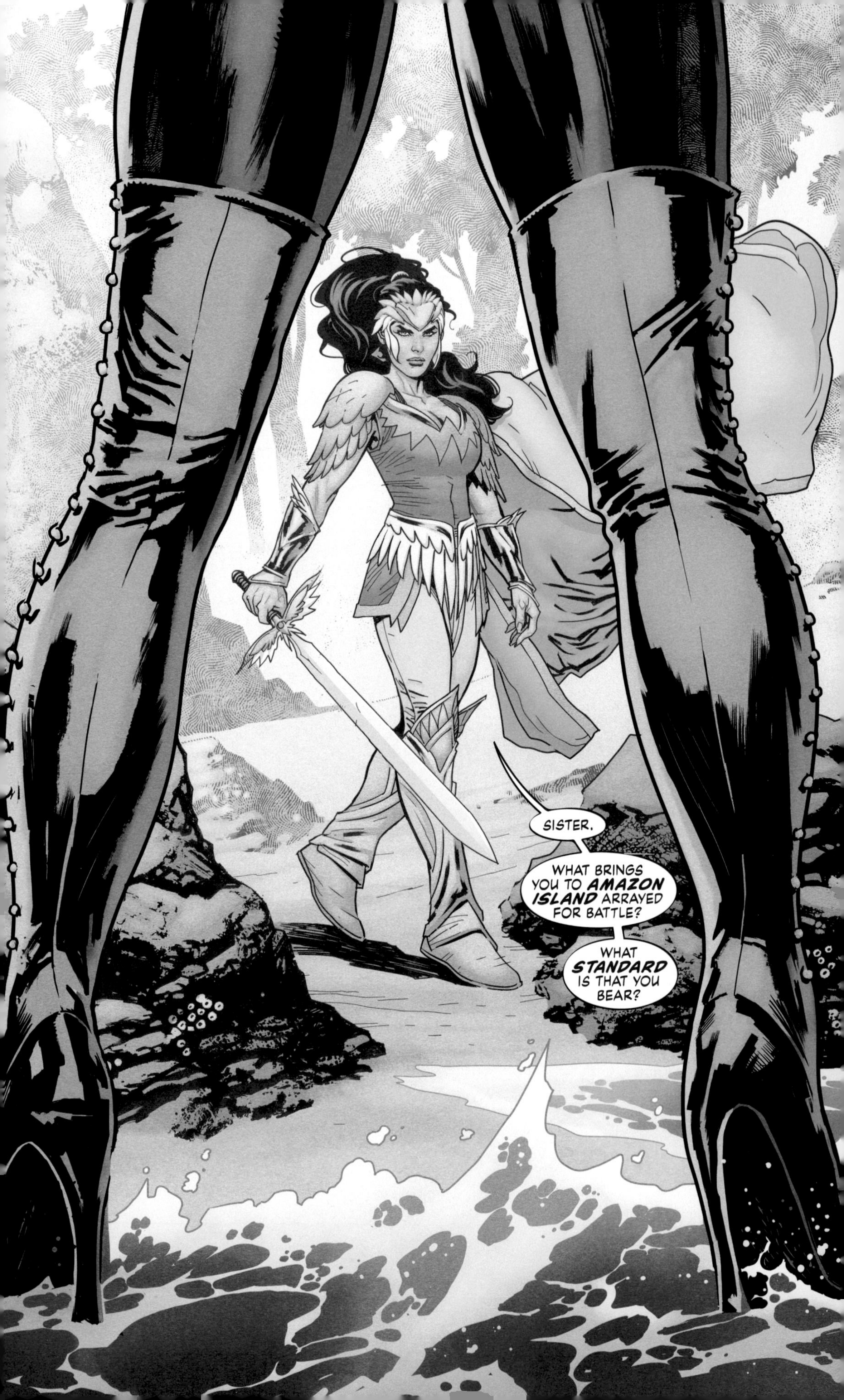
SISTER.
WHAT BRINGS YOU TO AMAZON ISLAND ARRAYED FOR BATTLE?
WHAT STANDARD IS THAT YOU BEAR?

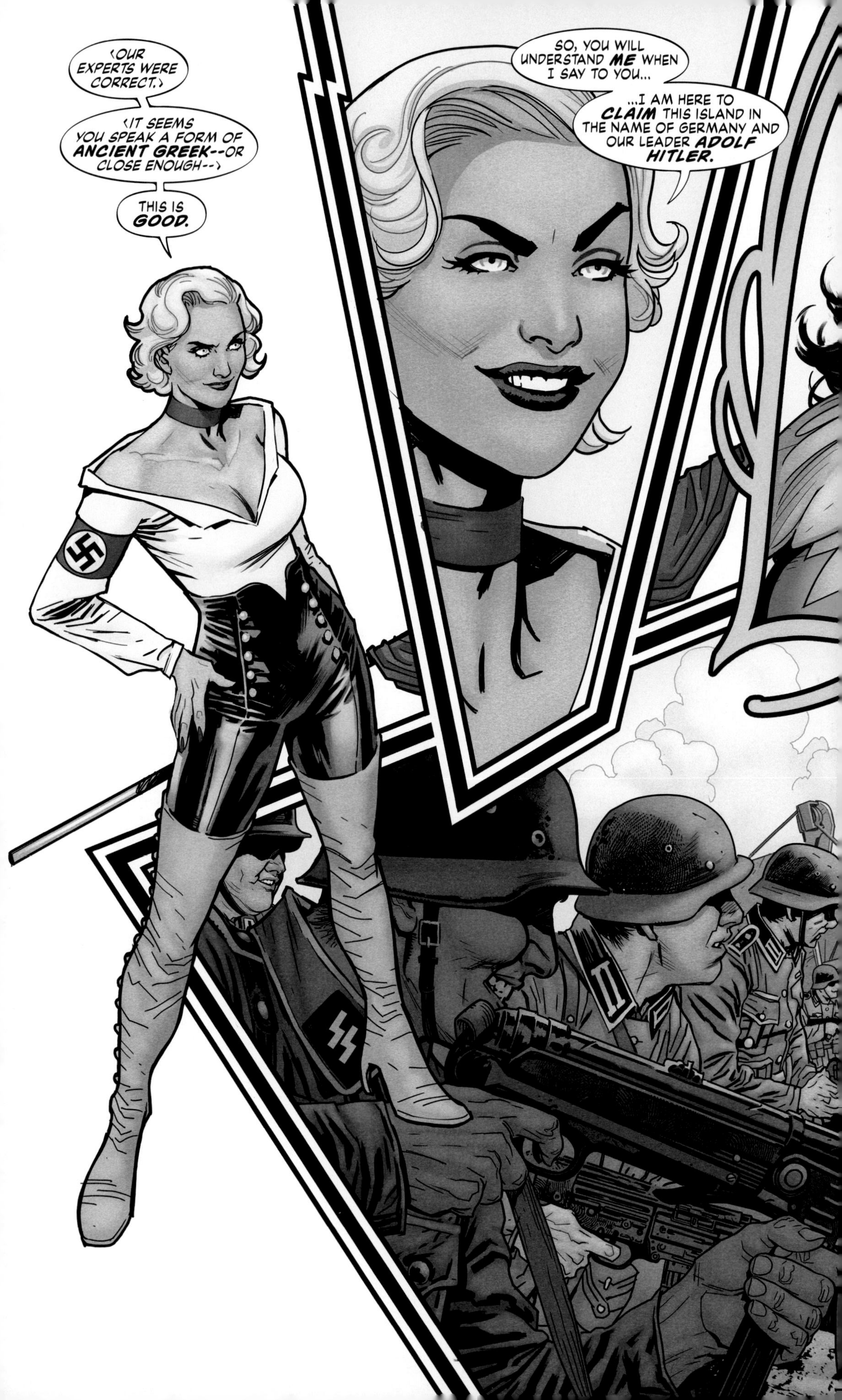

‹OUR EXPERTS WERE CORRECT.›
‹IT SEEMS YOU SPEAK A FORM OF ANCIENT GREEK--OR CLOSE ENOUGH--›
THIS IS GOOD.
SO, YOU WILL UNDERSTAND ME WHEN I SAY TO YOU...
...I AM HERE TO CLAIM THIS ISLAND IN THE NAME OF GERMANY AND OUR LEADER ADOLF HITLER.

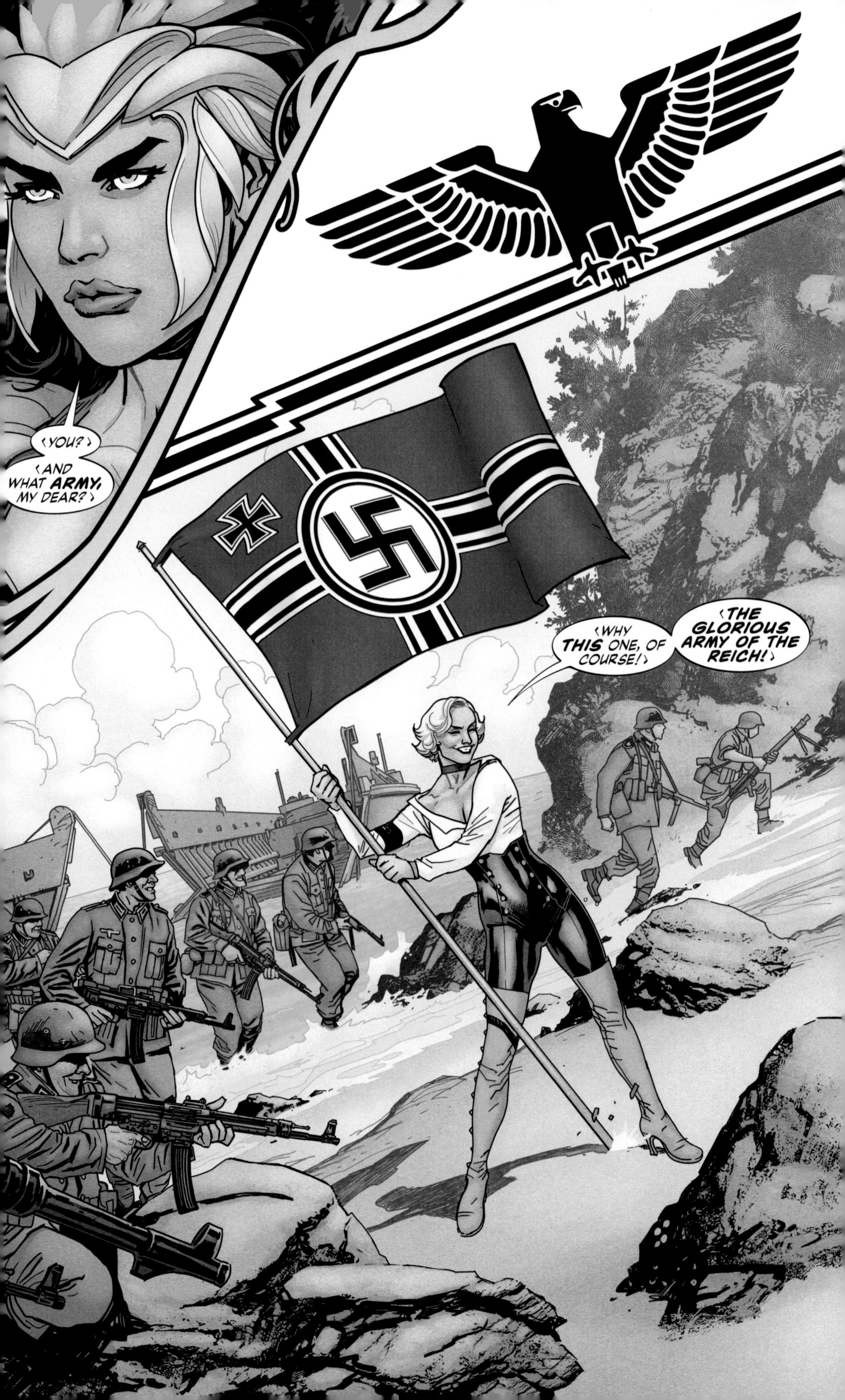
‹YOU?›
‹AND WHAT ARMY, MY DEAR?›
‹WHY THIS ONE, OF COURSE!›
‹THE GLORIOUS ARMY OF THE REICH!›

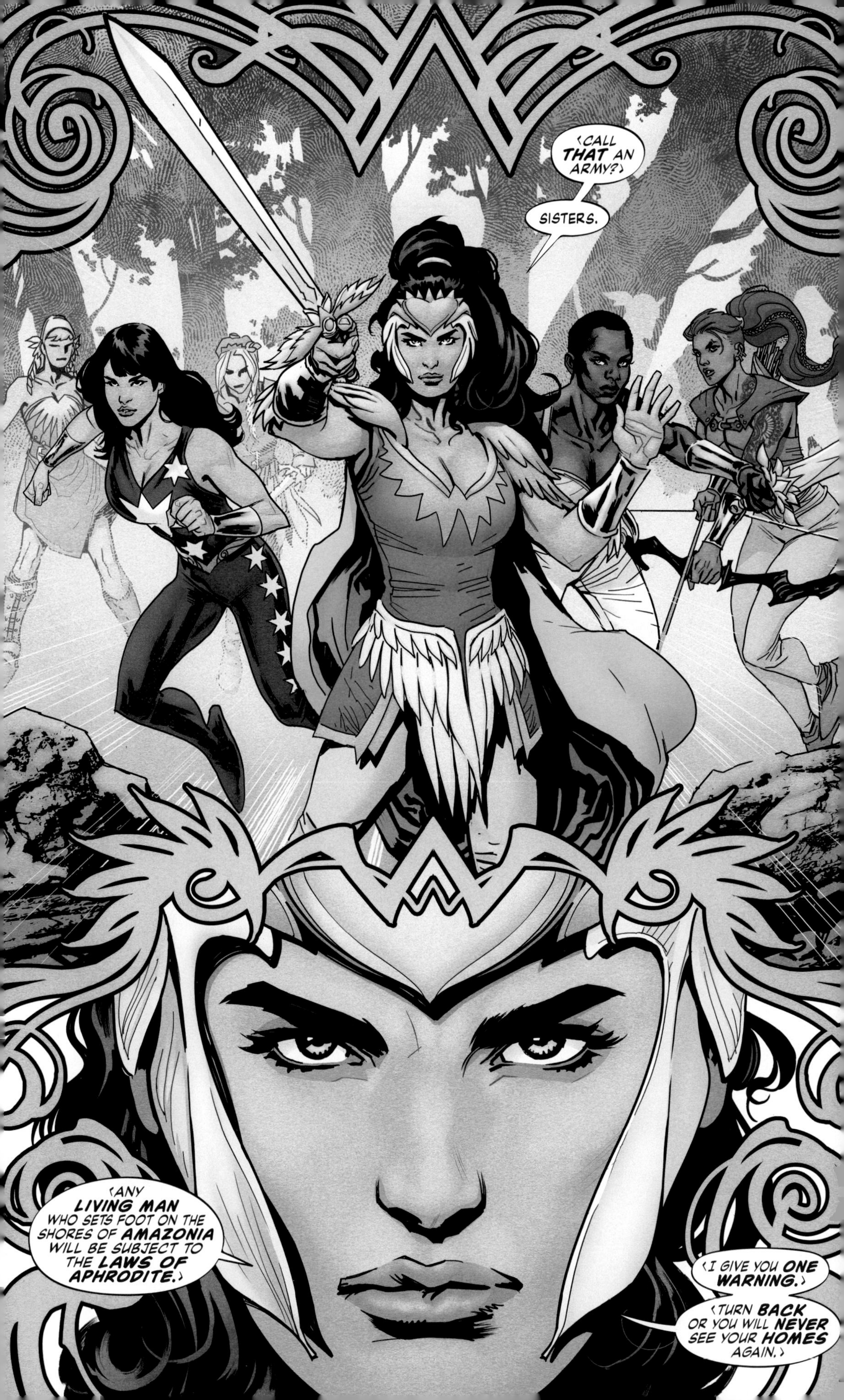
‹CALL THAT AN ARMY?›
SISTERS.
‹ANY LIVING MAN WHO SETS FOOT ON THE SHORES OF AMAZONIA WILL BE SUBJECT TO THE LAWS OF APHRODITE.›
‹I GIVE YOU ONE WARNING.›
‹TURN BACK OR YOU WILL NEVER SEE YOUR HOMES AGAIN.›

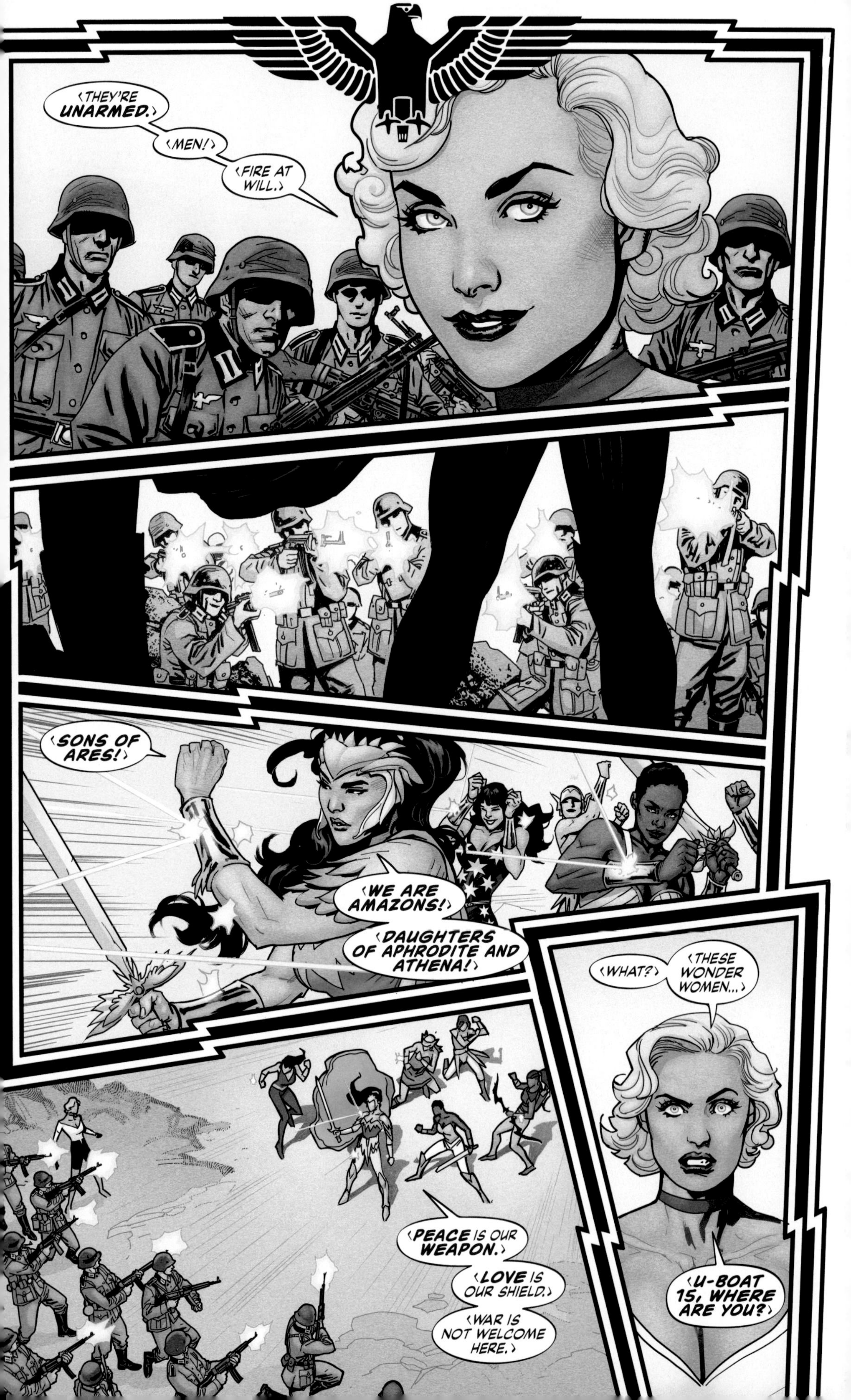
‹THEY'RE UNARMED.›
‹MEN!›
‹FIRE AT WILL.›
‹SONS OF ARES!›
‹WE ARE AMAZONS!›
‹DAUGHTERS OF APHRODITE AND ATHENA!›
‹WHAT?›
‹THESE WONDER WOMEN...›
‹PEACE IS OUR WEAPON.›
‹LOVE IS OUR SHIELD.›
‹WAR IS NOT WELCOME HERE.›
‹U-BOAT 15, WHERE ARE YOU?›

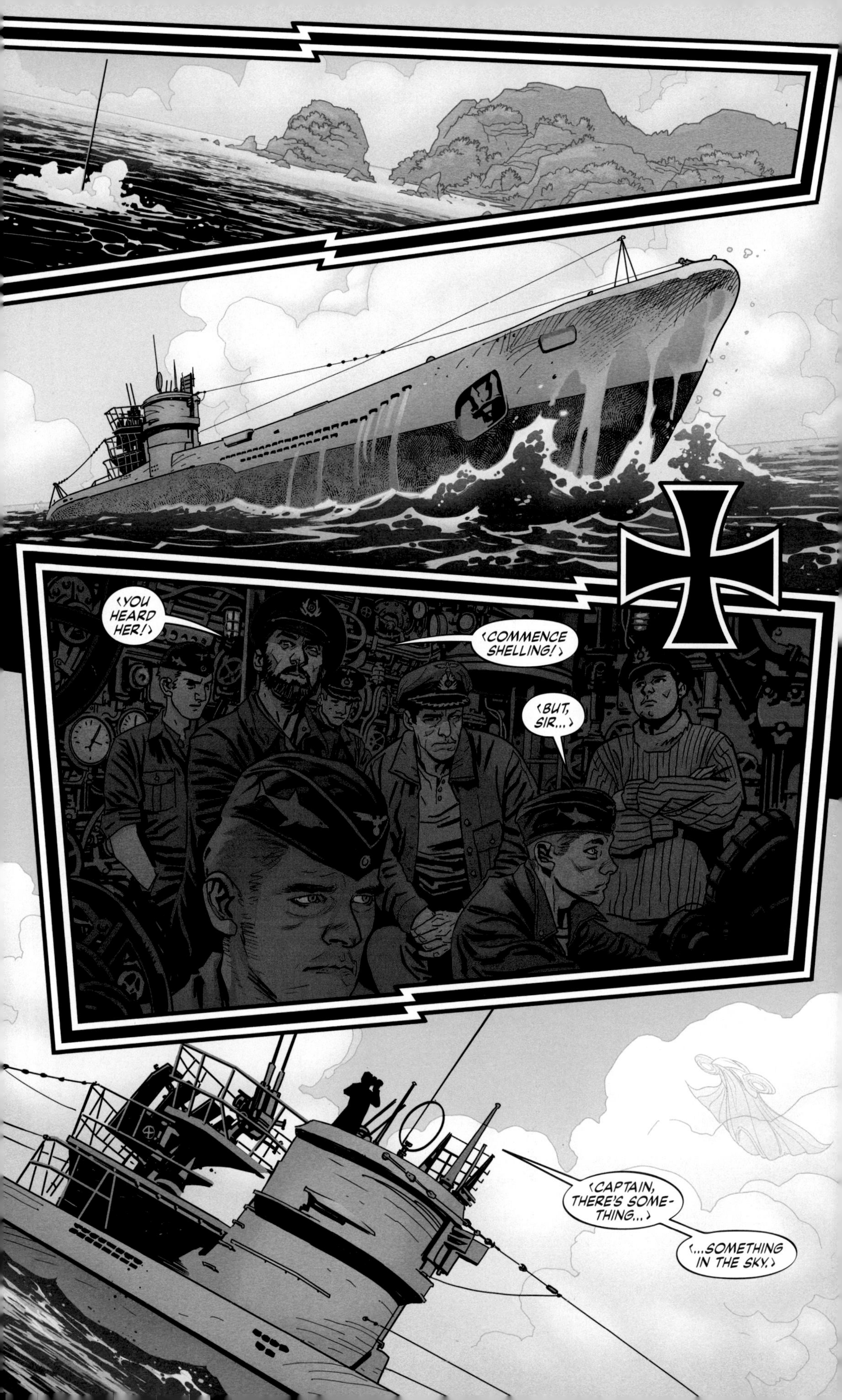
‹YOU HEARD HER!›
‹COMMENCE SHELLING!›
‹BUT, SIR...›
‹CAPTAIN, THERE'S SOME-THING...›
‹...SOMETHING IN THE SKY.›

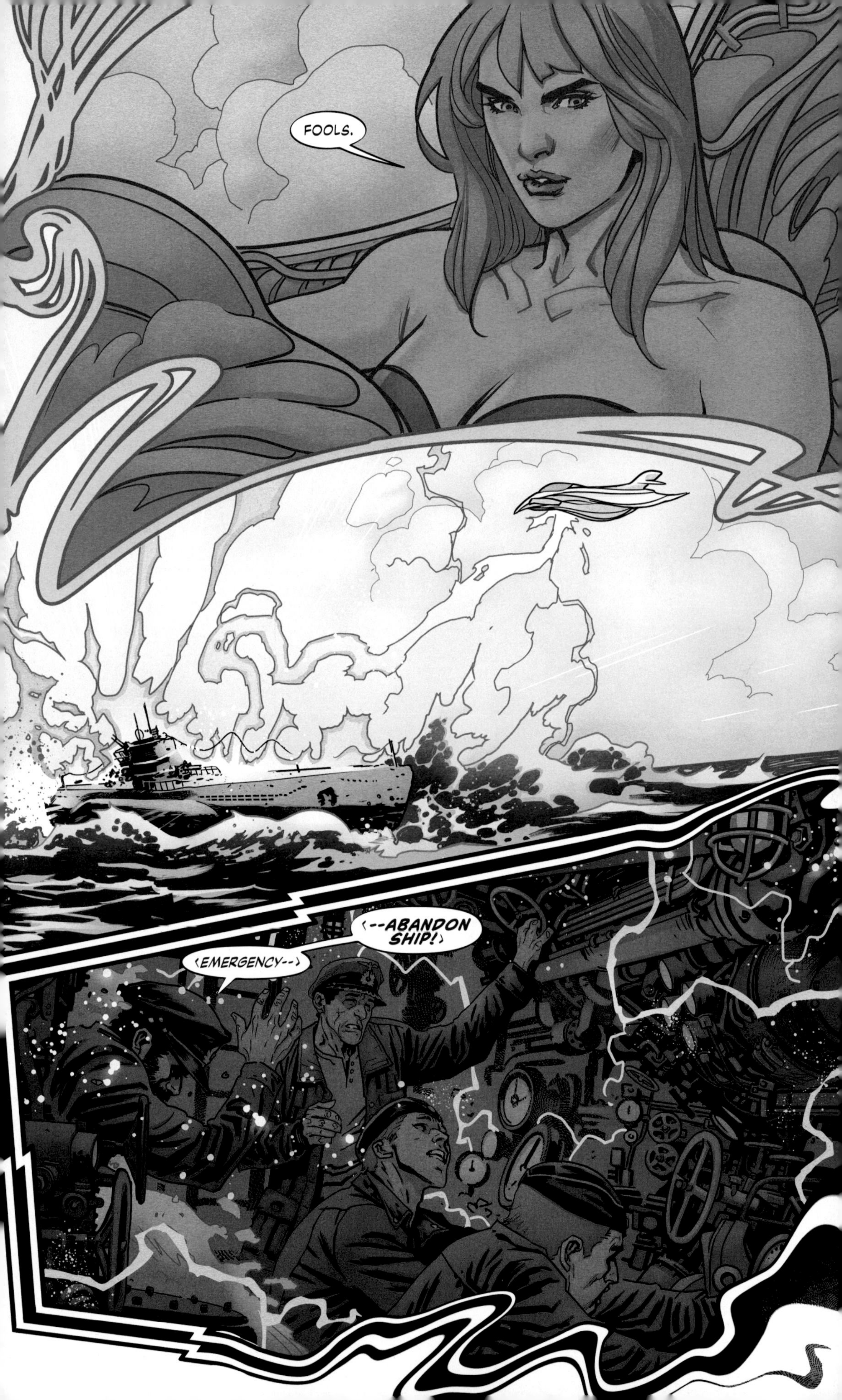
FOOLS.
‹EMERGENCY--›
‹--ABANDON SHIP!›

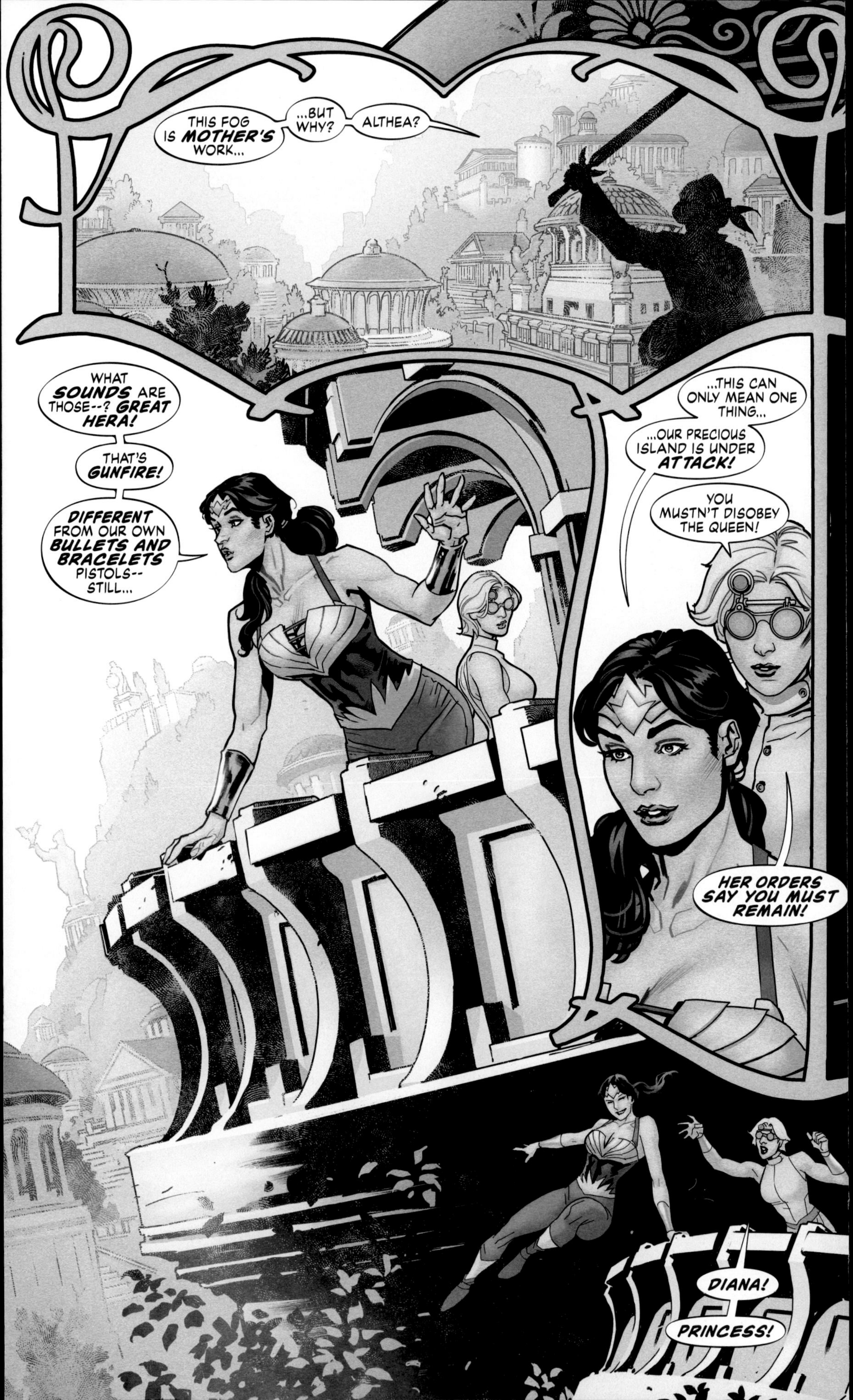
THIS FOG IS MOTHER'S WORK...
...BUT WHY?
ALTHEA?
WHAT SOUNDS ARE THOSE--? GREAT HERA!
THAT'S GUNFIRE!
DIFFERENT FROM OUR OWN BULLETS AND BRACELETS PISTOLS-- STILL...
...THIS CAN ONLY MEAN ONE THING...
...OUR PRECIOUS ISLAND IS UNDER ATTACK!
YOU MUSTN'T DISOBEY THE QUEEN!
HER ORDERS SAY YOU MUST REMAIN!
DIANA!
PRINCESS!

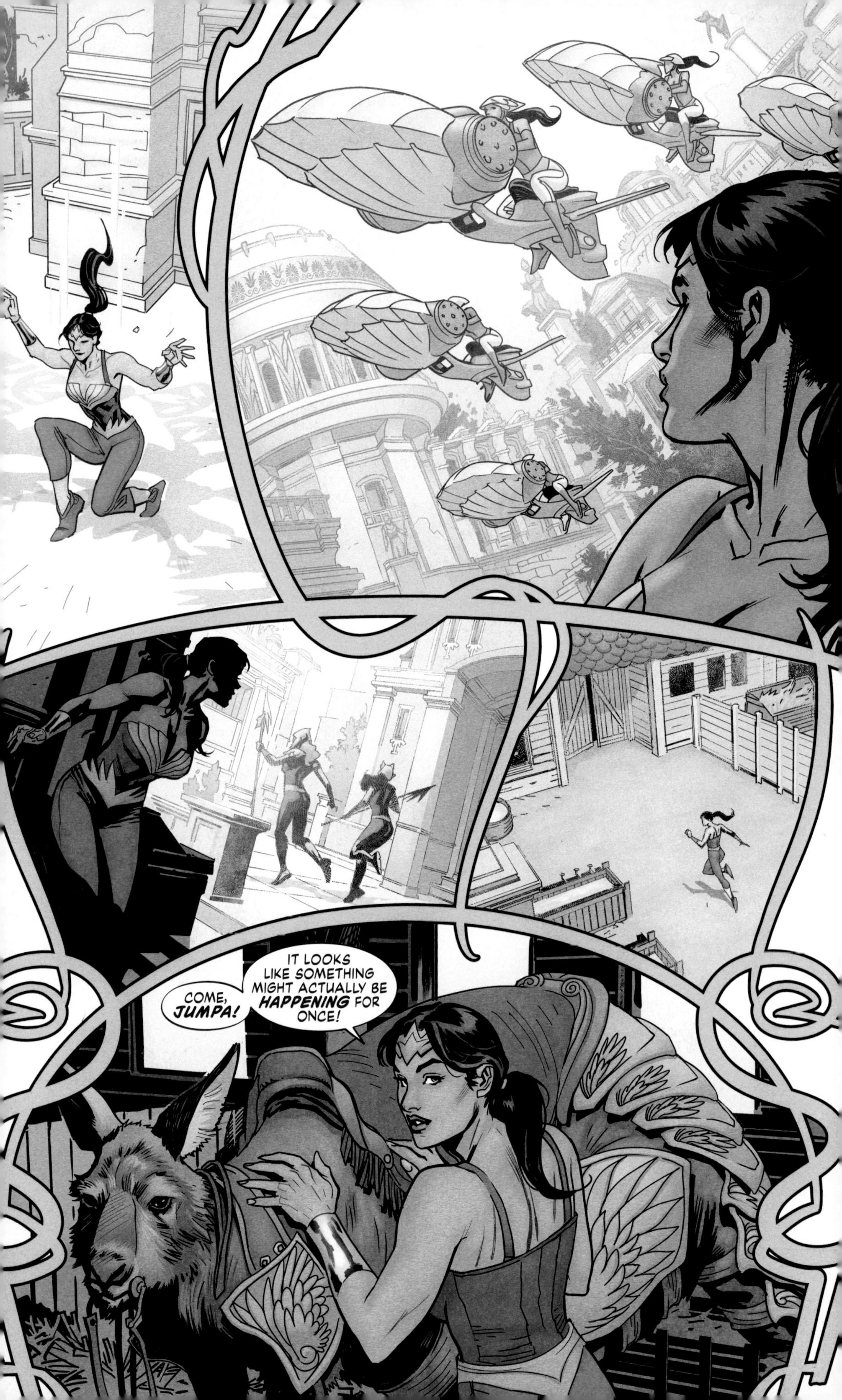
COME, JUMPA!
IT LOOKS LIKE SOMETHING MIGHT ACTUALLY BE HAPPENING FOR ONCE!

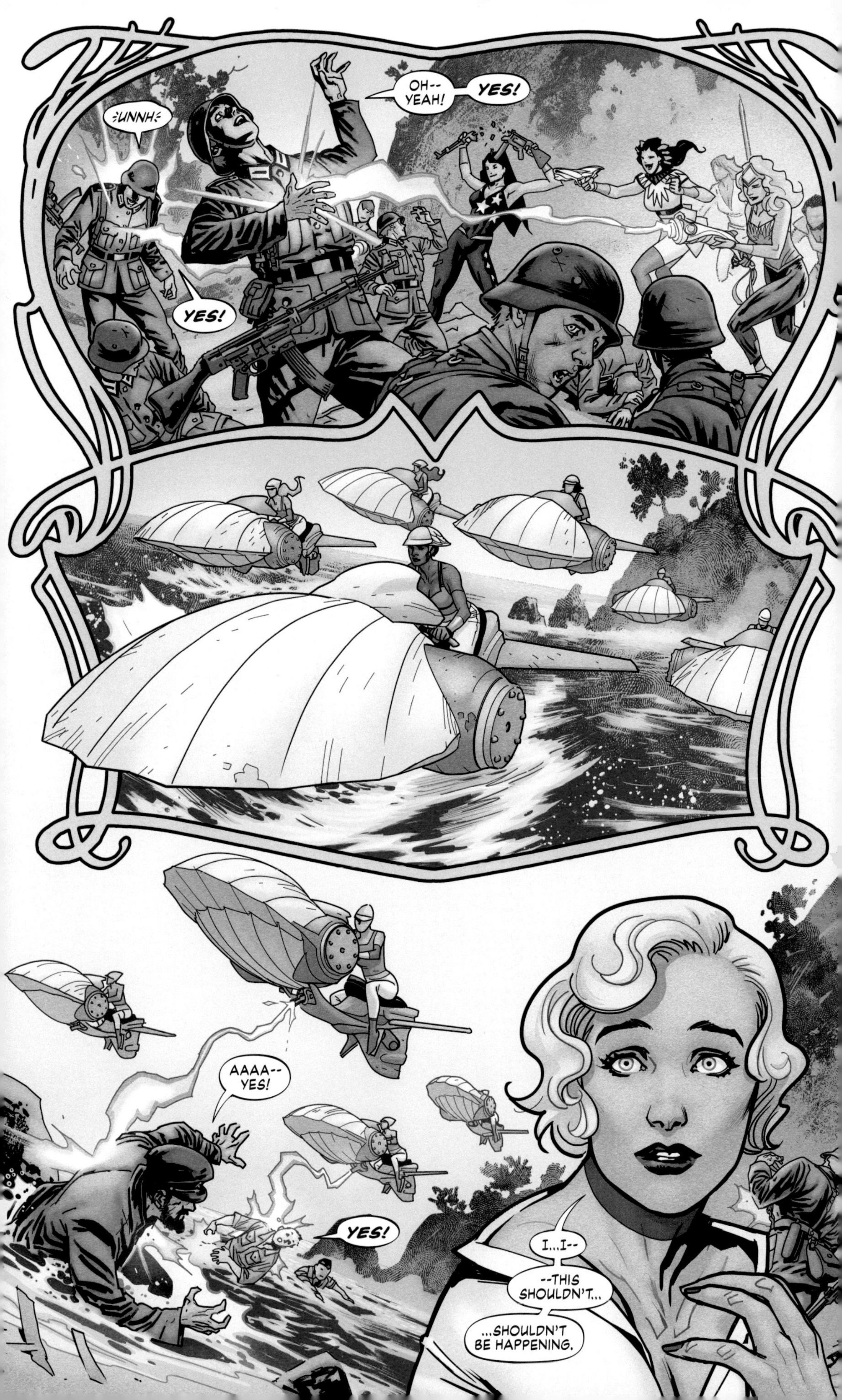
UNNH
OH-- YEAH!
YES!
YES!
AAAA-- YES!
YES!
I...I--
--THIS SHOULDN'T...
...SHOULDN'T BE HAPPENING.

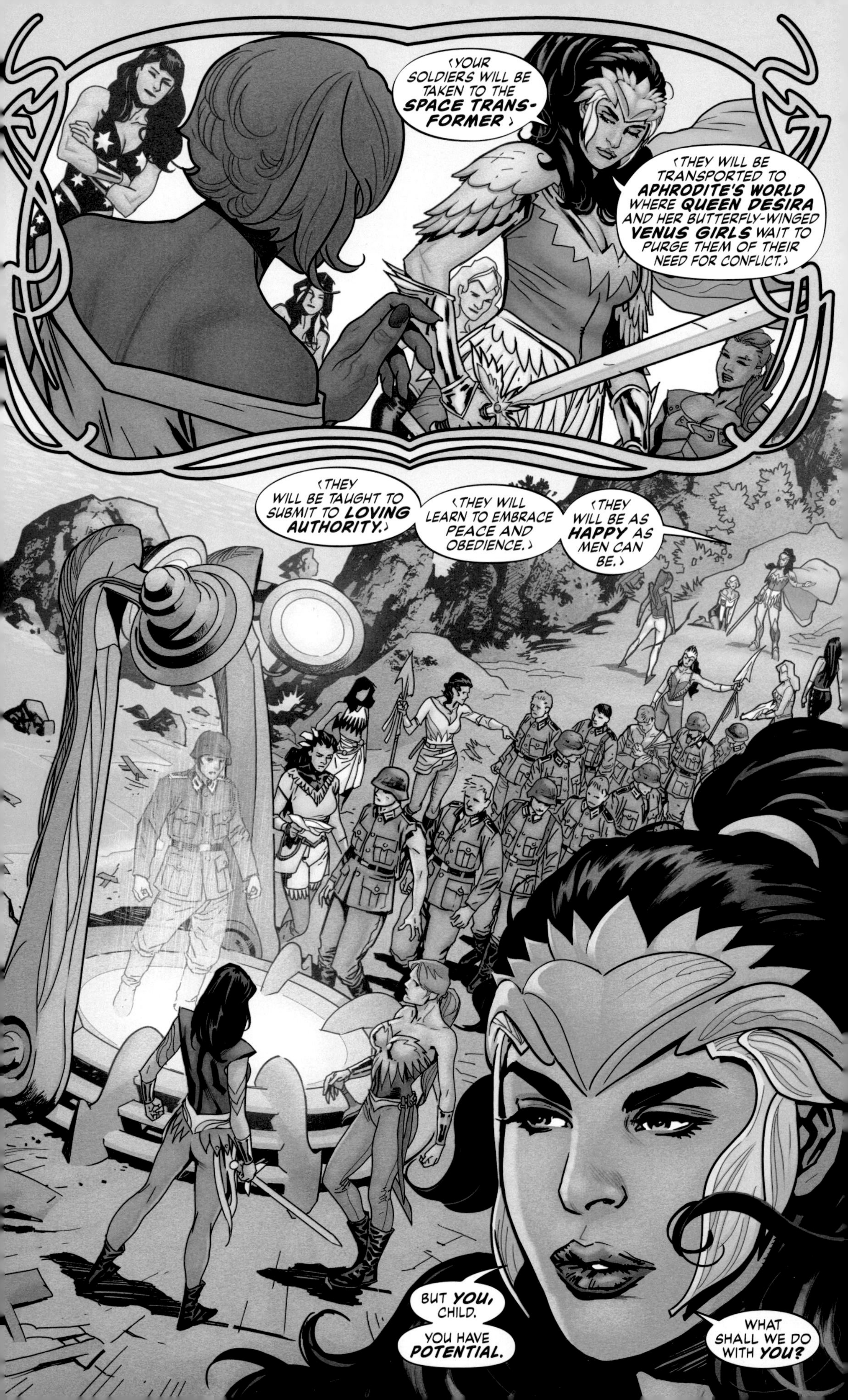
‹YOUR SOLDIERS WILL BE TAKEN TO THE SPACE TRANS-FORMER›
‹THEY WILL BE TRANSPORTED TO APHRODITE'S WORLD WHERE QUEEN DESIRA AND HER BUTTERFLY-WINGED VENUS GIRLS WAIT TO PURGE THEM OF THEIR NEED FOR CONFLICT.›
‹THEY WILL BE TAUGHT TO SUBMIT TO LOVING AUTHORITY.›
‹THEY WILL LEARN TO EMBRACE PEACE AND OBEDIENCE.›
‹THEY WILL BE AS HAPPY AS MEN CAN BE.›
BUT YOU, CHILD.
YOU HAVE POTENTIAL.
WHAT SHALL WE DO WITH YOU?

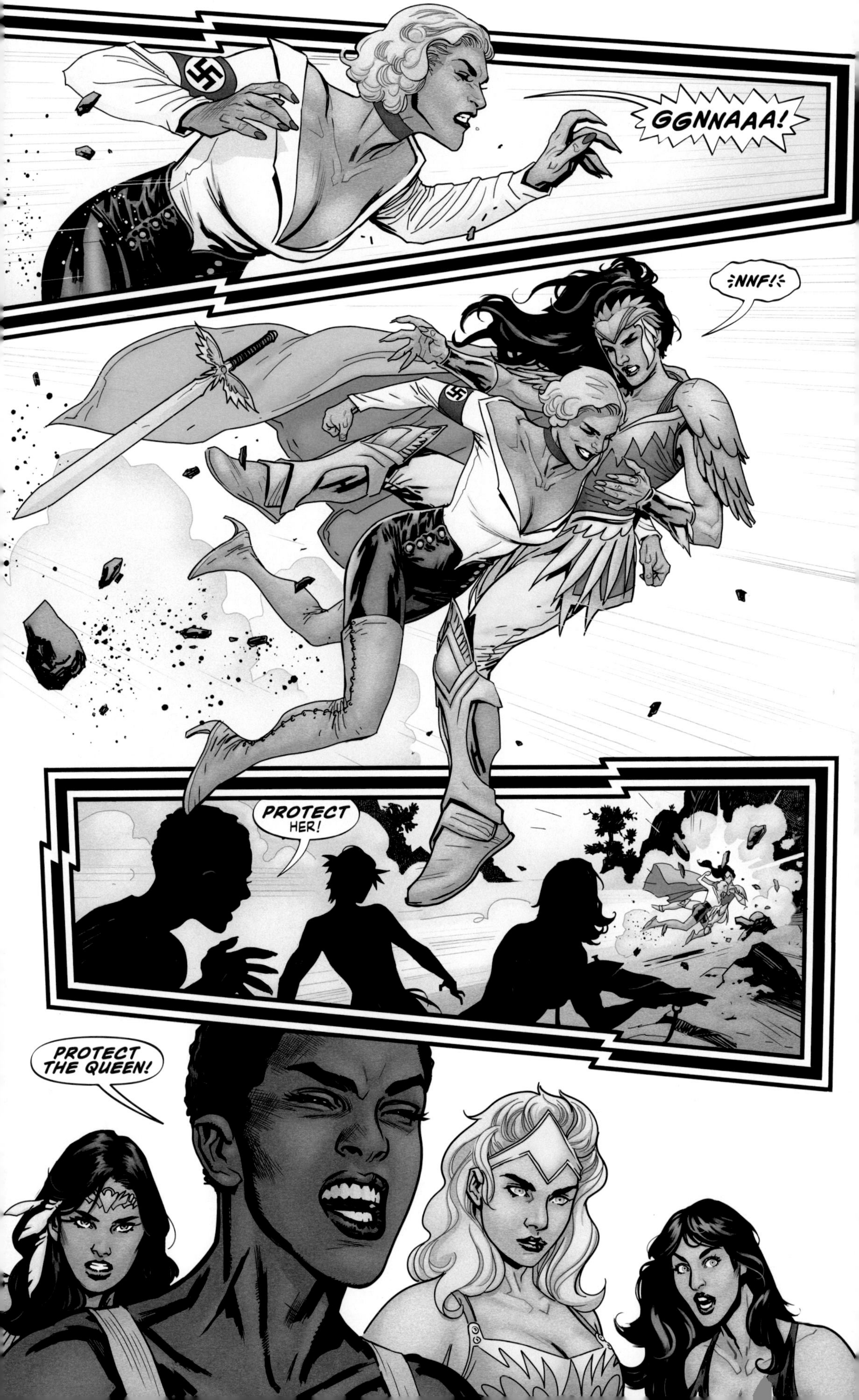
GGNNAAA!
NNF!
PROTECT HER!
PROTECT THE QUEEN!

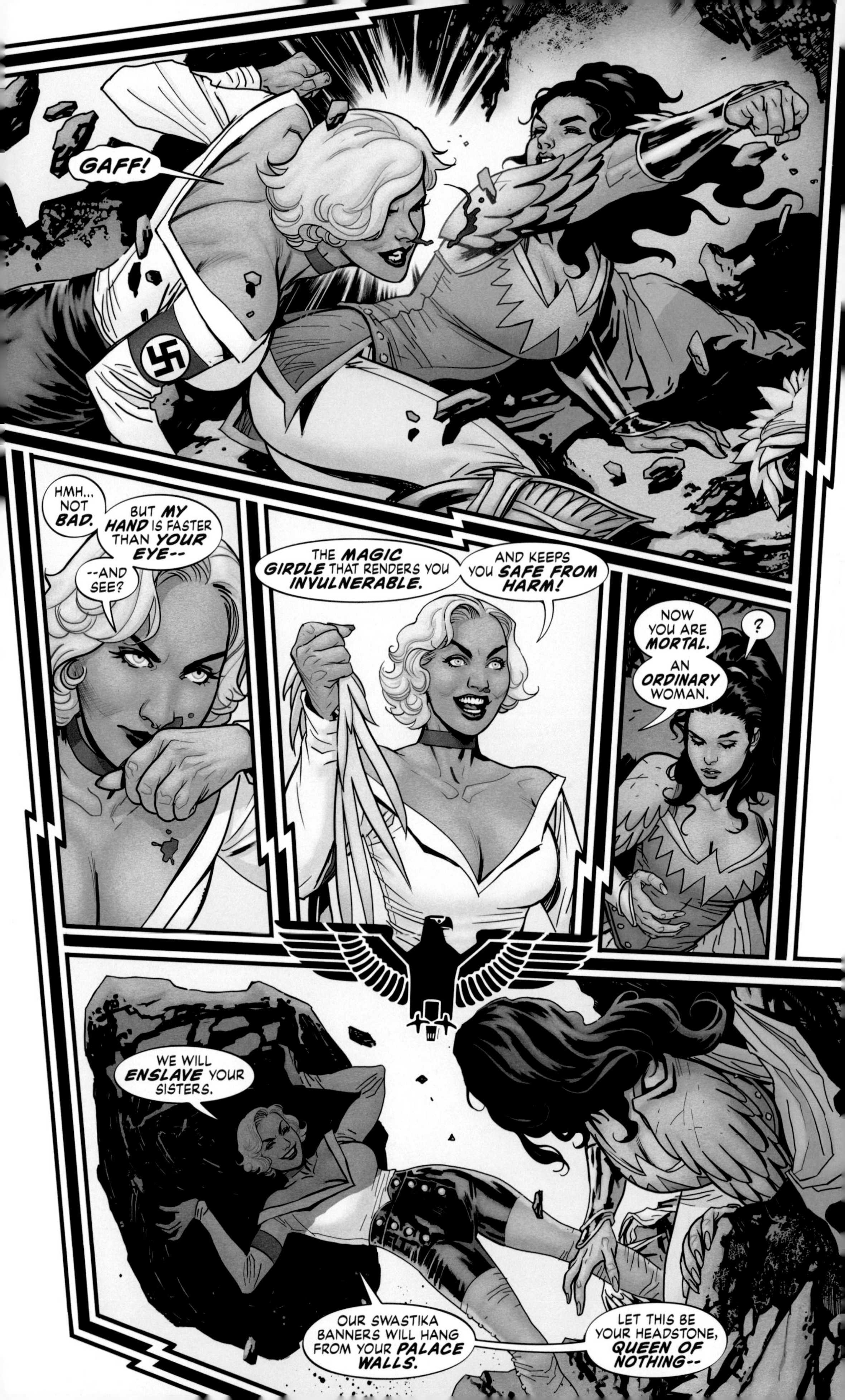
GAFF!
HMH... NOT BAD.
BUT MY HAND IS FASTER THAN YOUR EYE--
--AND SEE?
THE MAGIC GIRDLE THAT RENDERS YOU INVULNERABLE.
AND KEEPS YOU SAFE FROM HARM!
NOW YOU ARE MORTAL.
AN ORDINARY WOMAN.
?
WE WILL ENSLAVE YOUR SISTERS.
OUR SWASTIKA BANNERS WILL HANG FROM YOUR PALACE WALLS.
LET THIS BE YOUR HEADSTONE, QUEEN OF NOTHING--

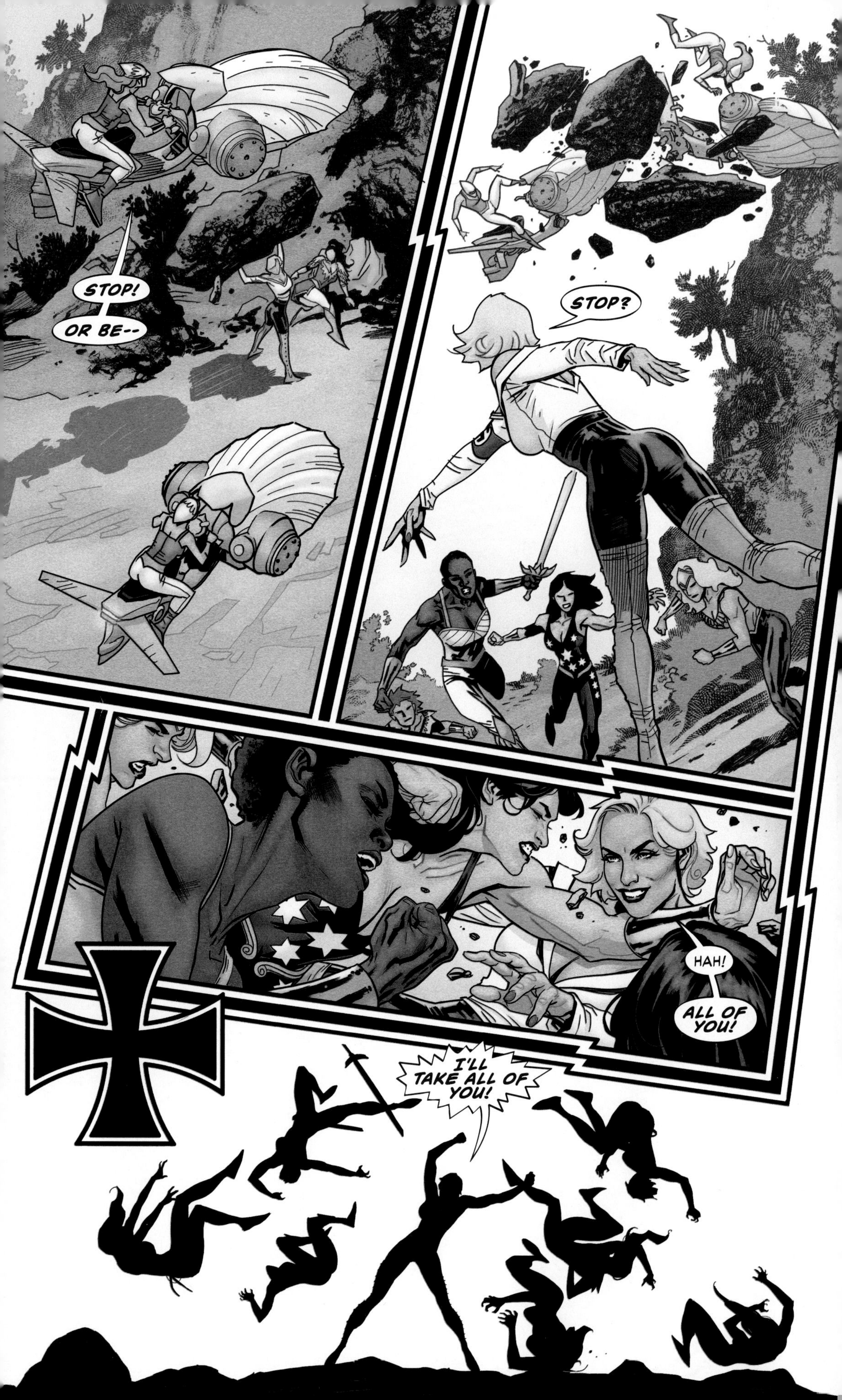
STOP!
OR BE--
STOP?
HAH!
ALL OF YOU!
I'LL TAKE ALL OF YOU!

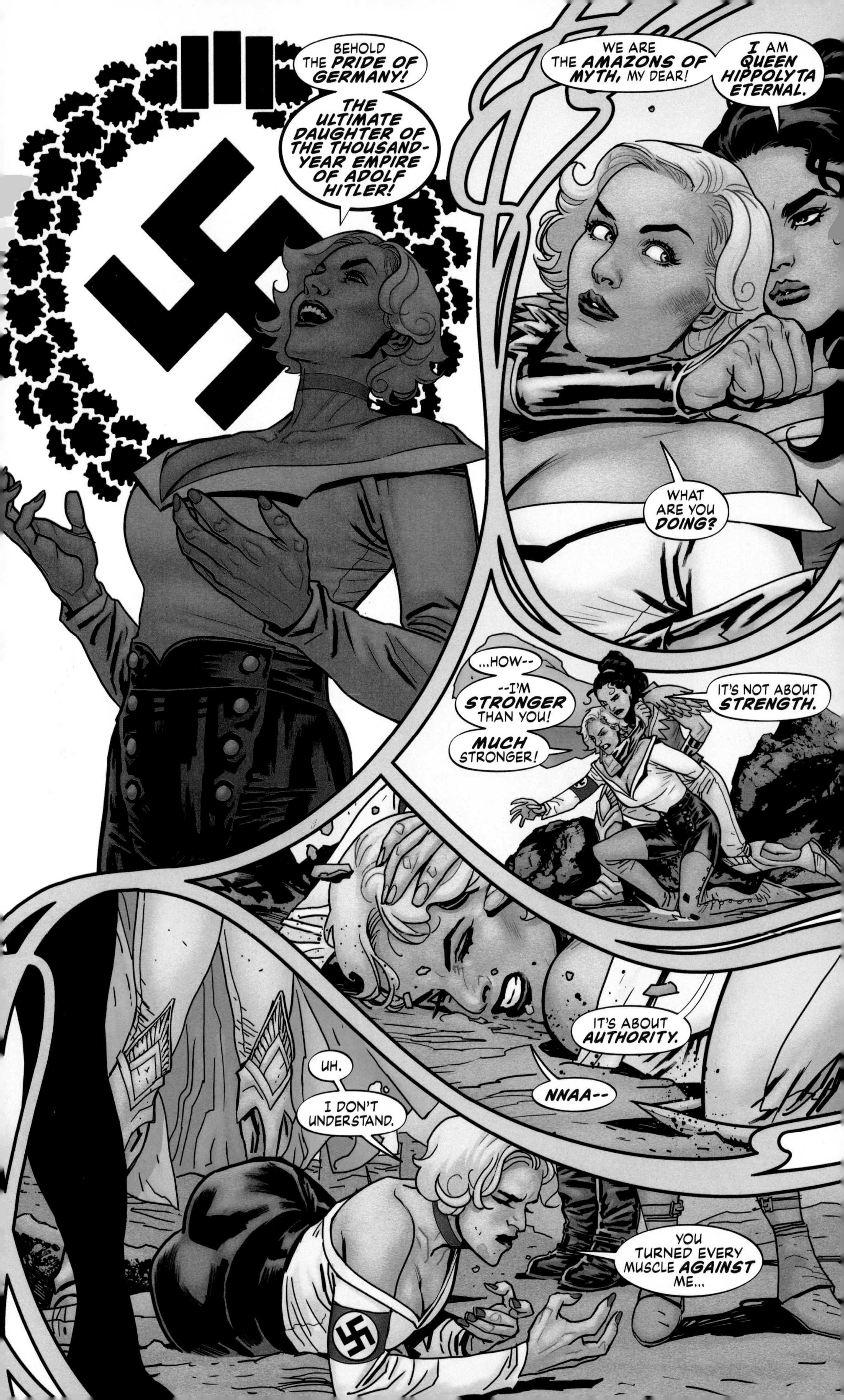

BEHOLD THE PRIDE OF GERMANY!
THE ULTIMATE DAUGHTER OF THE THOUSAND-YEAR EMPIRE OF ADOLF HITLER!
WE ARE THE AMAZONS OF MYTH, MY DEAR!
I AM QUEEN HIPPOLYTA ETERNAL.
WHAT ARE YOU DOING?
...HOW--
--I'M STRONGER THAN YOU!
MUCH STRONGER!
IT'S NOT ABOUT STRENGTH.
IT'S ABOUT AUTHORITY.
NNAA--
UH.
I DON'T UNDERSTAND.
YOU TURNED EVERY MUSCLE AGAINST ME...

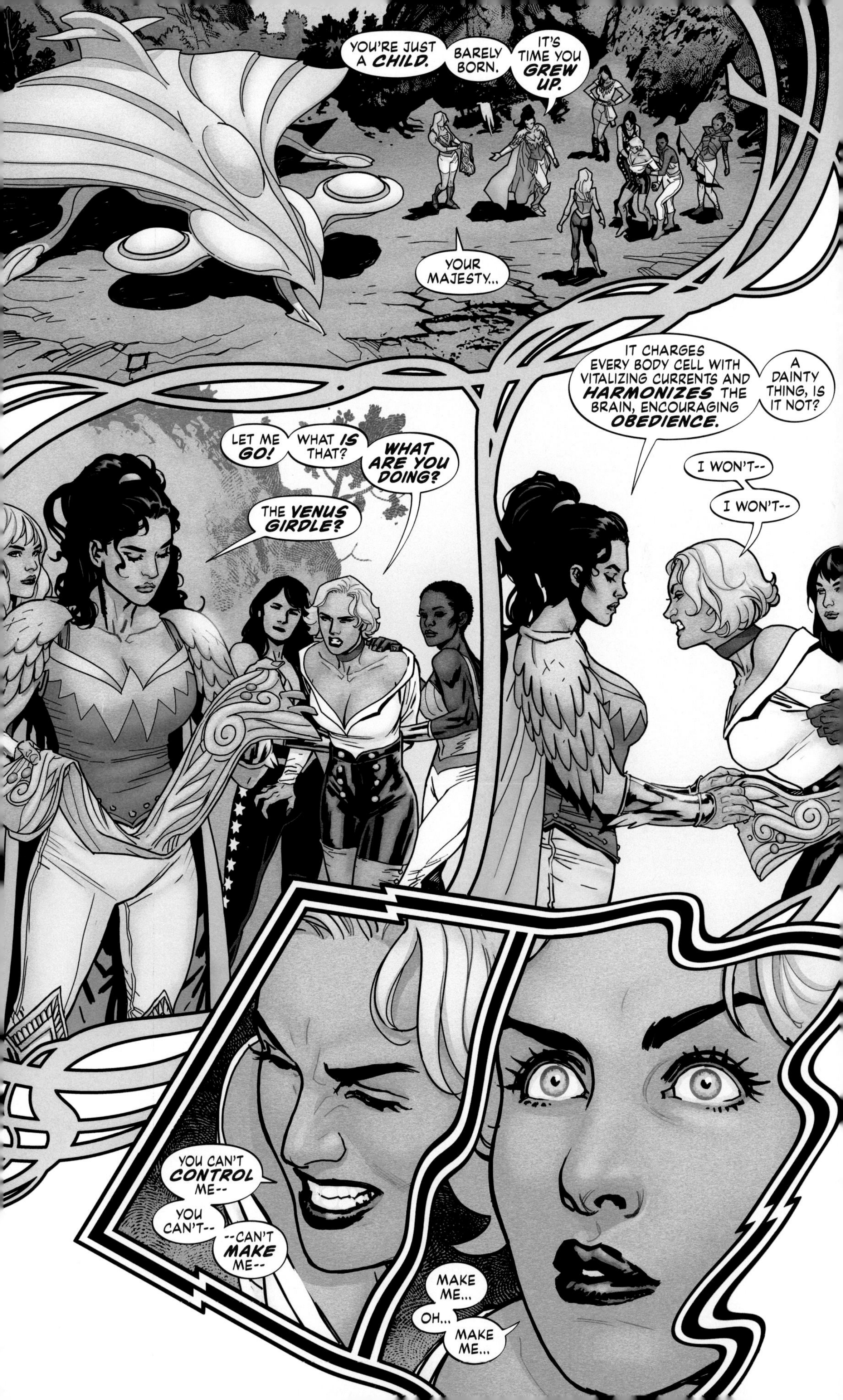
YOU'RE JUST A CHILD.
BARELY BORN.
IT'S TIME YOU GREW UP.
YOUR MAJESTY...
LET ME GO!
WHAT IS THAT?
WHAT ARE YOU DOING?
THE VENUS GIRDLE?
IT CHARGES EVERY BODY CELL WITH VITALIZING CURRENTS AND HARMONIZES THE BRAIN, ENCOURAGING OBEDIENCE.
A DAINTY THING, IS IT NOT?
I WON'T--
I WON'T--
YOU CAN'T CONTROL ME--
YOU CAN'T--
--CAN'T MAKE ME--
MAKE ME...
OH...
MAKE ME...

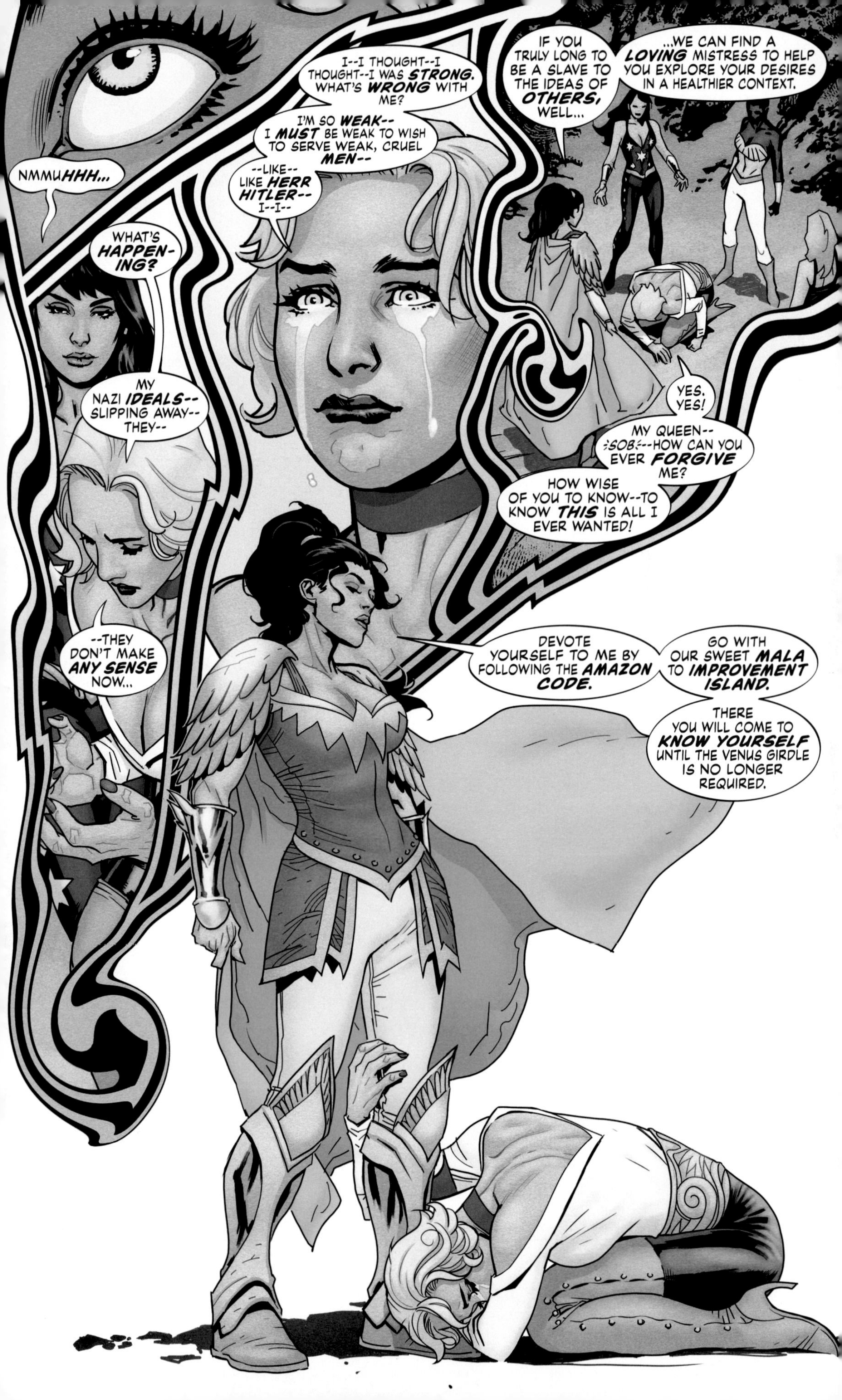

NMMUHHH...
WHAT'S HAPPENING?
MY NAZI IDEALS-- SLIPPING AWAY-- THEY--
--THEY DON'T MAKE ANY SENSE NOW...
I--I THOUGHT--I THOUGHT--I WAS STRONG. WHAT'S WRONG WITH ME?
I'M SO WEAK-- I MUST BE WEAK TO WISH TO SERVE WEAK, CRUEL MEN--
--LIKE-- LIKE HERR HITLER-- I--I--
IF YOU TRULY LONG TO BE A SLAVE TO THE IDEAS OF OTHERS, WELL...
...WE CAN FIND A LOVING MISTRESS TO HELP YOU EXPLORE YOUR DESIRES IN A HEALTHIER CONTEXT.
YES. YES!
MY QUEEN-- <SOB>--HOW CAN YOU EVER FORGIVE ME?
HOW WISE OF YOU TO KNOW--TO KNOW THIS IS ALL I EVER WANTED!
DEVOTE YOURSELF TO ME BY FOLLOWING THE AMAZON CODE.
GO WITH OUR SWEET MALA TO IMPROVEMENT ISLAND.
THERE YOU WILL COME TO KNOW YOURSELF UNTIL THE VENUS GIRDLE IS NO LONGER REQUIRED.

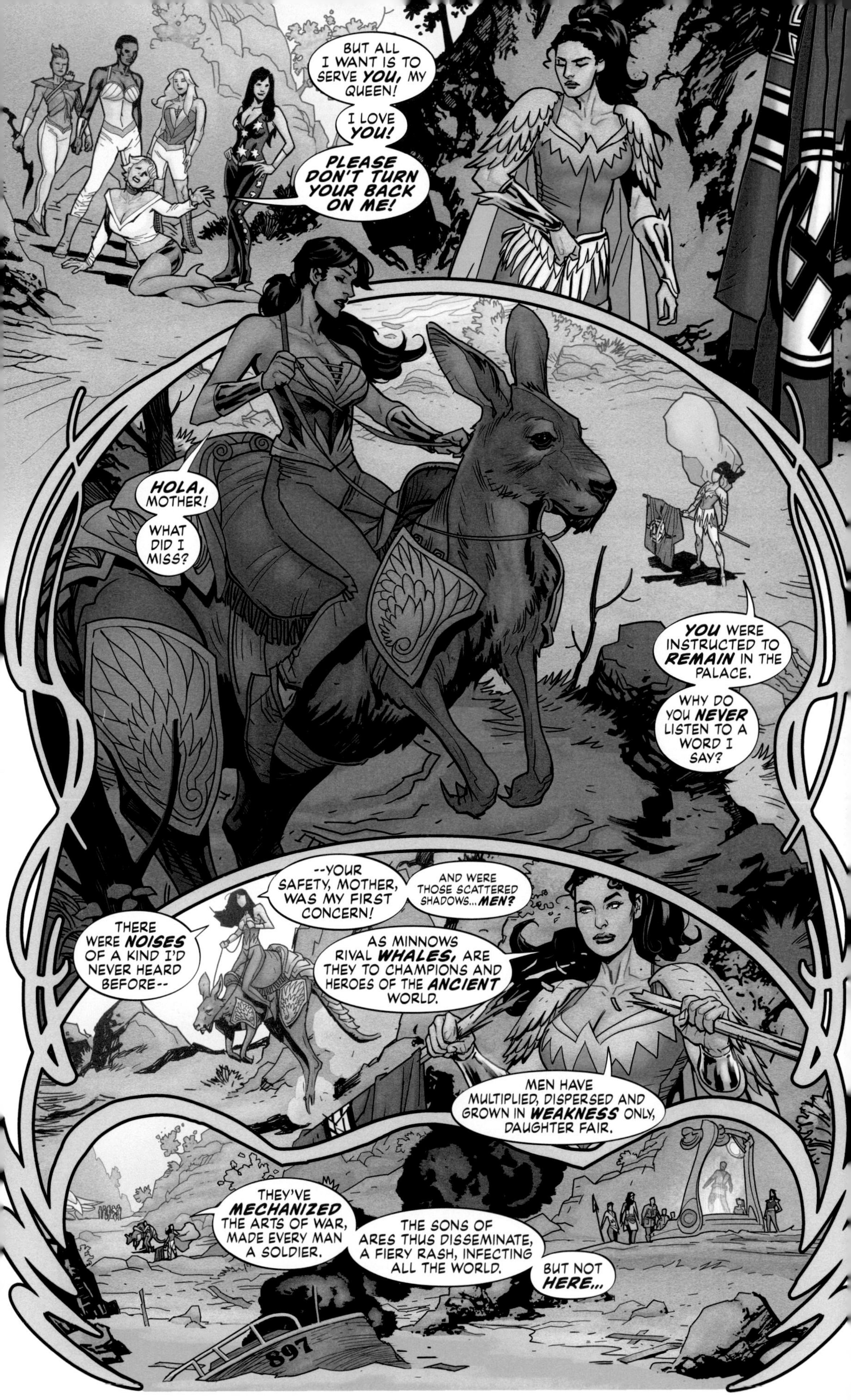

BUT ALL I WANT IS TO SERVE YOU, MY QUEEN!
I LOVE YOU!
PLEASE DON'T TURN YOUR BACK ON ME!
HOLA, MOTHER!
WHAT DID I MISS?
YOU WERE INSTRUCTED TO REMAIN IN THE PALACE.
WHY DO YOU NEVER LISTEN TO A WORD I SAY?
THERE WERE NOISES OF A KIND I'D NEVER HEARD BEFORE--
--YOUR SAFETY, MOTHER, WAS MY FIRST CONCERN!
AND WERE THOSE SCATTERED SHADOWS...MEN?
AS MINNOWS RIVAL WHALES, ARE THEY TO CHAMPIONS AND HEROES OF THE ANCIENT WORLD.
MEN HAVE MULTIPLIED, DISPERSED AND GROWN IN WEAKNESS ONLY, DAUGHTER FAIR.
THEY'VE MECHANIZED THE ARTS OF WAR, MADE EVERY MAN A SOLDIER.
THE SONS OF ARES THUS DISSEMINATE, A FIERY RASH, INFECTING ALL THE WORLD.
BUT NOT HERE...
897

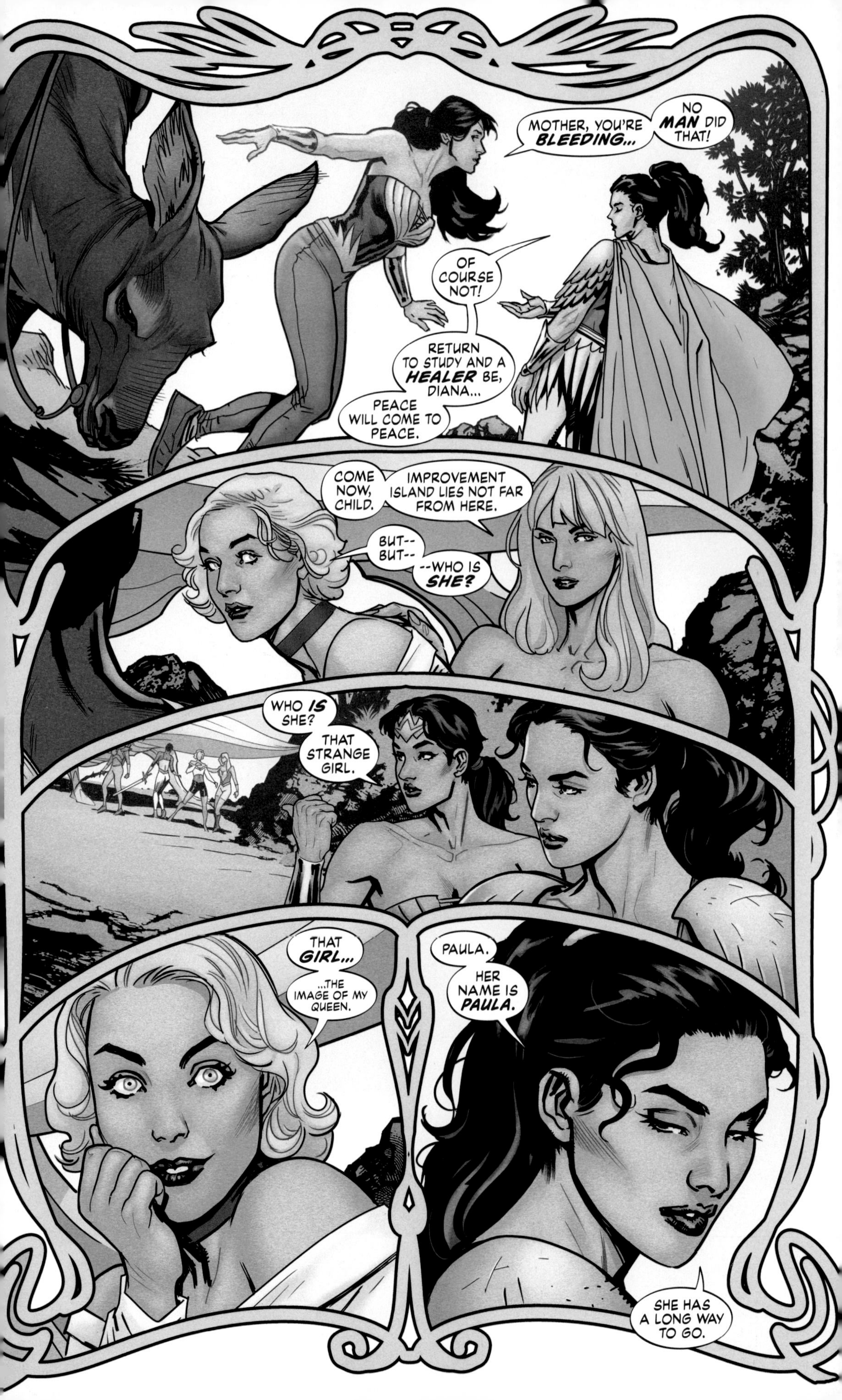

MOTHER, YOU'RE BLEEDING...
NO MAN DID THAT!
OF COURSE NOT!
RETURN TO STUDY AND A HEALER BE, DIANA...
PEACE WILL COME TO PEACE.
COME NOW, CHILD.
IMPROVEMENT ISLAND LIES NOT FAR FROM HERE.
BUT-- BUT--
--WHO IS SHE?
WHO IS SHE?
THAT STRANGE GIRL.
THAT GIRL...
...THE IMAGE OF MY QUEEN.
PAULA.
HER NAME IS PAULA.
SHE HAS A LONG WAY TO GO.

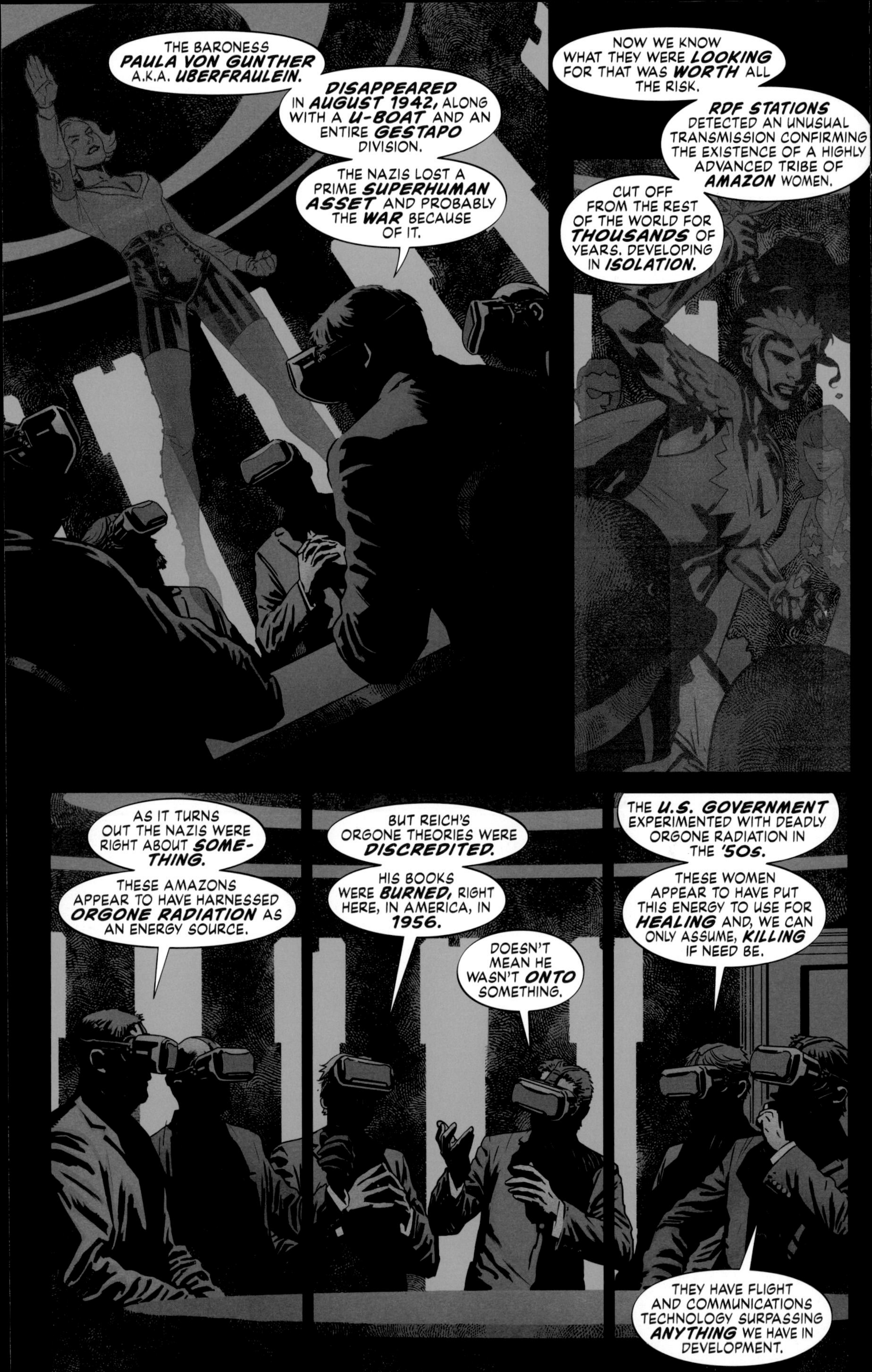
THE BARONESS PAULA VON GUNTHER A.K.A. UBERFRAULEIN.
DISAPPEARED IN AUGUST 1942, ALONG WITH A U-BOAT AND AN ENTIRE GESTAPO DIVISION.
THE NAZIS LOST A PRIME SUPERHUMAN ASSET AND PROBABLY THE WAR BECAUSE OF IT.
NOW WE KNOW WHAT THEY WERE LOOKING FOR THAT WAS WORTH ALL THE RISK.
RDF STATIONS DETECTED AN UNUSUAL TRANSMISSION CONFIRMING THE EXISTENCE OF A HIGHLY ADVANCED TRIBE OF AMAZON WOMEN.
CUT OFF FROM THE REST OF THE WORLD FOR THOUSANDS OF YEARS, DEVELOPING IN ISOLATION.
AS IT TURNS OUT THE NAZIS WERE RIGHT ABOUT SOME-THING.
THESE AMAZONS APPEAR TO HAVE HARNESSED ORGONE RADIATION AS AN ENERGY SOURCE.
BUT REICH'S ORGONE THEORIES WERE DISCREDITED.
HIS BOOKS WERE BURNED, RIGHT HERE, IN AMERICA, IN 1956.
DOESN'T MEAN HE WASN'T ONTO SOMETHING.
THE U.S. GOVERNMENT EXPERIMENTED WITH DEADLY ORGONE RADIATION IN THE '50s.
THESE WOMEN APPEAR TO HAVE PUT THIS ENERGY TO USE FOR HEALING AND, WE CAN ONLY ASSUME, KILLING IF NEED BE.
THEY HAVE FLIGHT AND COMMUNICATIONS TECHNOLOGY SURPASSING ANYTHING WE HAVE IN DEVELOPMENT.

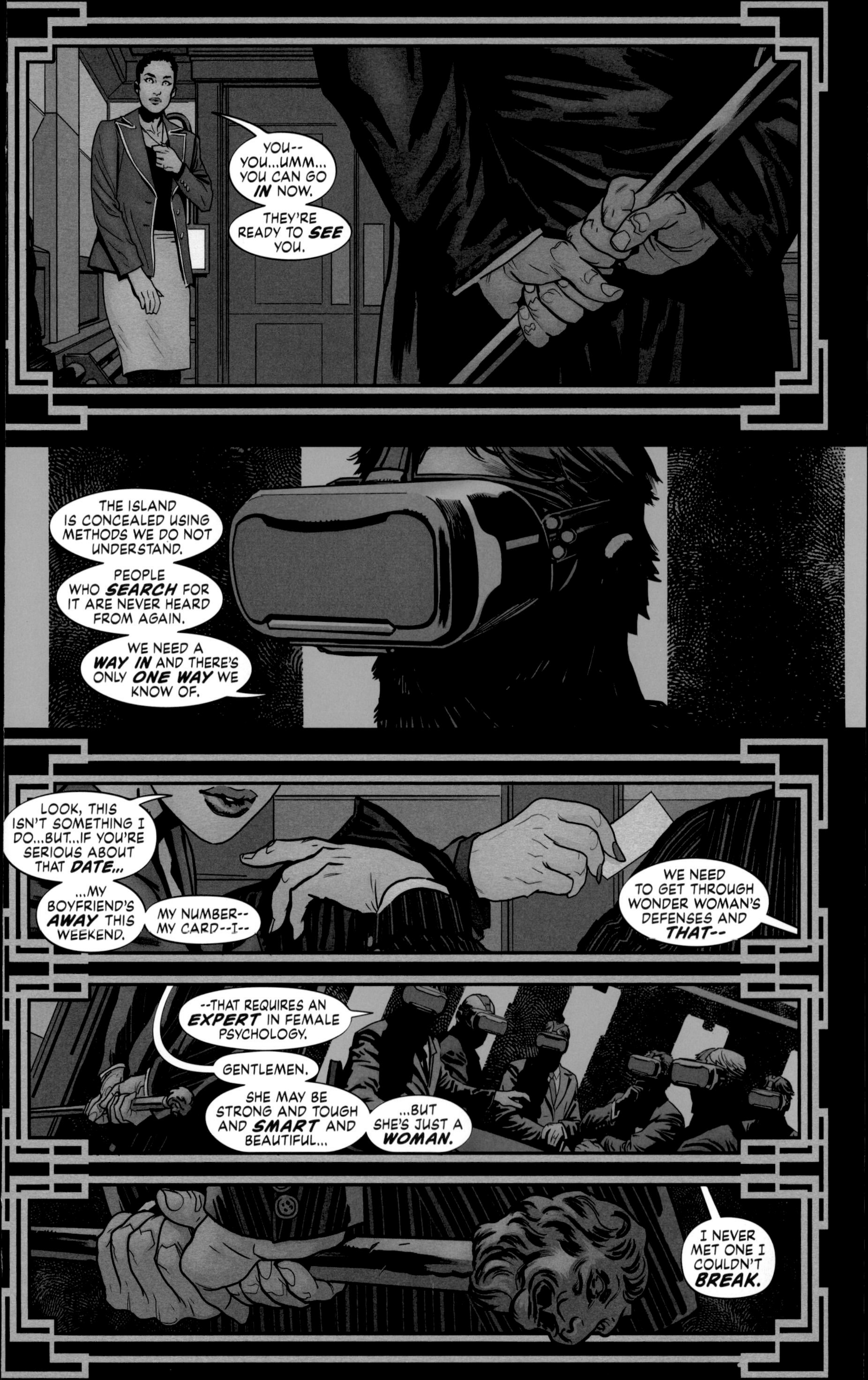
YOU--
YOU...UMM...
YOU CAN GO
IN NOW.
THEY'RE
READY TO SEE
YOU.
THE ISLAND
IS CONCEALED USING
METHODS WE DO NOT
UNDERSTAND.
PEOPLE
WHO SEARCH FOR
IT ARE NEVER HEARD
FROM AGAIN.
WE NEED A
WAY IN AND THERE'S
ONLY ONE WAY WE
KNOW OF.
LOOK, THIS
ISN'T SOMETHING I
DO...BUT...IF YOU'RE
SERIOUS ABOUT
THAT DATE...
...MY
BOYFRIEND'S
AWAY THIS
WEEKEND.
MY NUMBER--
MY CARD--I--
WE NEED
TO GET THROUGH
WONDER WOMAN'S
DEFENSES AND
THAT--
--THAT REQUIRES AN
EXPERT IN FEMALE
PSYCHOLOGY.
GENTLEMEN.
SHE MAY BE
STRONG AND TOUGH
AND SMART AND
BEAUTIFUL...
...BUT
SHE'S JUST A
WOMAN.
I NEVER
MET ONE I
COULDN'T
BREAK.

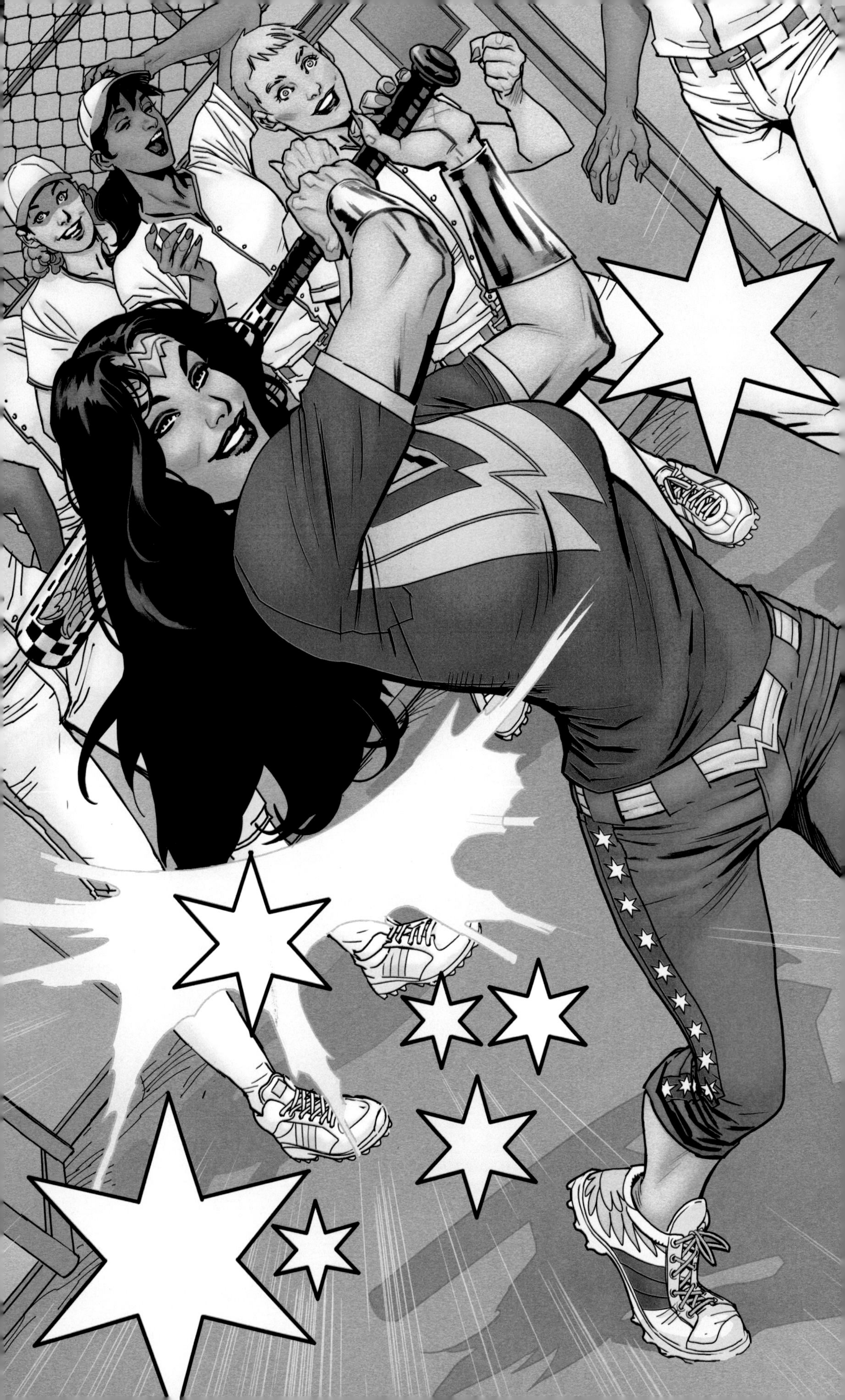

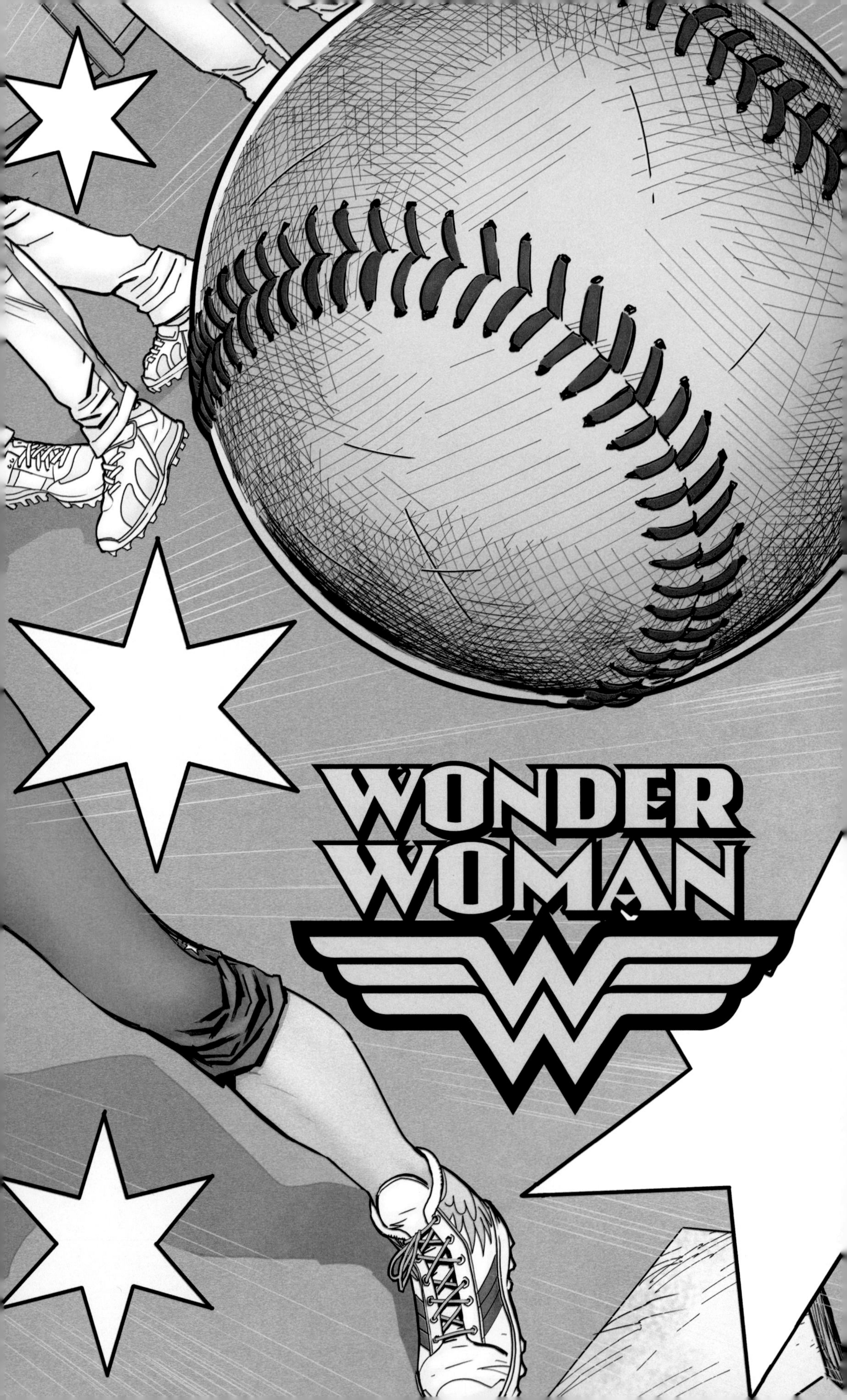
WONDER
WOMAN

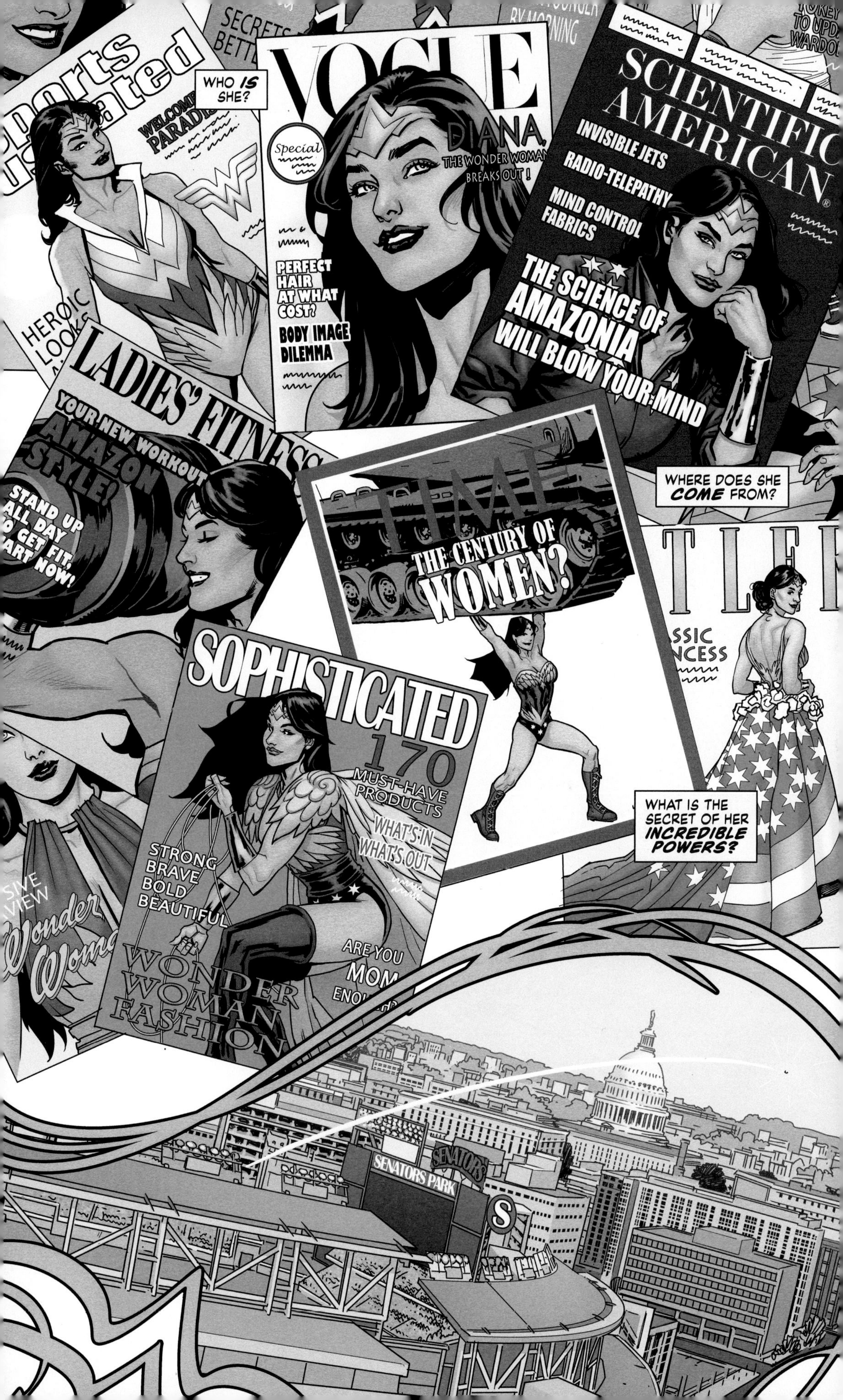

Sports Illustrated
WHO IS SHE?
WELCOME PARADISE
HEROIC LOOKS
VOGUE
Special
DIANA, THE WONDER WOMAN BREAKS OUT!
PERFECT HAIR AT WHAT COST?
BODY IMAGE DILEMMA
SCIENTIFIC AMERICAN
INVISIBLE JETS
RADIO-TELEPATHY
MIND CONTROL FABRICS
THE SCIENCE OF AMAZONIA WILL BLOW YOUR MIND
LADIES' FITNESS
YOUR NEW WORKOUT AMAZON STYLE!
TIME
THE CENTURY OF WOMEN?
WHERE DOES SHE COME FROM?
SOPHISTICATED
170 MUST-HAVE PRODUCTS
WHAT'S IN WHAT'S OUT
STRONG BRAVE BOLD BEAUTIFUL
WONDER WOMAN FASHION
WHAT IS THE SECRET OF HER INCREDIBLE POWERS?
Wonder Woman
SENATORS PARK
SENATORS

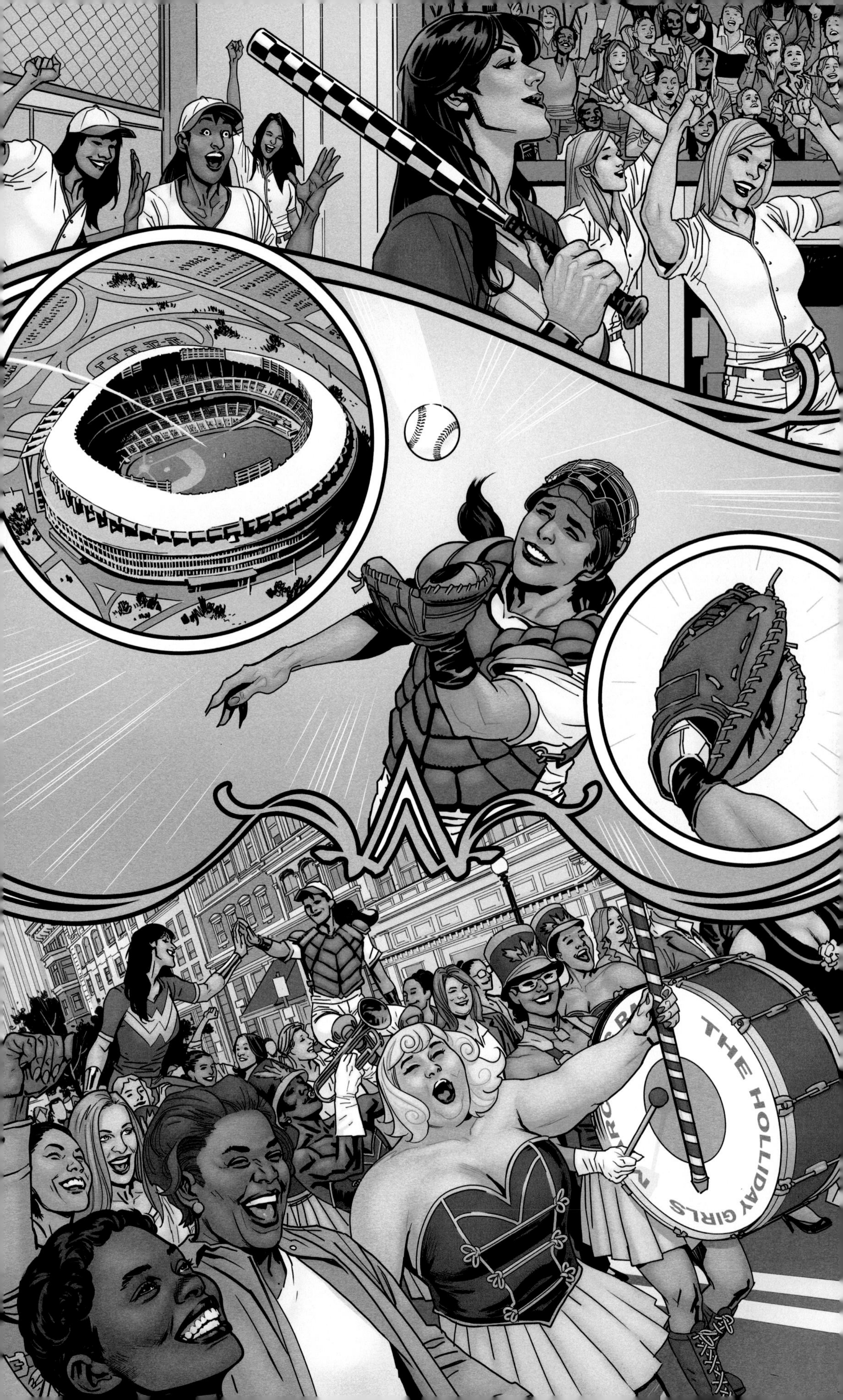
THE HOLLIDAY GIRLS

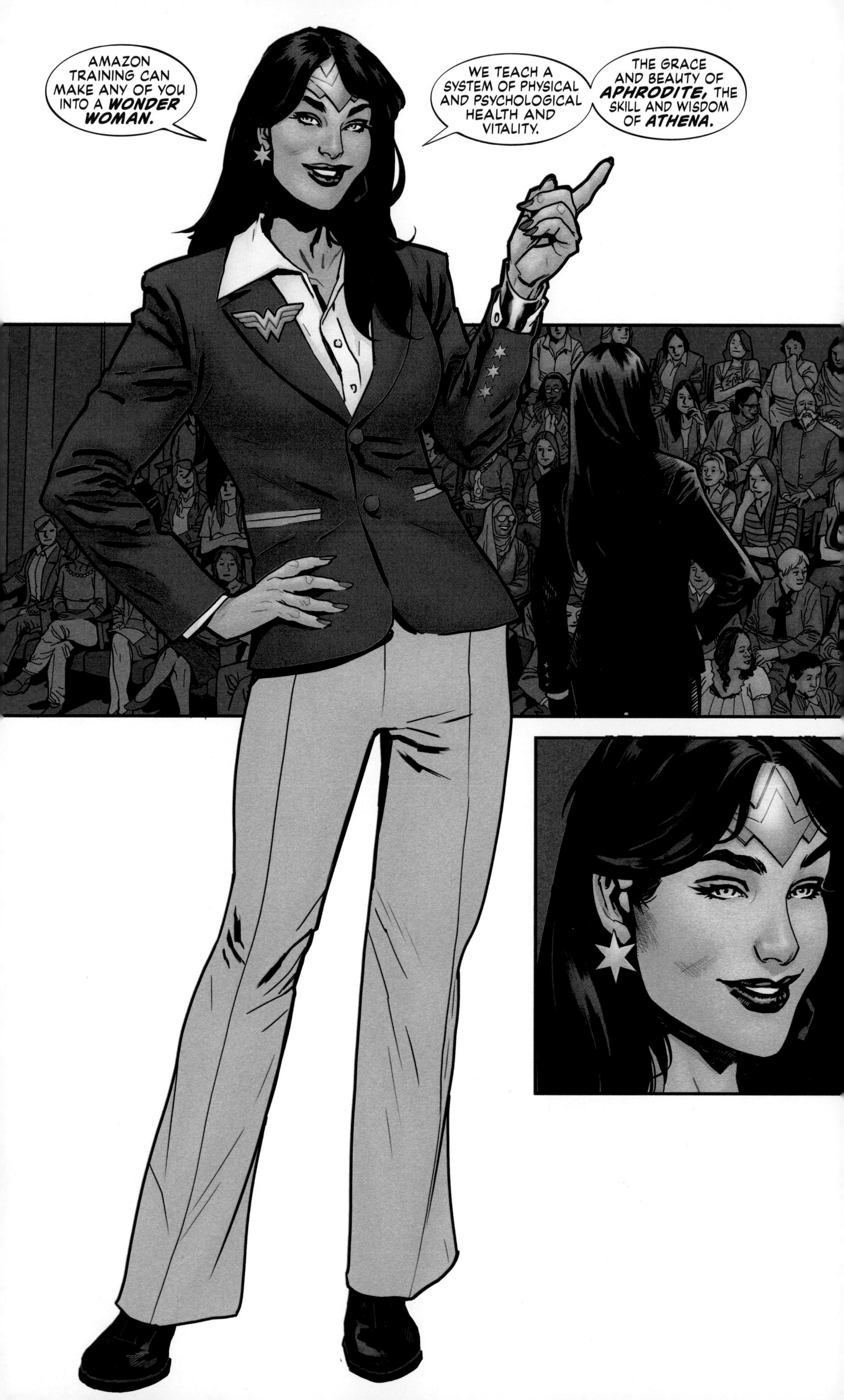
AMAZON TRAINING CAN MAKE ANY OF YOU INTO A WONDER WOMAN.
WE TEACH A SYSTEM OF PHYSICAL AND PSYCHOLOGICAL HEALTH AND VITALITY.
THE GRACE AND BEAUTY OF APHRODITE, THE SKILL AND WISDOM OF ATHENA.

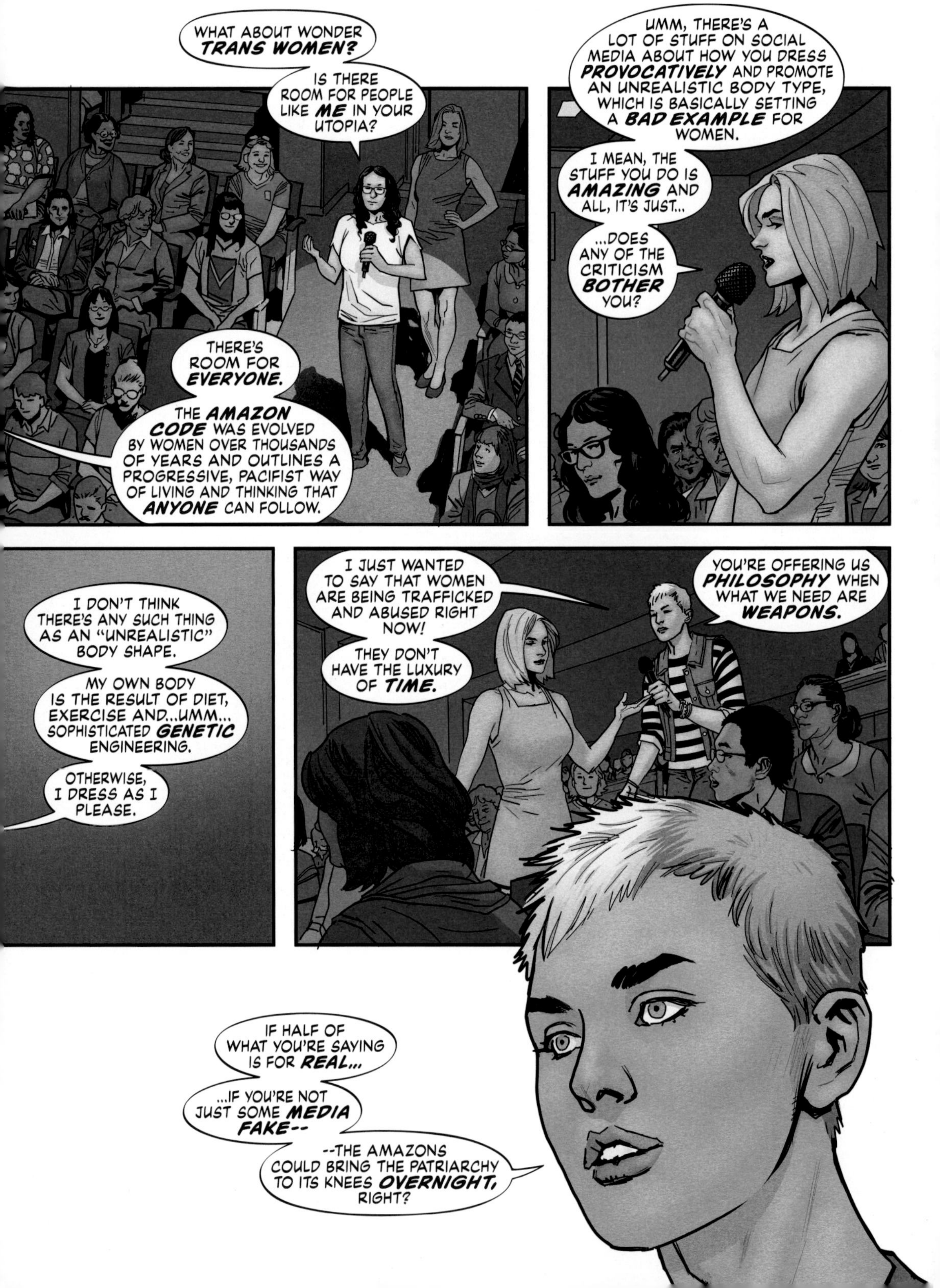
WHAT ABOUT WONDER TRANS WOMEN?
IS THERE ROOM FOR PEOPLE LIKE ME IN YOUR UTOPIA?
THERE'S ROOM FOR EVERYONE.
THE AMAZON CODE WAS EVOLVED BY WOMEN OVER THOUSANDS OF YEARS AND OUTLINES A PROGRESSIVE, PACIFIST WAY OF LIVING AND THINKING THAT ANYONE CAN FOLLOW.
UMM, THERE'S A LOT OF STUFF ON SOCIAL MEDIA ABOUT HOW YOU DRESS PROVOCATIVELY AND PROMOTE AN UNREALISTIC BODY TYPE, WHICH IS BASICALLY SETTING A BAD EXAMPLE FOR WOMEN.
I MEAN, THE STUFF YOU DO IS AMAZING AND ALL, IT'S JUST...
...DOES ANY OF THE CRITICISM BOTHER YOU?
I DON'T THINK THERE'S ANY SUCH THING AS AN "UNREALISTIC" BODY SHAPE.
MY OWN BODY IS THE RESULT OF DIET, EXERCISE AND...UMM... SOPHISTICATED GENETIC ENGINEERING.
OTHERWISE, I DRESS AS I PLEASE.
I JUST WANTED TO SAY THAT WOMEN ARE BEING TRAFFICKED AND ABUSED RIGHT NOW!
THEY DON'T HAVE THE LUXURY OF TIME.
YOU'RE OFFERING US PHILOSOPHY WHEN WHAT WE NEED ARE WEAPONS.
IF HALF OF WHAT YOU'RE SAYING IS FOR REAL...
...IF YOU'RE NOT JUST SOME MEDIA FAKE--
--THE AMAZONS COULD BRING THE PATRIARCHY TO ITS KNEES OVERNIGHT, RIGHT?

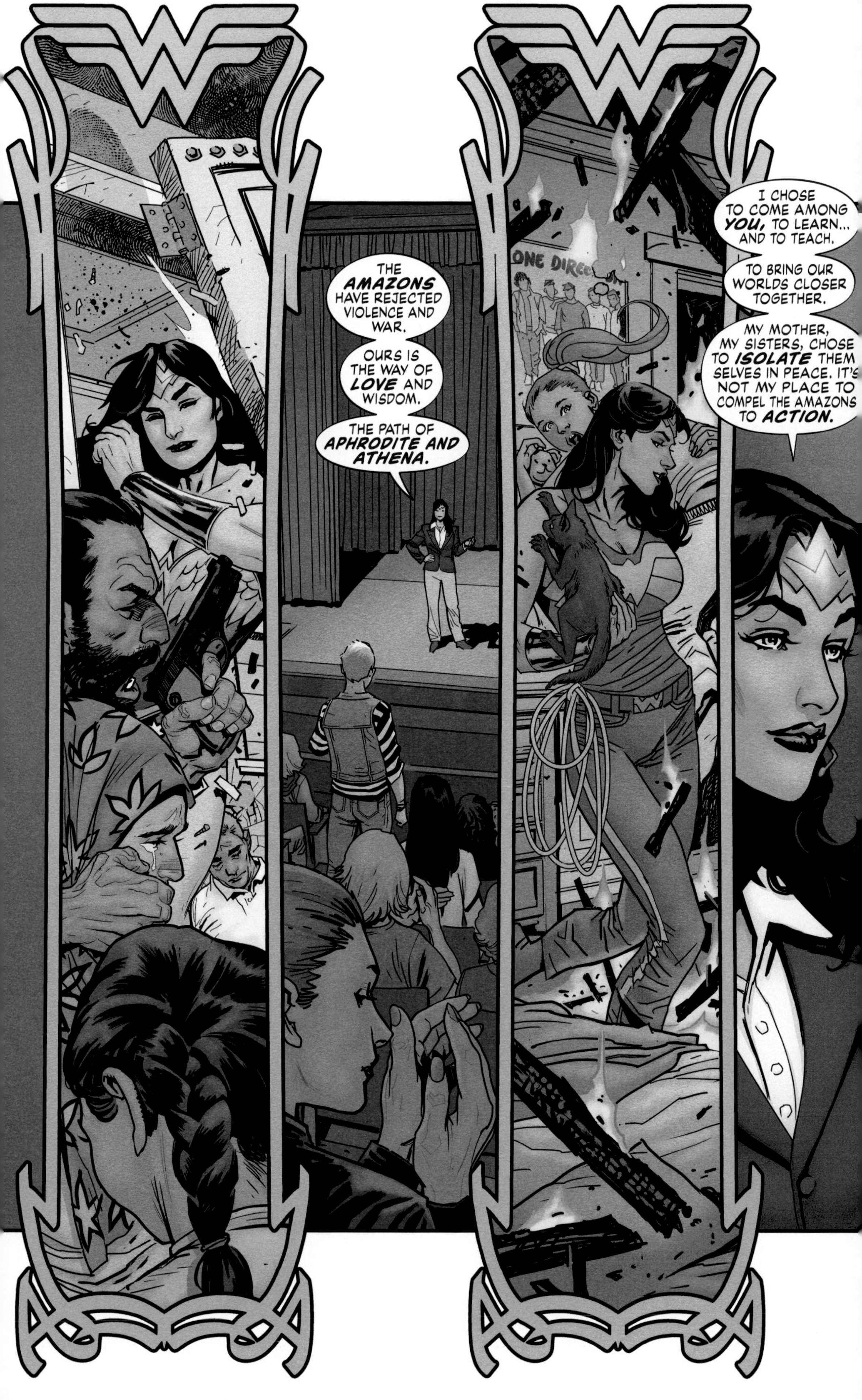
THE AMAZONS HAVE REJECTED VIOLENCE AND WAR.
OURS IS THE WAY OF LOVE AND WISDOM.
THE PATH OF APHRODITE AND ATHENA.
ONE DIREC
I CHOSE TO COME AMONG YOU, TO LEARN... AND TO TEACH.
TO BRING OUR WORLDS CLOSER TOGETHER.
MY MOTHER, MY SISTERS, CHOSE TO ISOLATE THEM SELVES IN PEACE. IT'S NOT MY PLACE TO COMPEL THE AMAZONS TO ACTION.

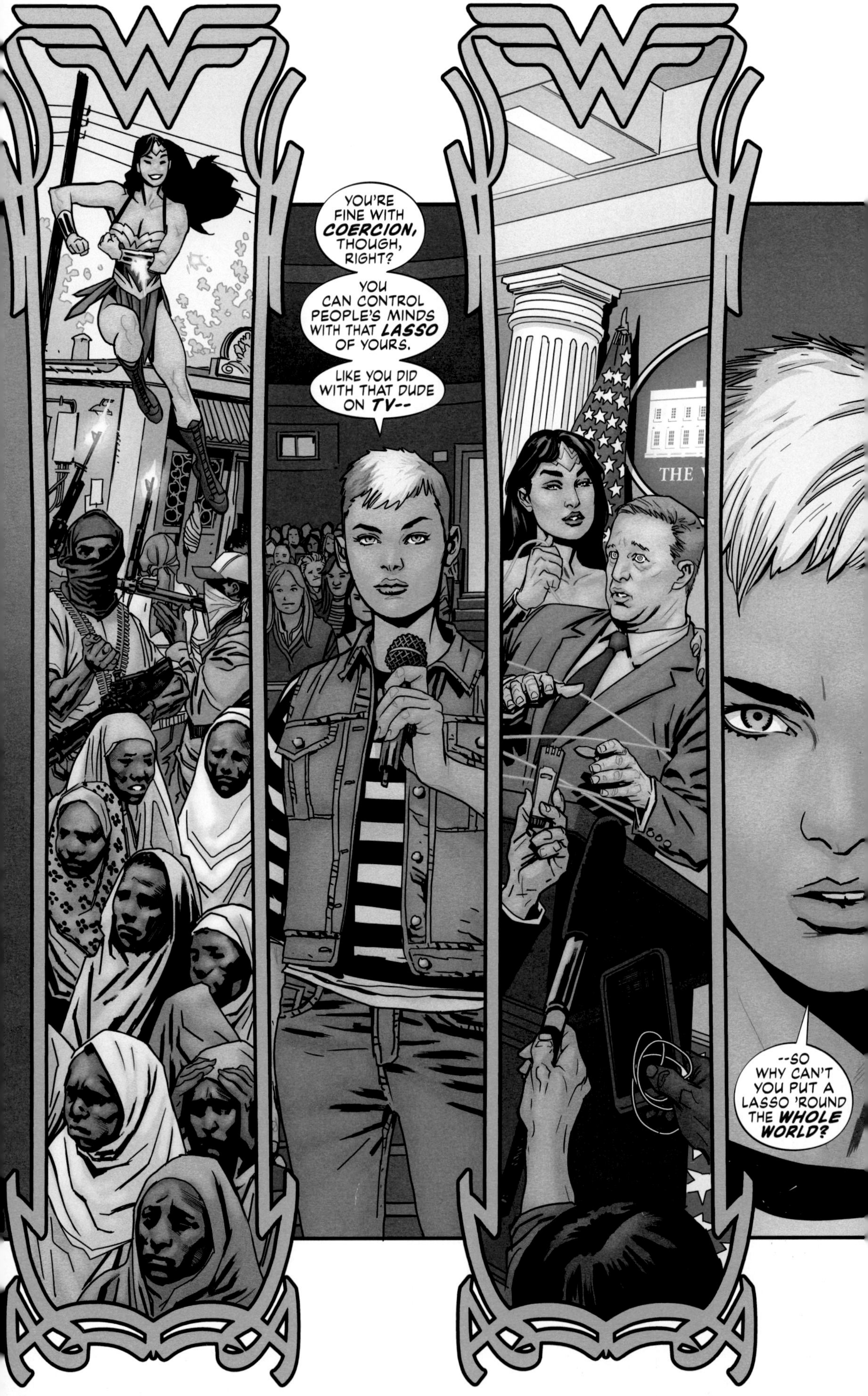
YOU'RE FINE WITH COERCION, THOUGH, RIGHT?
YOU CAN CONTROL PEOPLE'S MINDS WITH THAT LASSO OF YOURS.
LIKE YOU DID WITH THAT DUDE ON TV--
THE W
--SO WHY CAN'T YOU PUT A LASSO 'ROUND THE WHOLE WORLD?

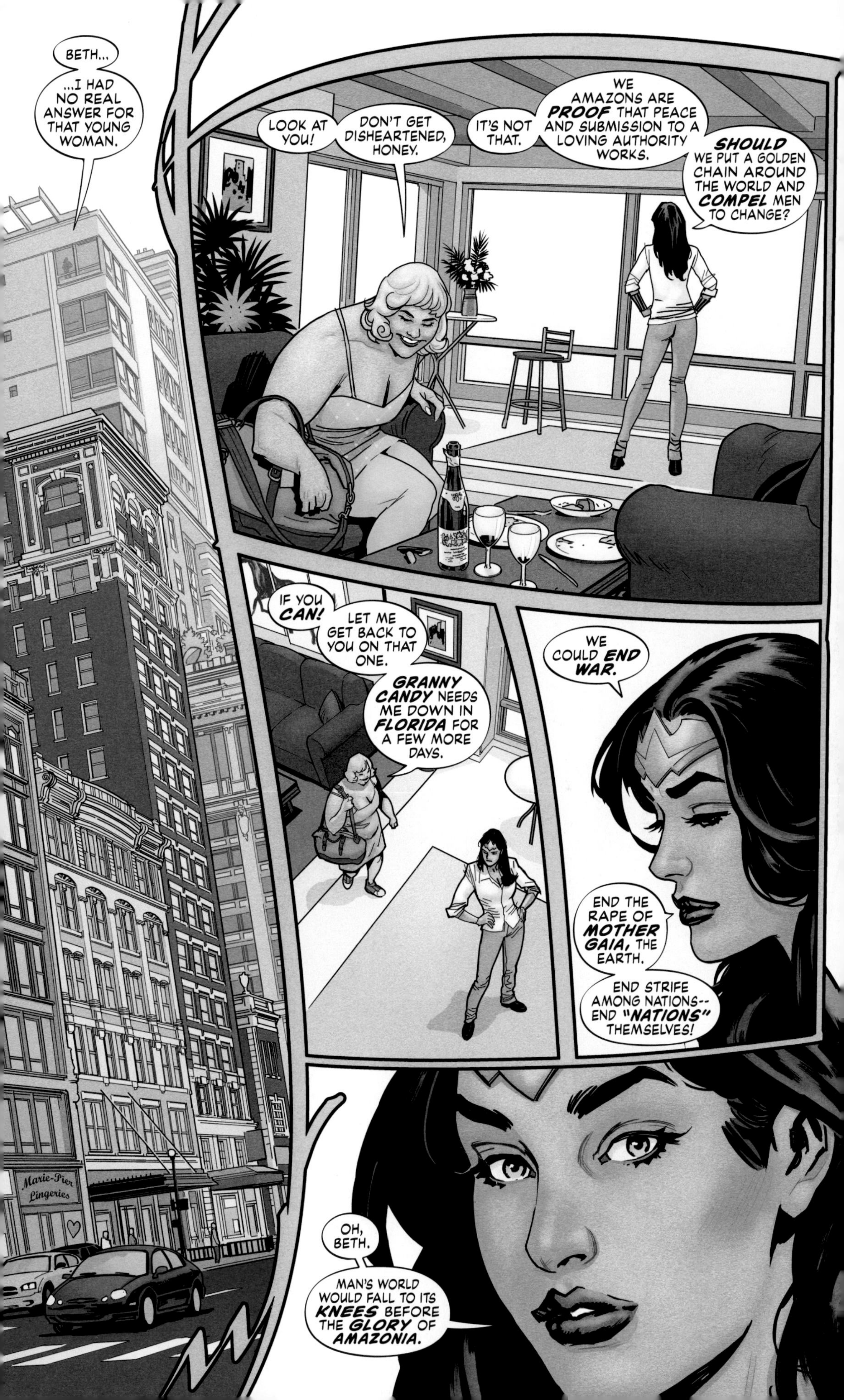
BETH...
...I HAD NO REAL ANSWER FOR THAT YOUNG WOMAN.
LOOK AT YOU!
DON'T GET DISHEARTENED, HONEY.
IT'S NOT THAT.
WE AMAZONS ARE PROOF THAT PEACE AND SUBMISSION TO A LOVING AUTHORITY WORKS.
SHOULD WE PUT A GOLDEN CHAIN AROUND THE WORLD AND COMPEL MEN TO CHANGE?
IF YOU CAN!
LET ME GET BACK TO YOU ON THAT ONE.
GRANNY CANDY NEEDS ME DOWN IN FLORIDA FOR A FEW MORE DAYS.
WE COULD END WAR.
END THE RAPE OF MOTHER GAIA, THE EARTH.
END STRIFE AMONG NATIONS--END "NATIONS" THEMSELVES!
OH, BETH.
MAN'S WORLD WOULD FALL TO ITS KNEES BEFORE THE GLORY OF AMAZONIA.
Marie-Pier Lingeries

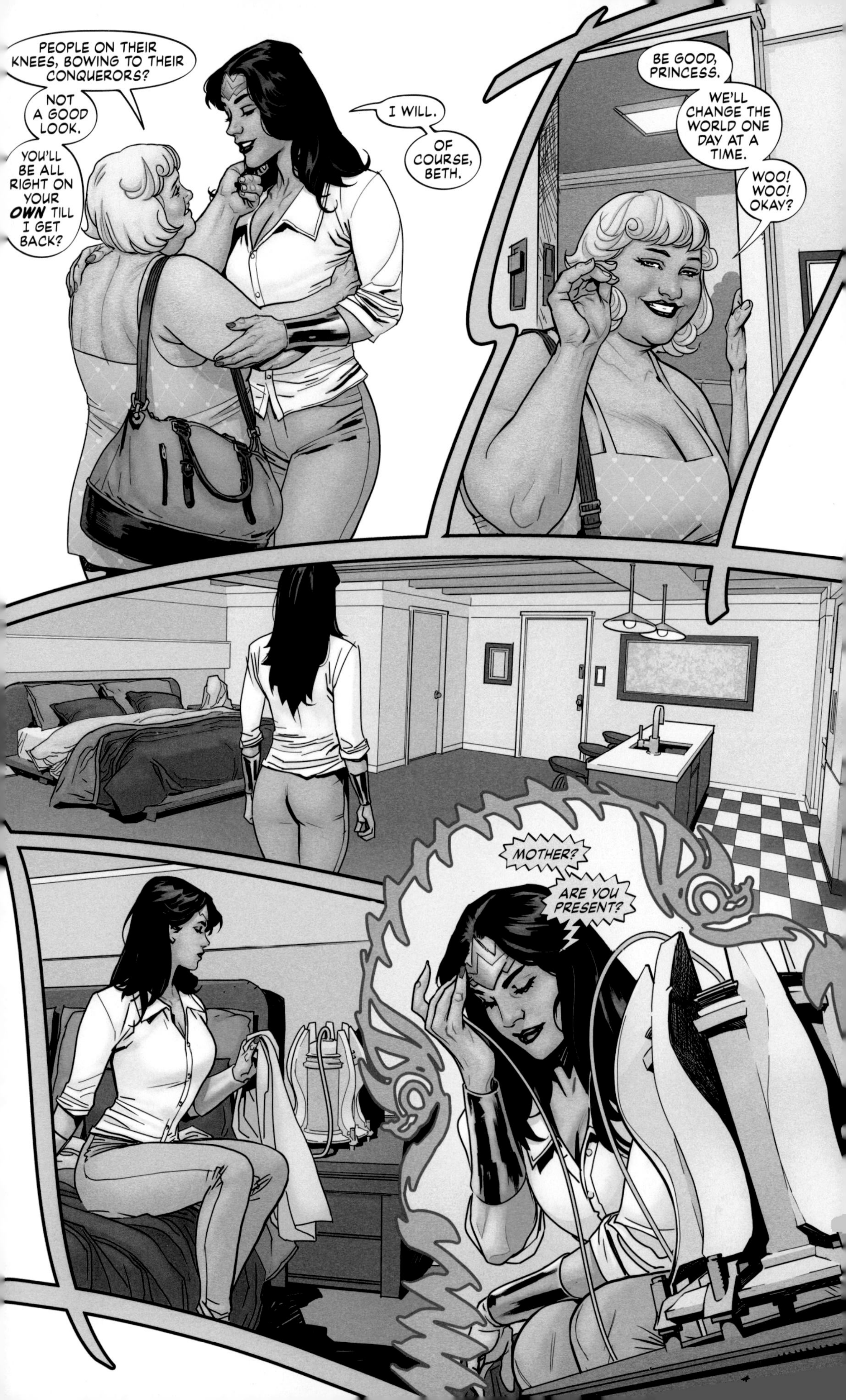
PEOPLE ON THEIR KNEES, BOWING TO THEIR CONQUERORS?
NOT A GOOD LOOK.
YOU'LL BE ALL RIGHT ON YOUR **OWN** TILL I GET BACK?
I WILL.
OF COURSE, BETH.
BE GOOD, PRINCESS.
WE'LL CHANGE THE WORLD ONE DAY AT A TIME.
WOO! WOO! OKAY?
MOTHER?
ARE YOU PRESENT?

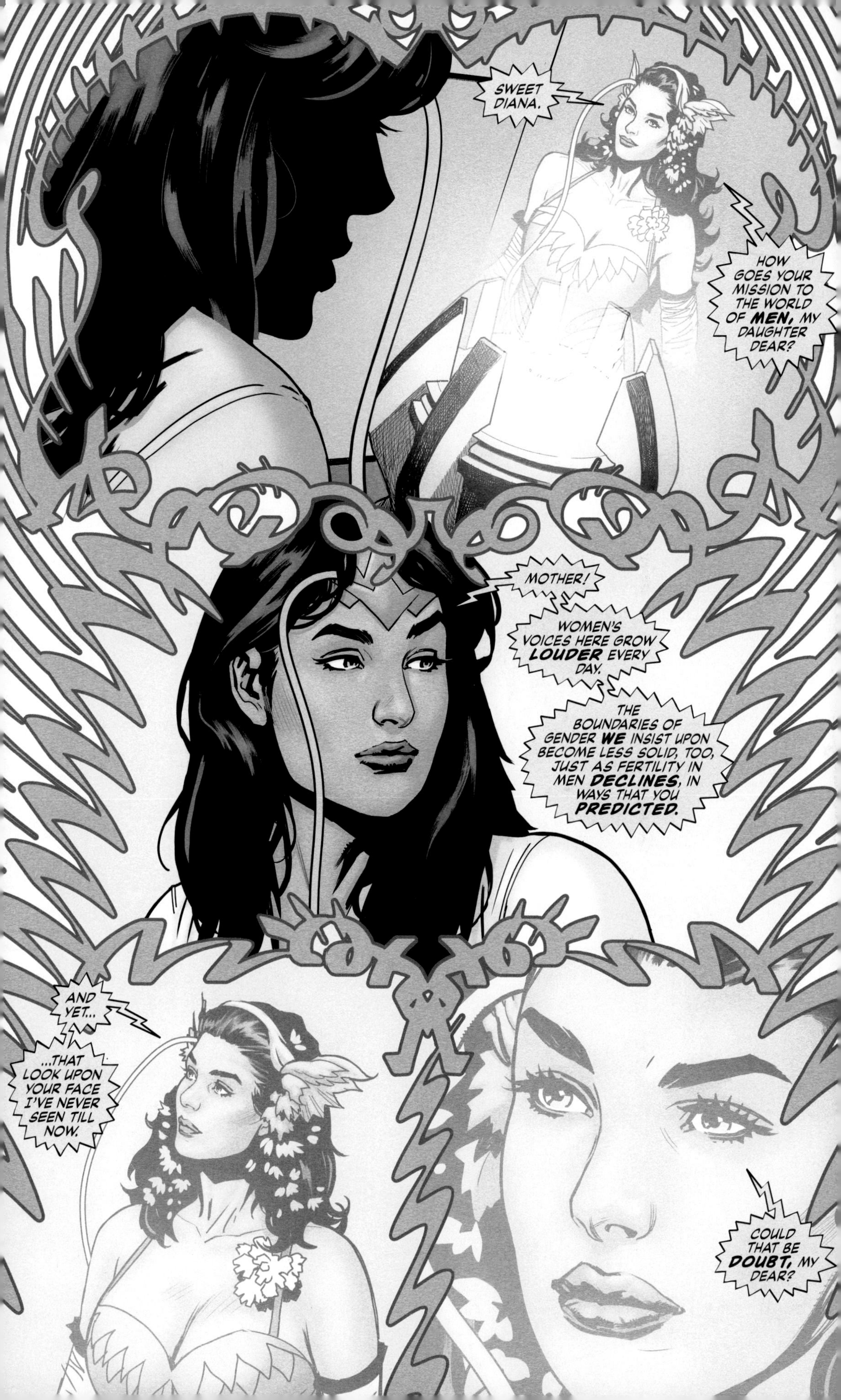
SWEET DIANA.
HOW GOES YOUR MISSION TO THE WORLD OF **MEN,** MY DAUGHTER DEAR?
MOTHER!
WOMEN'S VOICES HERE GROW **LOUDER** EVERY DAY.
THE BOUNDARIES OF GENDER **WE** INSIST UPON BECOME LESS SOLID, TOO, JUST AS FERTILITY IN MEN **DECLINES**, IN WAYS THAT YOU **PREDICTED.**
AND YET...
...THAT LOOK UPON YOUR FACE I'VE NEVER SEEN TILL NOW.
COULD THAT BE **DOUBT,** MY DEAR?

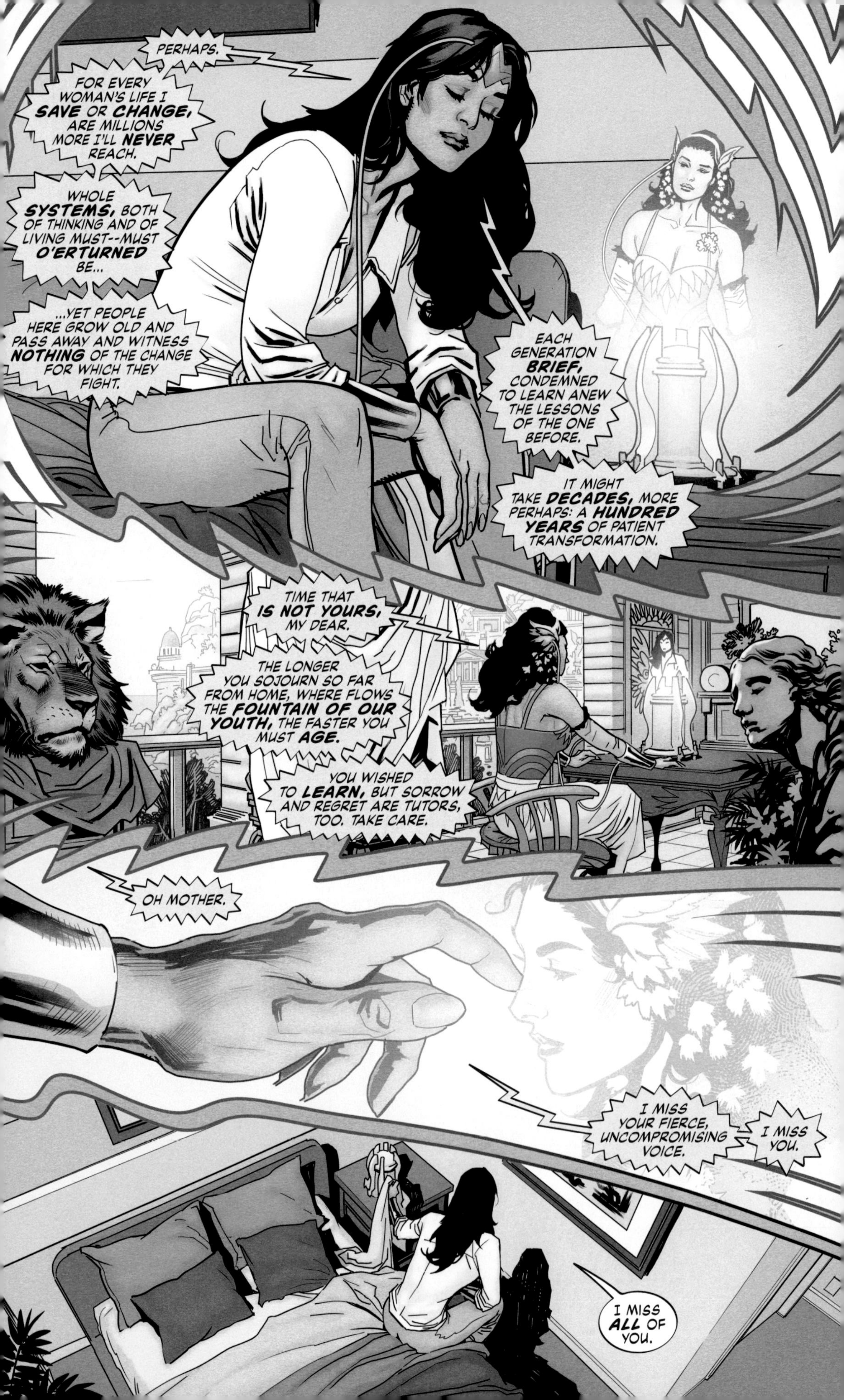
PERHAPS.
FOR EVERY WOMAN'S LIFE I SAVE OR CHANGE, ARE MILLIONS MORE I'LL NEVER REACH.
WHOLE SYSTEMS, BOTH OF THINKING AND OF LIVING MUST--MUST O'ERTURNED BE...
...YET PEOPLE HERE GROW OLD AND PASS AWAY AND WITNESS NOTHING OF THE CHANGE FOR WHICH THEY FIGHT.
EACH GENERATION BRIEF, CONDEMNED TO LEARN ANEW THE LESSONS OF THE ONE BEFORE.
IT MIGHT TAKE DECADES, MORE PERHAPS: A HUNDRED YEARS OF PATIENT TRANSFORMATION.
TIME THAT IS NOT YOURS, MY DEAR.
THE LONGER YOU SOJOURN SO FAR FROM HOME, WHERE FLOWS THE FOUNTAIN OF OUR YOUTH, THE FASTER YOU MUST AGE.
YOU WISHED TO LEARN, BUT SORROW AND REGRET ARE TUTORS, TOO. TAKE CARE.
OH MOTHER.
I MISS YOUR FIERCE, UNCOMPROMISING VOICE.
I MISS YOU.
I MISS ALL OF YOU.

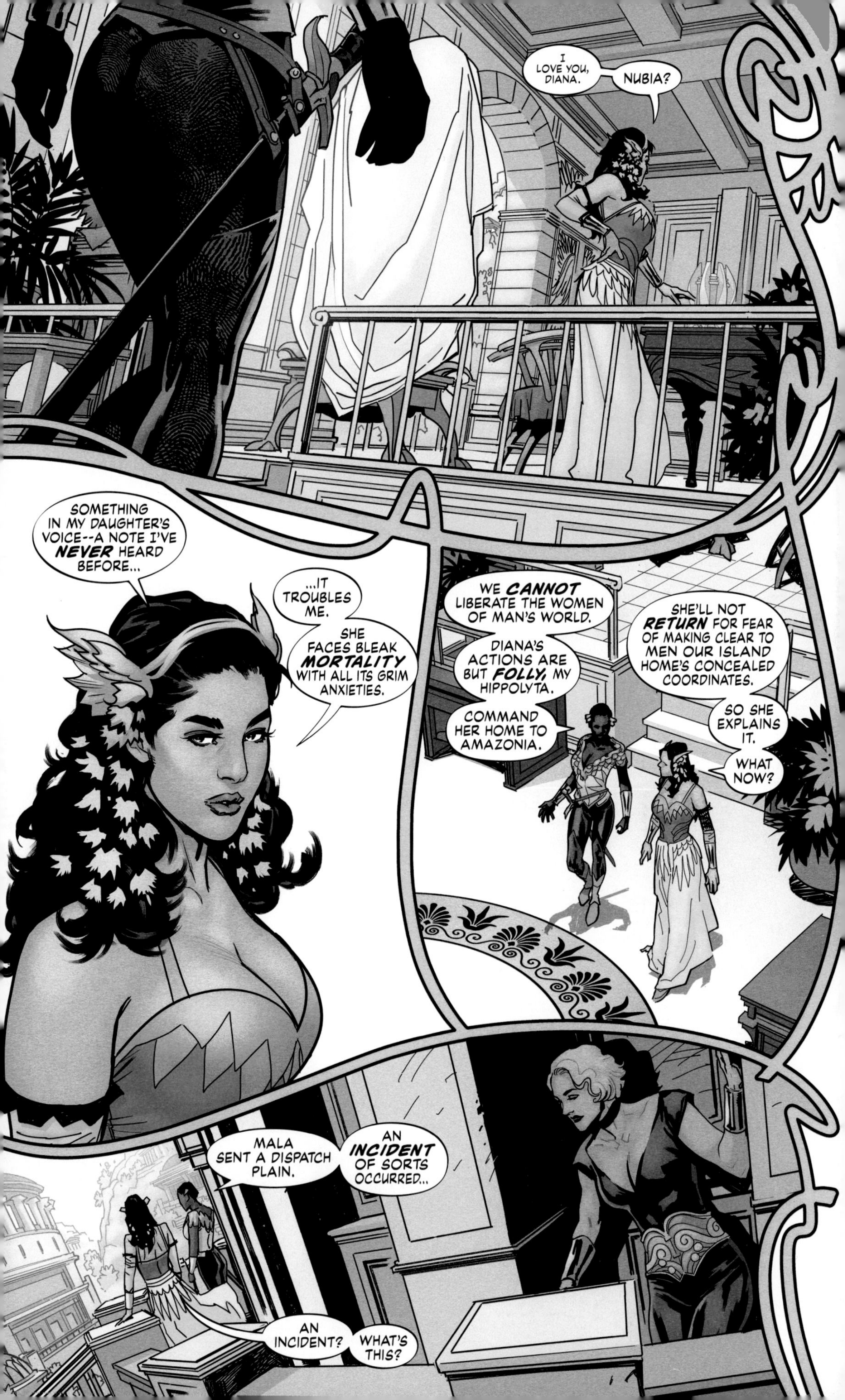
I LOVE YOU, DIANA.
NUBIA?
SOMETHING IN MY DAUGHTER'S VOICE--A NOTE I'VE NEVER HEARD BEFORE...
...IT TROUBLES ME.
SHE FACES BLEAK MORTALITY WITH ALL ITS GRIM ANXIETIES.
WE CANNOT LIBERATE THE WOMEN OF MAN'S WORLD.
DIANA'S ACTIONS ARE BUT FOLLY, MY HIPPOLYTA.
COMMAND HER HOME TO AMAZONIA.
SHE'LL NOT RETURN FOR FEAR OF MAKING CLEAR TO MEN OUR ISLAND HOME'S CONCEALED COORDINATES.
SO SHE EXPLAINS IT.
WHAT NOW?
MALA SENT A DISPATCH PLAIN.
AN INCIDENT OF SORTS OCCURRED...
AN INCIDENT?
WHAT'S THIS?

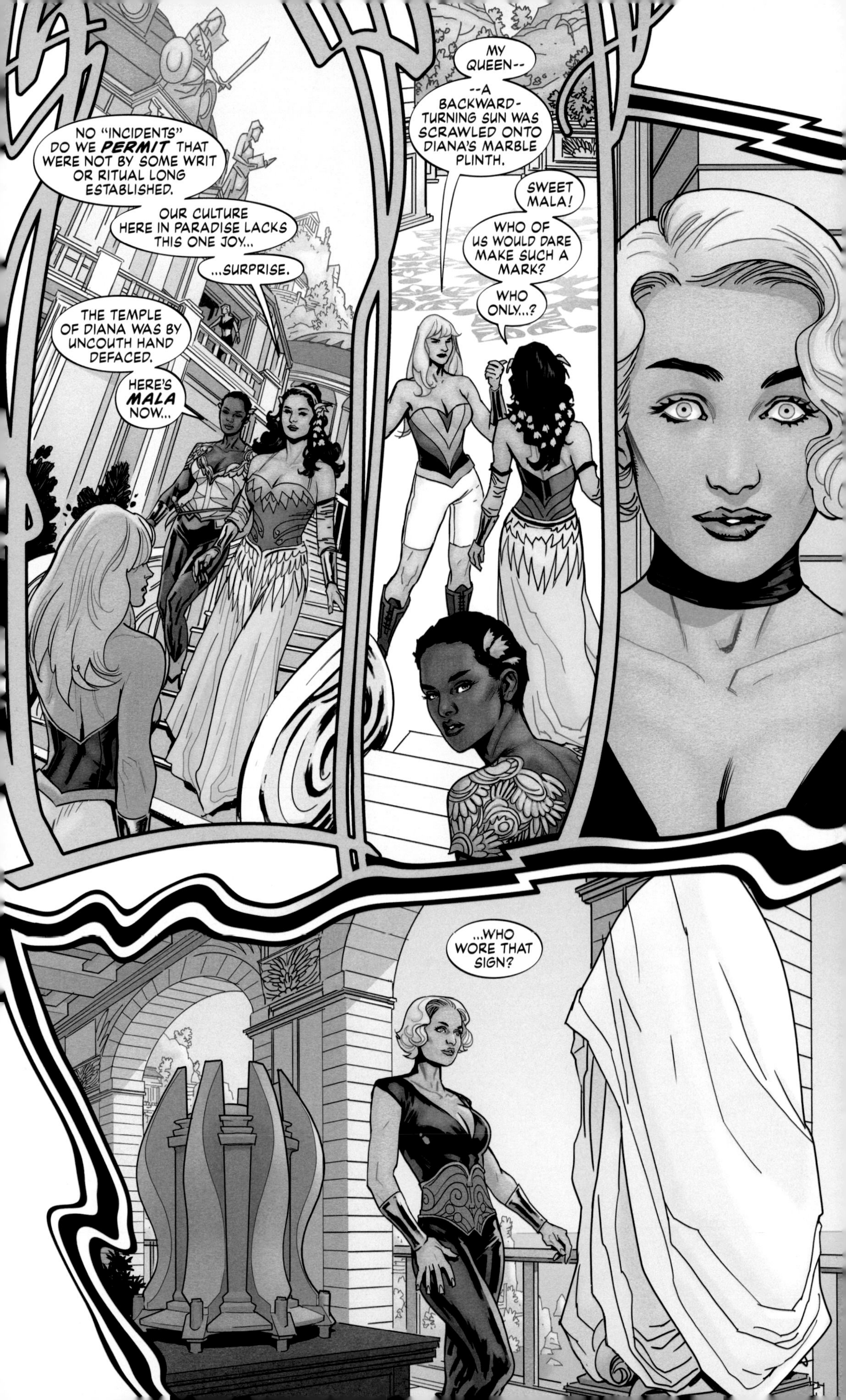
NO "INCIDENTS" DO WE PERMIT THAT WERE NOT BY SOME WRIT OR RITUAL LONG ESTABLISHED.
OUR CULTURE HERE IN PARADISE LACKS THIS ONE JOY...
...SURPRISE.
THE TEMPLE OF DIANA WAS BY UNCOUTH HAND DEFACED.
HERE'S MALA NOW...
MY QUEEN--
--A BACKWARD-TURNING SUN WAS SCRAWLED ONTO DIANA'S MARBLE PLINTH.
SWEET MALA!
WHO OF US WOULD DARE MAKE SUCH A MARK?
WHO ONLY...?
...WHO WORE THAT SIGN?

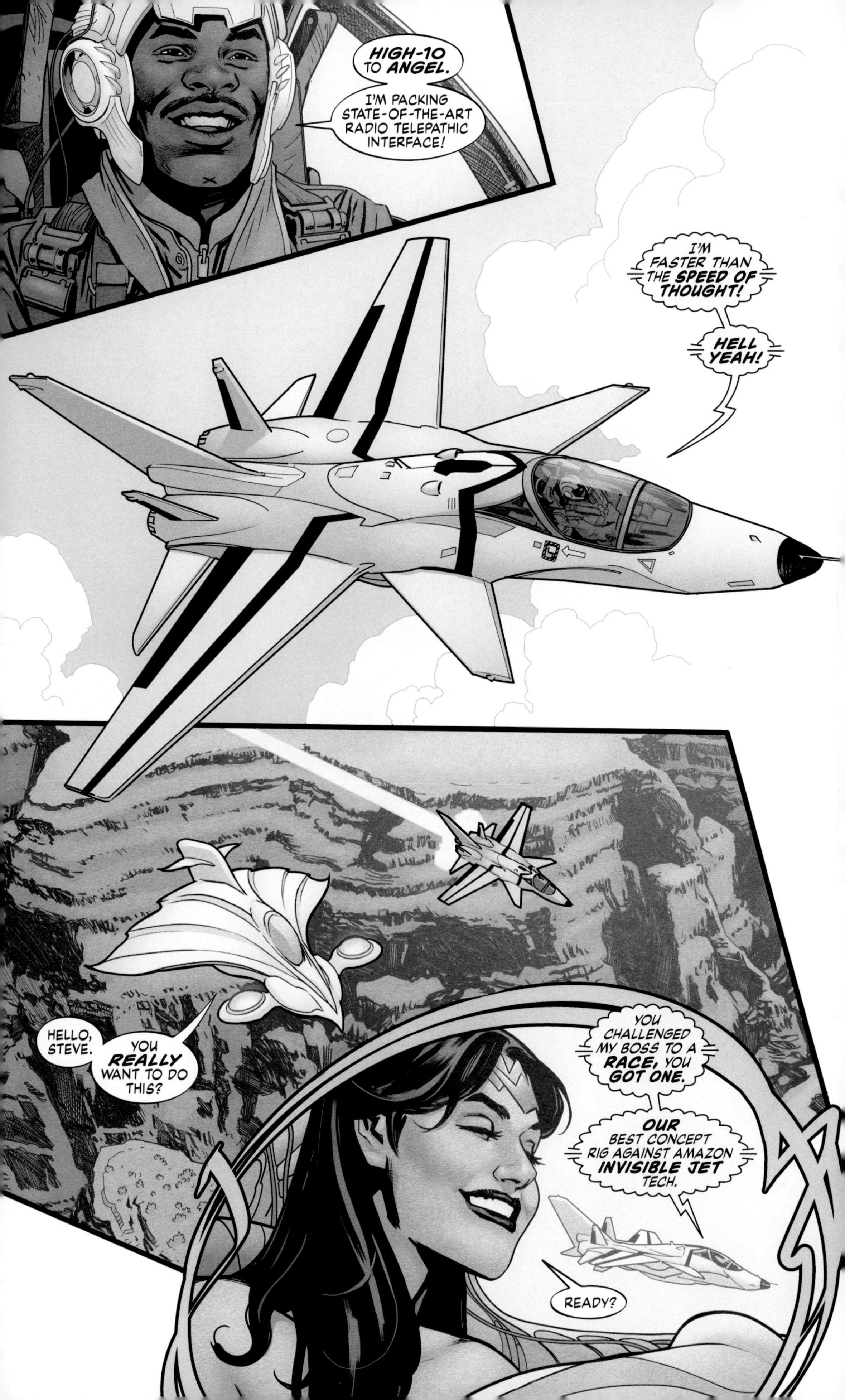

HIGH-10 TO ANGEL.
I'M PACKING STATE-OF-THE-ART RADIO TELEPATHIC INTERFACE!
I'M FASTER THAN THE SPEED OF THOUGHT!
HELL YEAH!
HELLO, STEVE.
YOU REALLY WANT TO DO THIS?
YOU CHALLENGED MY BOSS TO A RACE, YOU GOT ONE.
OUR BEST CONCEPT RIG AGAINST AMAZON INVISIBLE JET TECH.
READY?

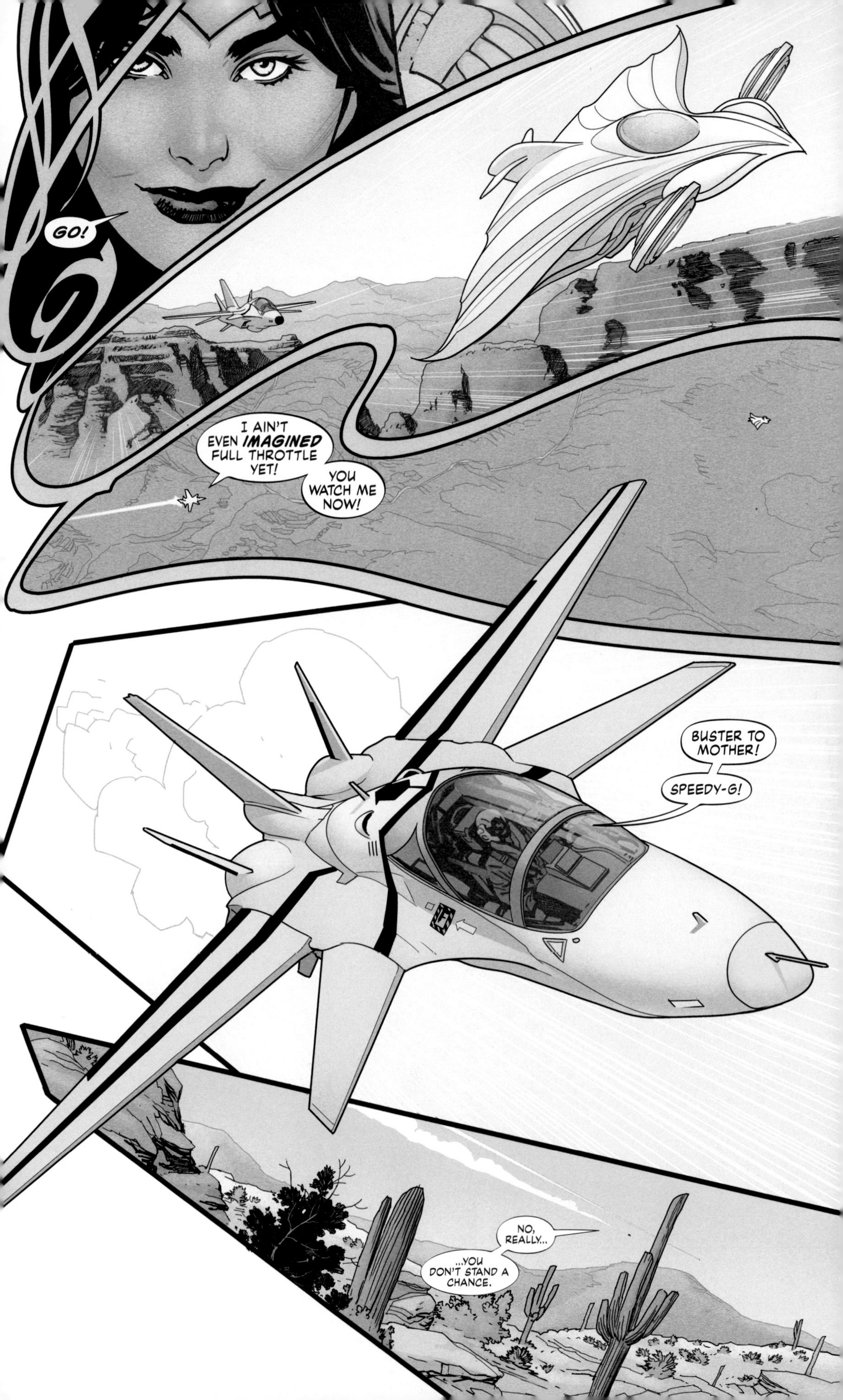
GO!
I AIN'T EVEN *IMAGINED* FULL THROTTLE YET!
YOU WATCH ME NOW!
BUSTER TO MOTHER!
SPEEDY-G!
NO, REALLY...
...YOU DON'T STAND A CHANCE.

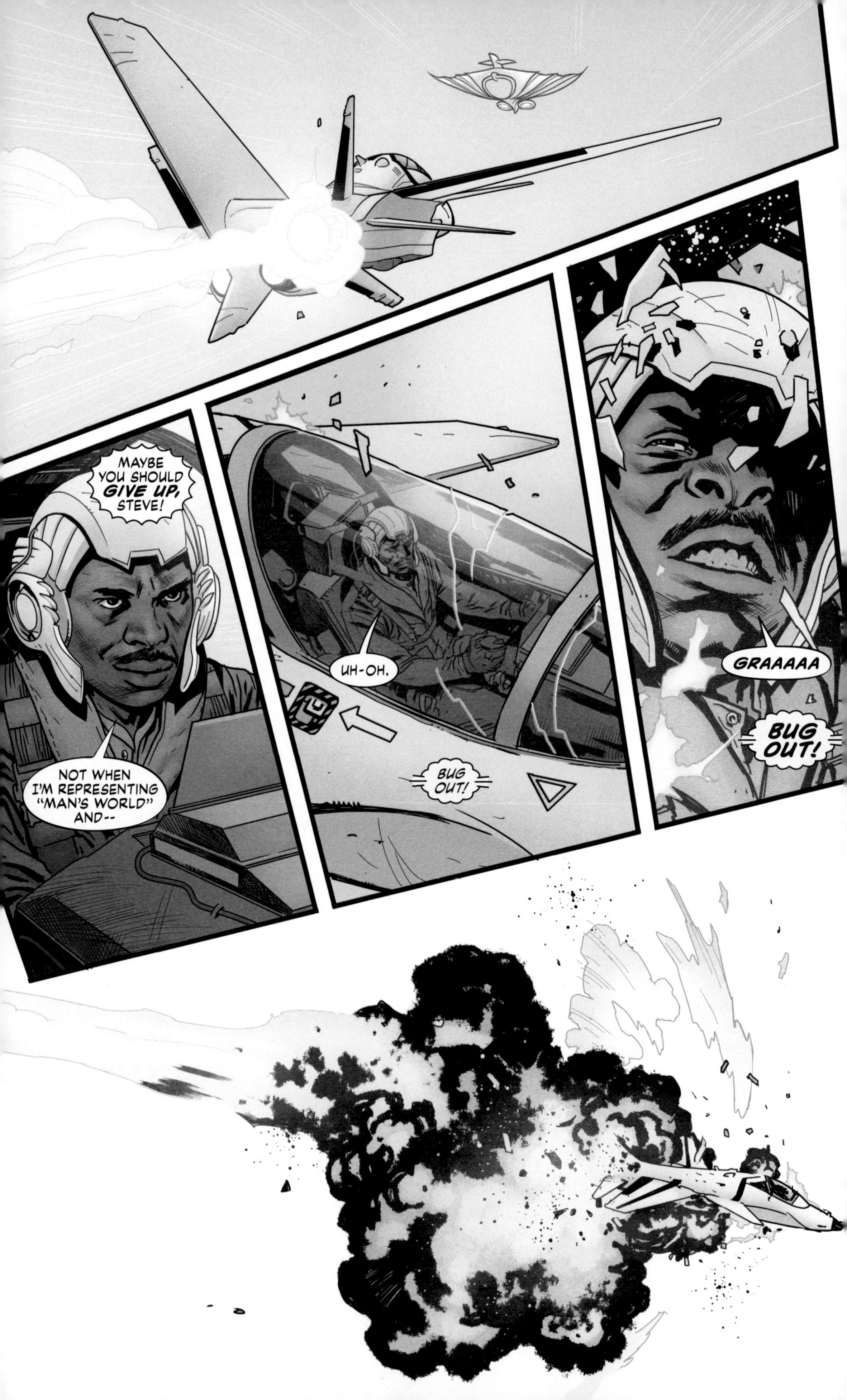
MAYBE YOU SHOULD GIVE UP, STEVE!
NOT WHEN I'M REPRESENTING "MAN'S WORLD" AND--
UH-OH.
BUG OUT!
GRAAAAA
BUG OUT!

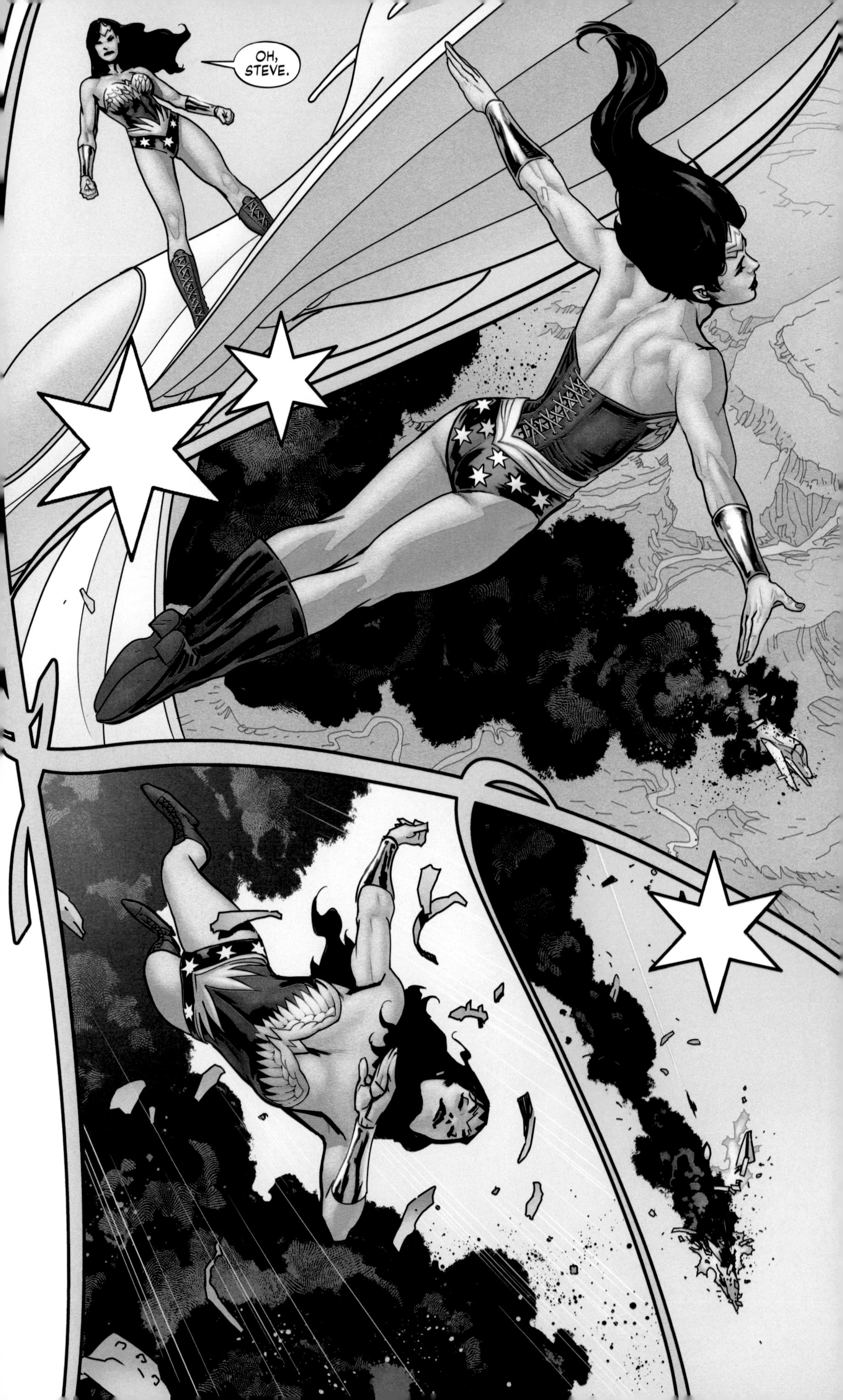
OH, STEVE.

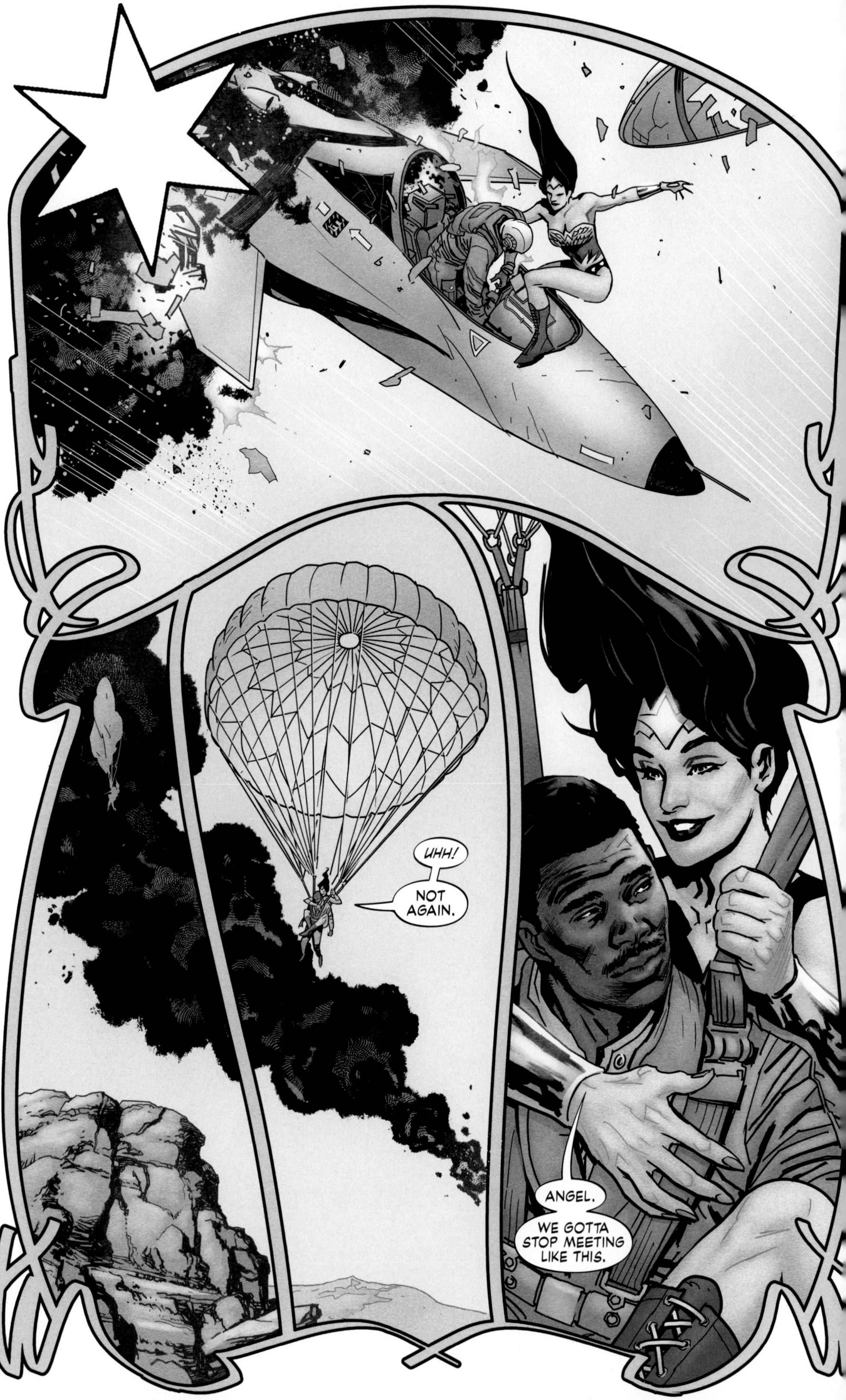
UHH!
NOT AGAIN.
ANGEL.
WE GOTTA STOP MEETING LIKE THIS.

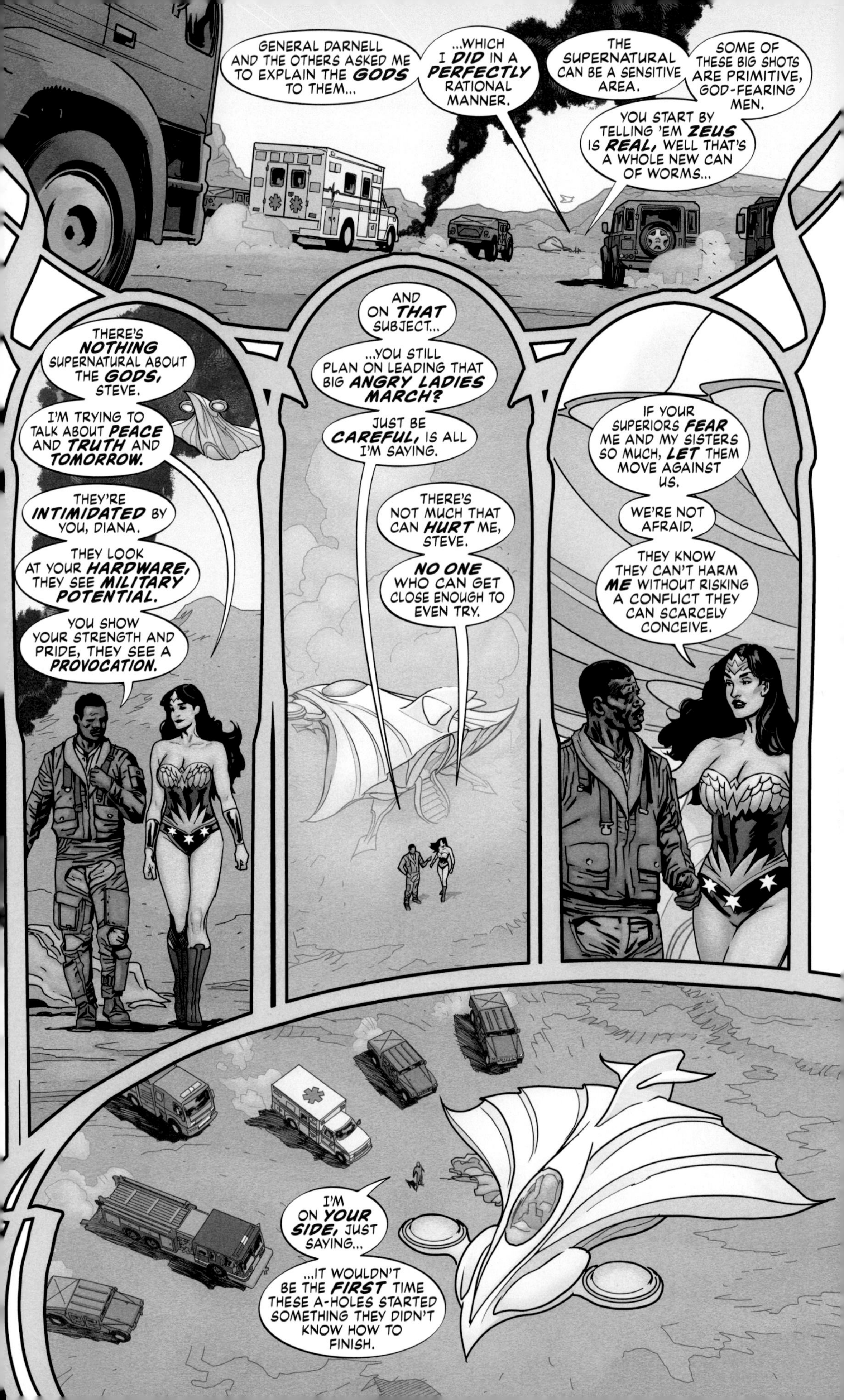
GENERAL DARNELL AND THE OTHERS ASKED ME TO EXPLAIN THE GODS TO THEM...
...WHICH I DID IN A PERFECTLY RATIONAL MANNER.
THE SUPERNATURAL CAN BE A SENSITIVE AREA.
SOME OF THESE BIG SHOTS ARE PRIMITIVE, GOD-FEARING MEN.
YOU START BY TELLING 'EM ZEUS IS REAL, WELL THAT'S A WHOLE NEW CAN OF WORMS...
THERE'S NOTHING SUPERNATURAL ABOUT THE GODS, STEVE.
I'M TRYING TO TALK ABOUT PEACE AND TRUTH AND TOMORROW.
THEY'RE INTIMIDATED BY YOU, DIANA.
THEY LOOK AT YOUR HARDWARE, THEY SEE MILITARY POTENTIAL.
YOU SHOW YOUR STRENGTH AND PRIDE, THEY SEE A PROVOCATION.
AND ON THAT SUBJECT...
...YOU STILL PLAN ON LEADING THAT BIG ANGRY LADIES MARCH?
JUST BE CAREFUL, IS ALL I'M SAYING.
THERE'S NOT MUCH THAT CAN HURT ME, STEVE.
NO ONE WHO CAN GET CLOSE ENOUGH TO EVEN TRY.
IF YOUR SUPERIORS FEAR ME AND MY SISTERS SO MUCH, LET THEM MOVE AGAINST US.
WE'RE NOT AFRAID.
THEY KNOW THEY CAN'T HARM ME WITHOUT RISKING A CONFLICT THEY CAN SCARCELY CONCEIVE.
I'M ON YOUR SIDE, JUST SAYING...
...IT WOULDN'T BE THE FIRST TIME THESE A-HOLES STARTED SOMETHING THEY DIDN'T KNOW HOW TO FINISH.

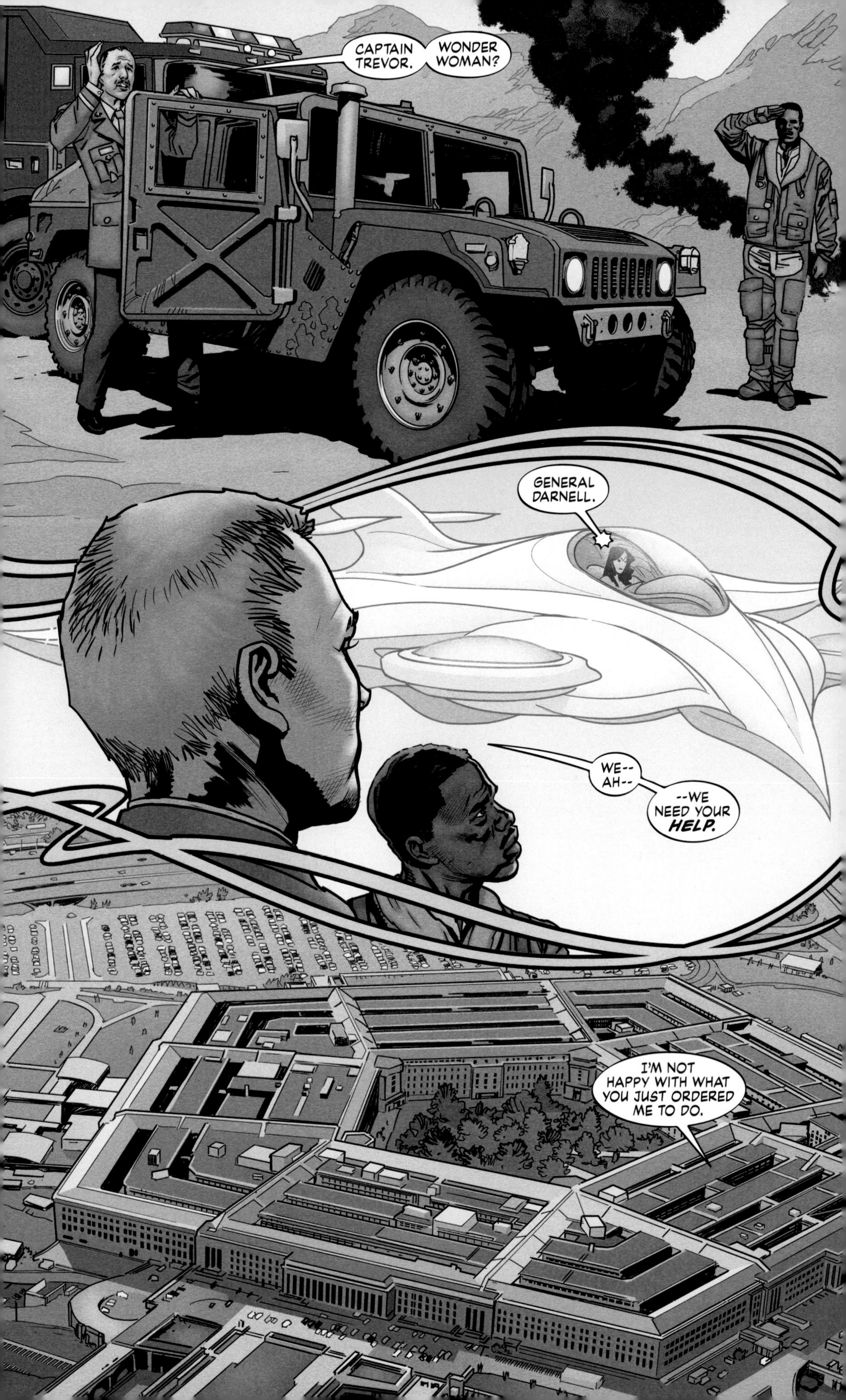
CAPTAIN TREVOR.
WONDER WOMAN?
GENERAL DARNELL.
WE-- AH--
--WE NEED YOUR HELP.
I'M NOT HAPPY WITH WHAT YOU JUST ORDERED ME TO DO.

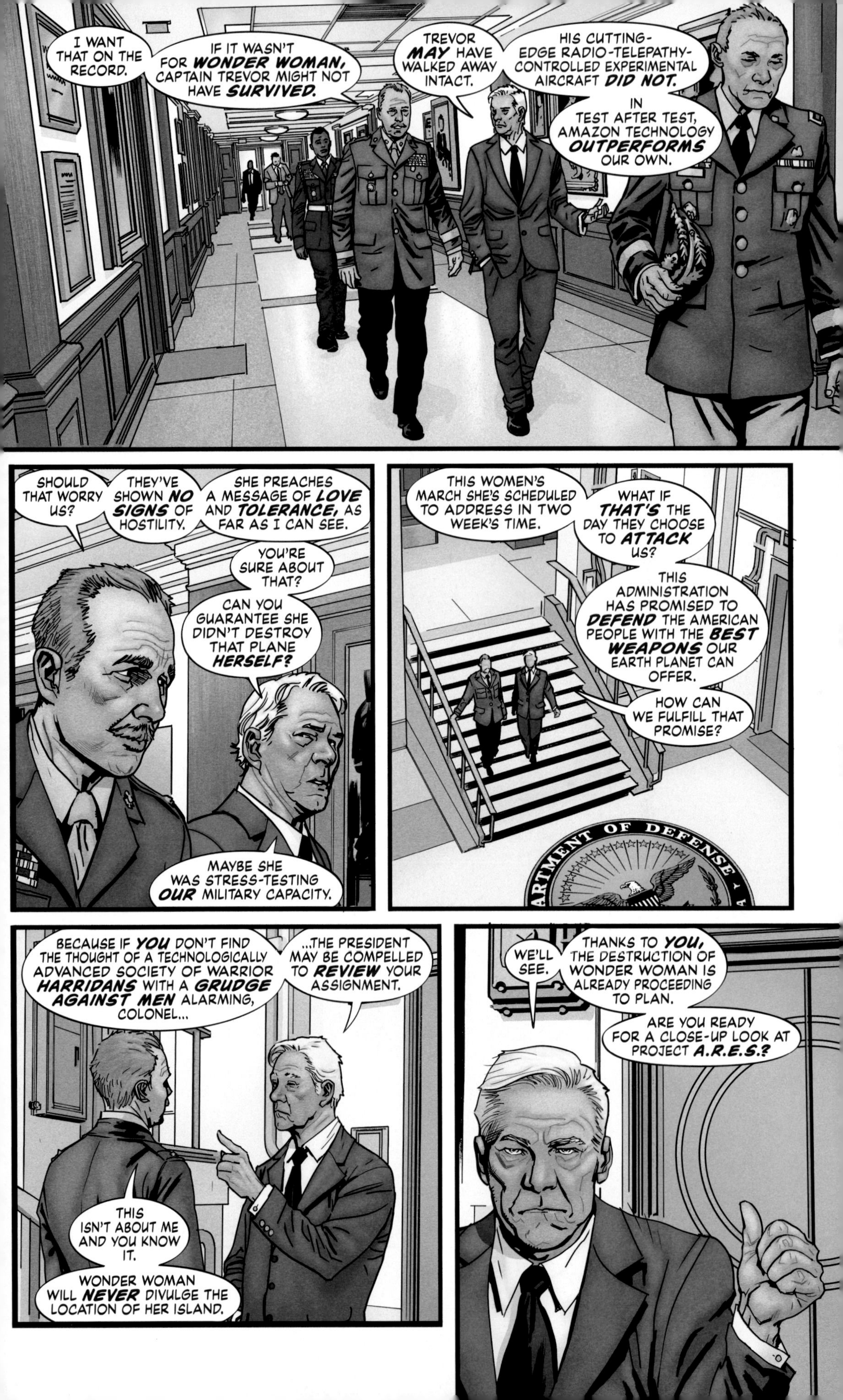
I WANT THAT ON THE RECORD.
IF IT WASN'T FOR WONDER WOMAN, CAPTAIN TREVOR MIGHT NOT HAVE SURVIVED.
TREVOR MAY HAVE WALKED AWAY INTACT.
HIS CUTTING-EDGE RADIO-TELEPATHY-CONTROLLED EXPERIMENTAL AIRCRAFT DID NOT.
IN TEST AFTER TEST, AMAZON TECHNOLOGY OUTPERFORMS OUR OWN.
SHOULD THAT WORRY US?
THEY'VE SHOWN NO SIGNS OF HOSTILITY.
SHE PREACHES A MESSAGE OF LOVE AND TOLERANCE, AS FAR AS I CAN SEE.
YOU'RE SURE ABOUT THAT?
CAN YOU GUARANTEE SHE DIDN'T DESTROY THAT PLANE HERSELF?
MAYBE SHE WAS STRESS-TESTING OUR MILITARY CAPACITY.
THIS WOMEN'S MARCH SHE'S SCHEDULED TO ADDRESS IN TWO WEEK'S TIME.
WHAT IF THAT'S THE DAY THEY CHOOSE TO ATTACK US?
THIS ADMINISTRATION HAS PROMISED TO DEFEND THE AMERICAN PEOPLE WITH THE BEST WEAPONS OUR EARTH PLANET CAN OFFER.
HOW CAN WE FULFILL THAT PROMISE?
DEPARTMENT OF DEFENSE
BECAUSE IF YOU DON'T FIND THE THOUGHT OF A TECHNOLOGICALLY ADVANCED SOCIETY OF WARRIOR HARRIDANS WITH A GRUDGE AGAINST MEN ALARMING, COLONEL...
...THE PRESIDENT MAY BE COMPELLED TO REVIEW YOUR ASSIGNMENT.
THIS ISN'T ABOUT ME AND YOU KNOW IT.
WONDER WOMAN WILL NEVER DIVULGE THE LOCATION OF HER ISLAND.
WE'LL SEE.
THANKS TO YOU, THE DESTRUCTION OF WONDER WOMAN IS ALREADY PROCEEDING TO PLAN.
ARE YOU READY FOR A CLOSE-UP LOOK AT PROJECT A.R.E.S.?

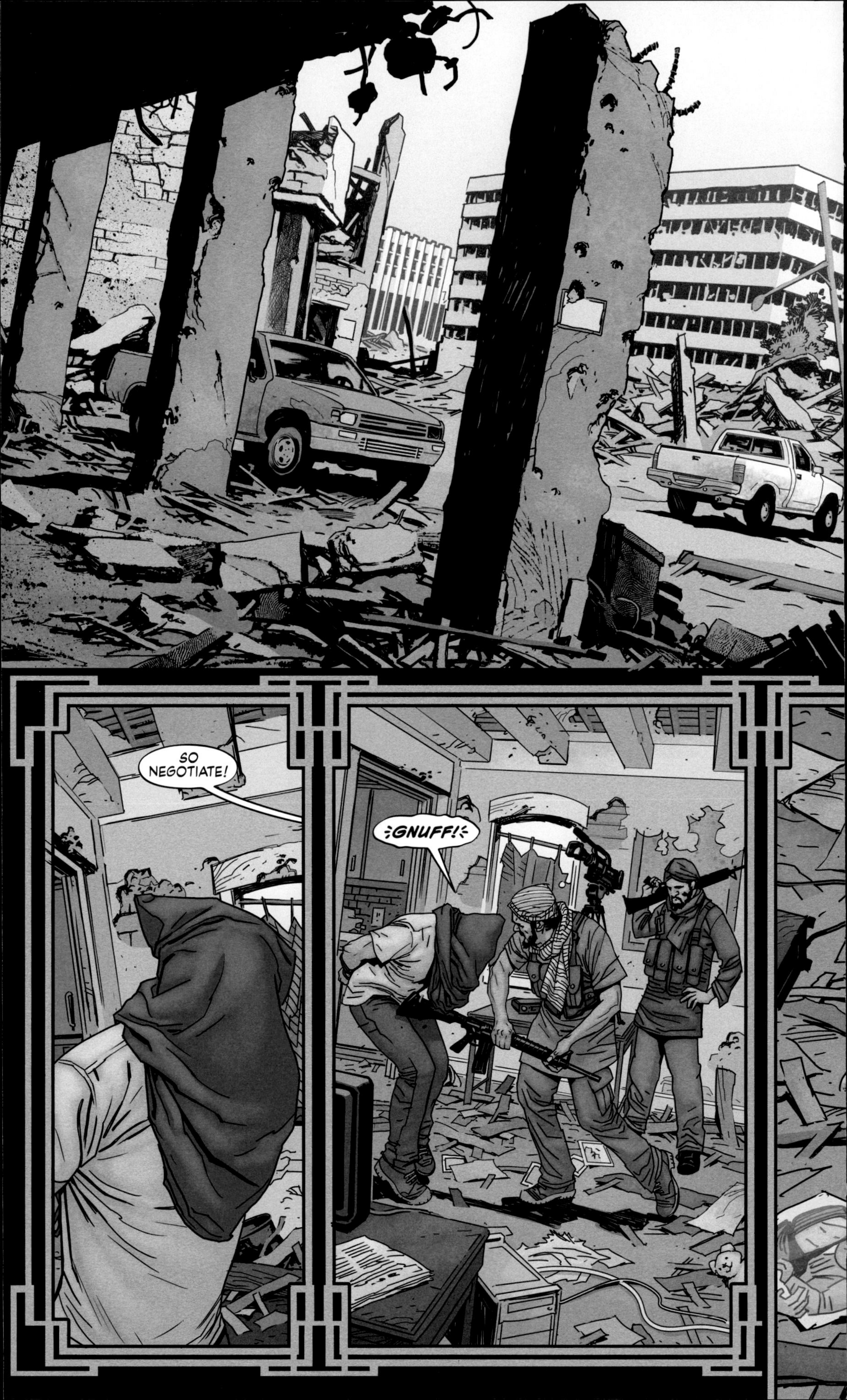
SO NEGOTIATE!
GNUFF!

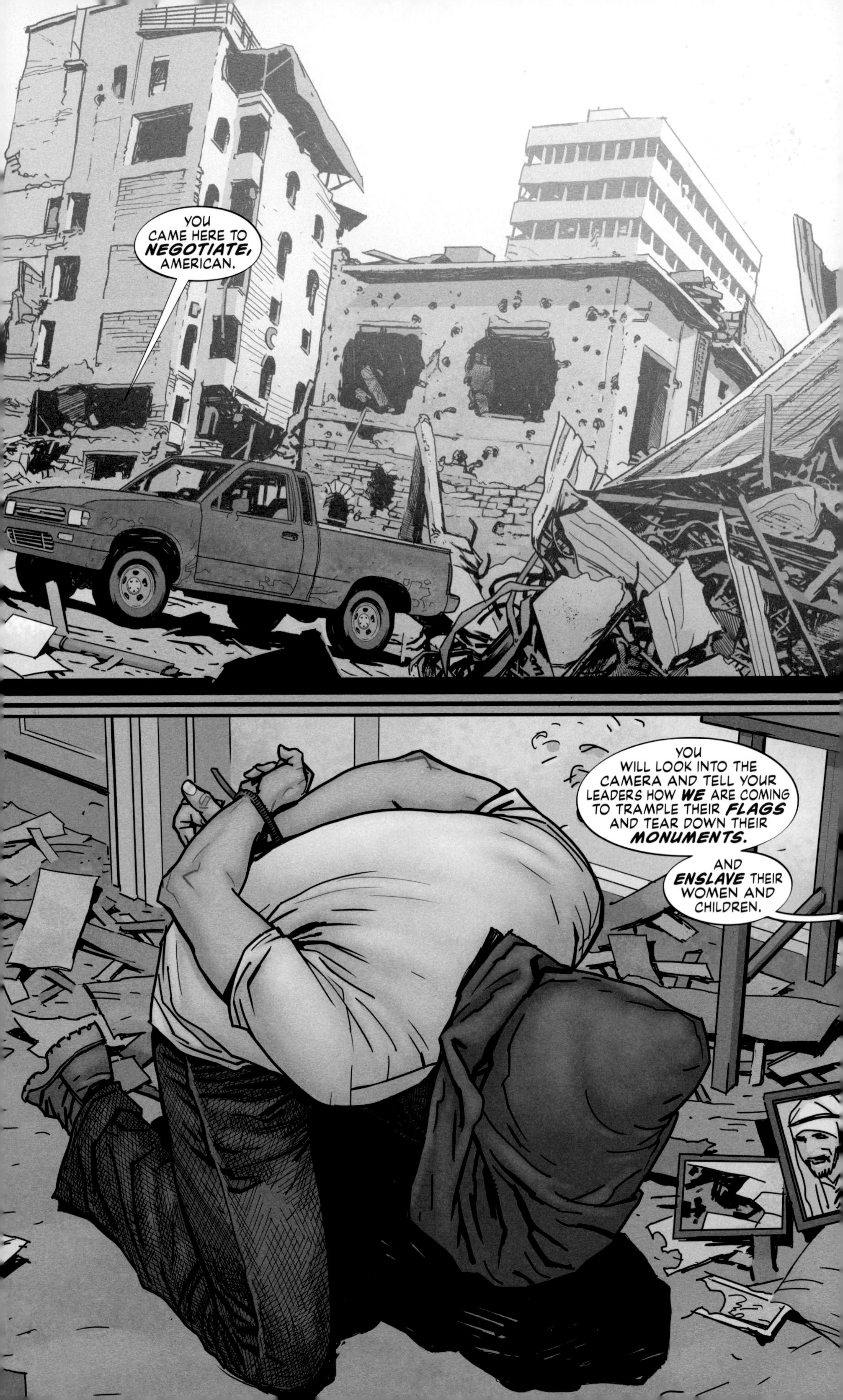
YOU CAME HERE TO NEGOTIATE, AMERICAN.
YOU WILL LOOK INTO THE CAMERA AND TELL YOUR LEADERS HOW WE ARE COMING TO TRAMPLE THEIR FLAGS AND TEAR DOWN THEIR MONUMENTS.
AND ENSLAVE THEIR WOMEN AND CHILDREN.

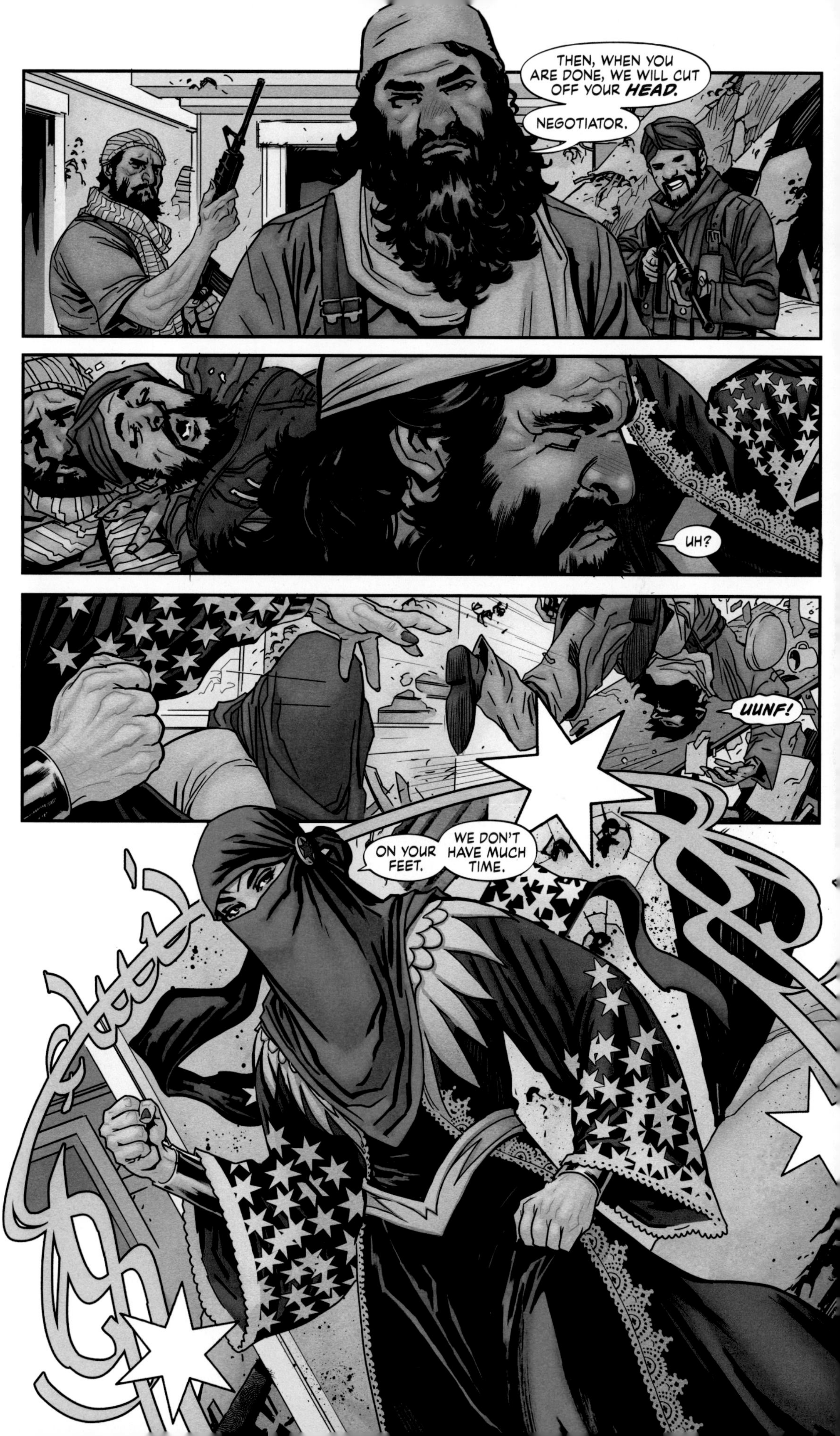
THEN, WHEN YOU ARE DONE, WE WILL CUT OFF YOUR **HEAD.**
NEGOTIATOR.
UH?
UUNF!
ON YOUR FEET.
WE DON'T HAVE MUCH TIME.

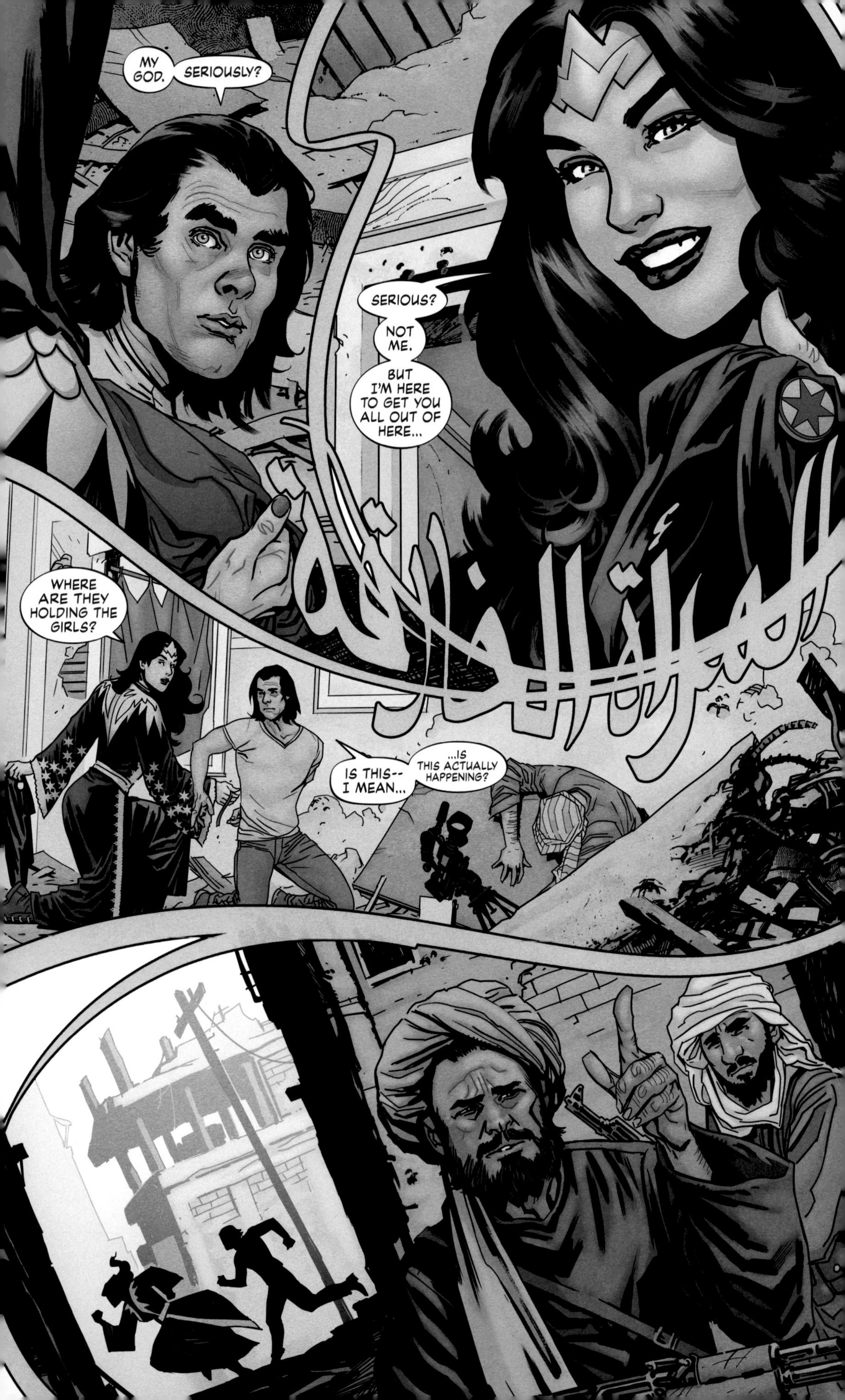
MY GOD.
SERIOUSLY?
SERIOUS?
NOT ME.
BUT I'M HERE TO GET YOU ALL OUT OF HERE...
WHERE ARE THEY HOLDING THE GIRLS?
IS THIS-- I MEAN...
...IS THIS ACTUALLY HAPPENING?

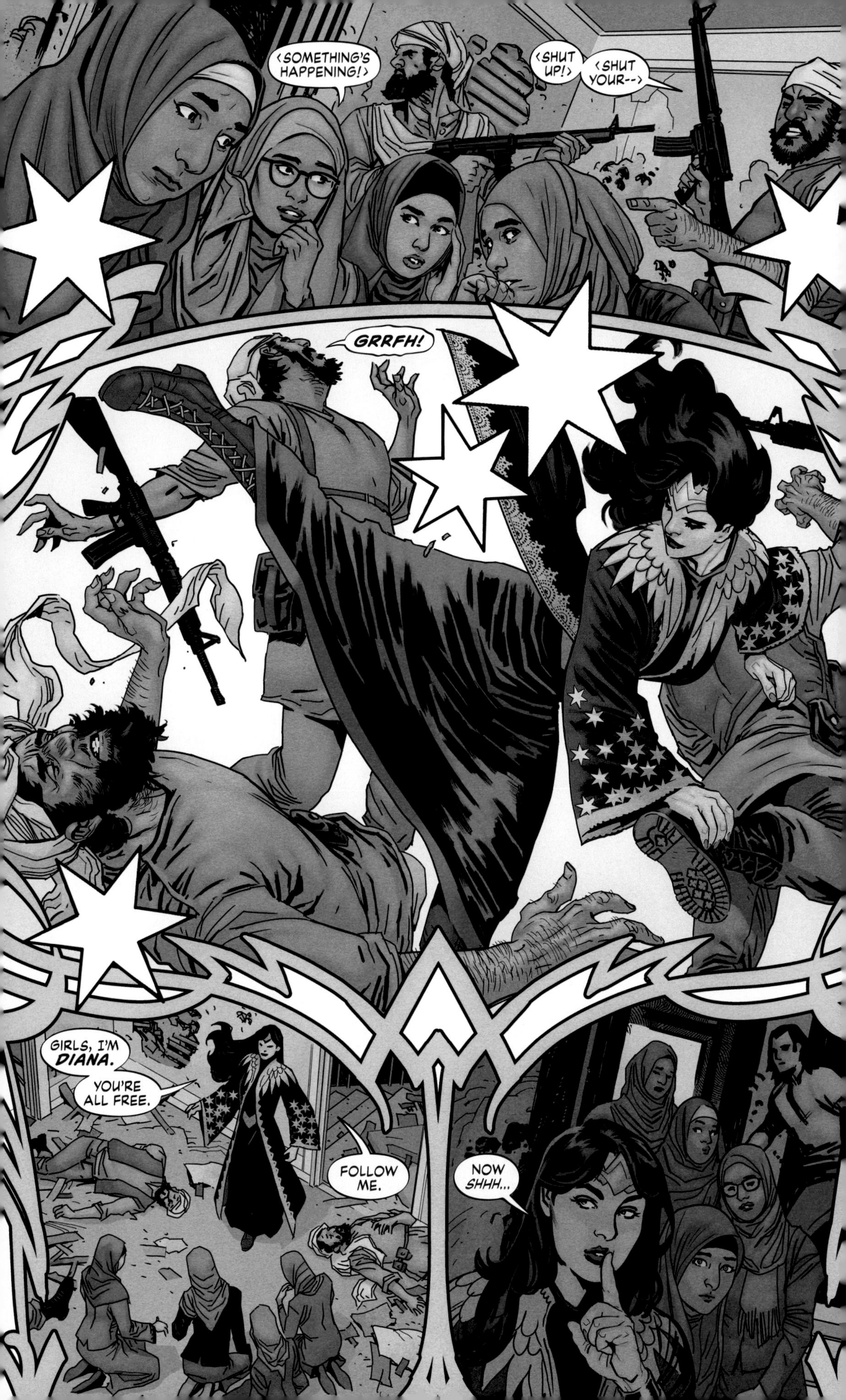
‹SOMETHING'S HAPPENING!›
‹SHUT UP!›
‹SHUT YOUR--›
GRRFH!
GIRLS, I'M DIANA.
YOU'RE ALL FREE.
FOLLOW ME.
NOW SHHH...

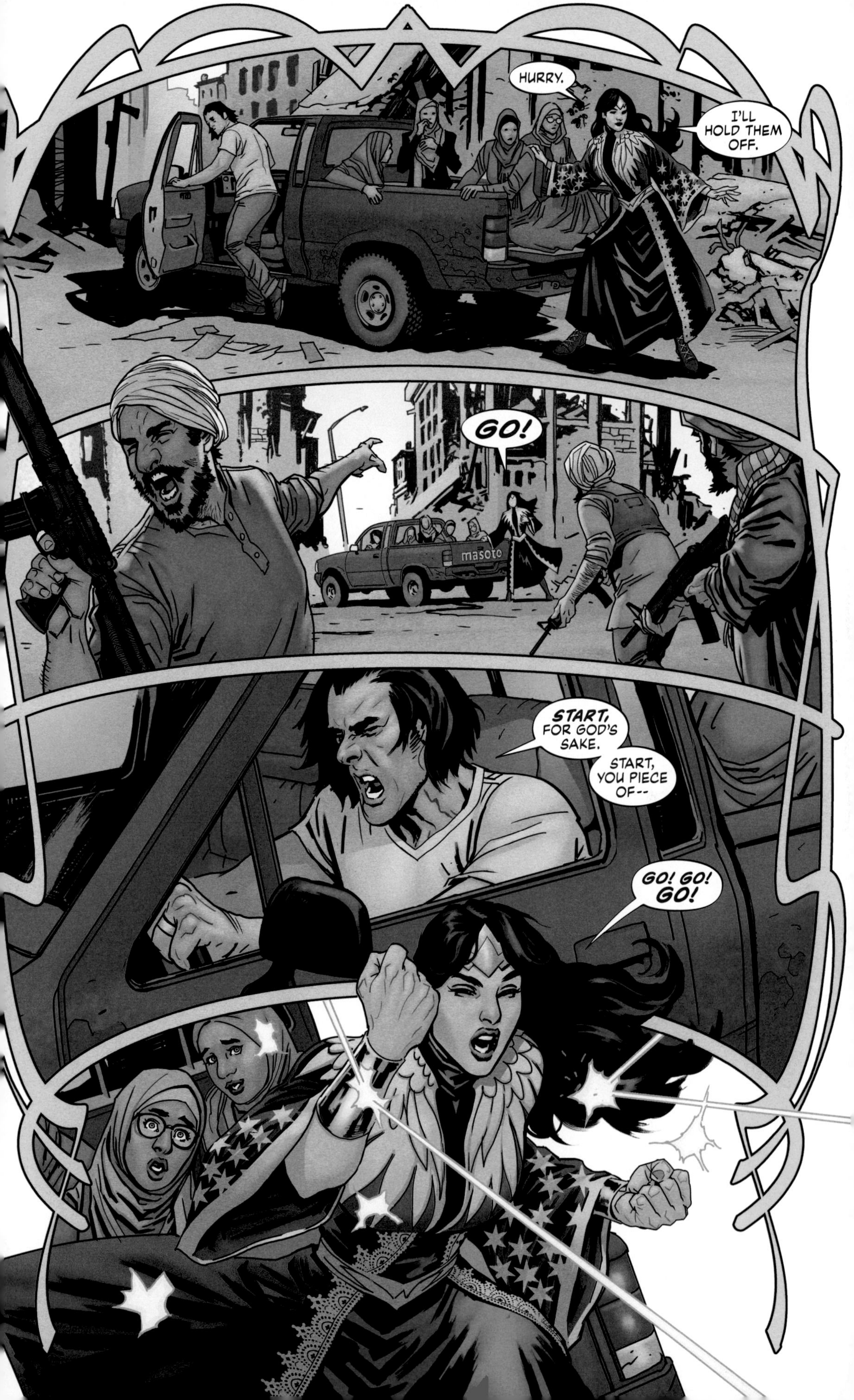
HURRY.
I'LL HOLD THEM OFF.
GO!
START, FOR GOD'S SAKE.
START, YOU PIECE OF--
GO! GO! GO!

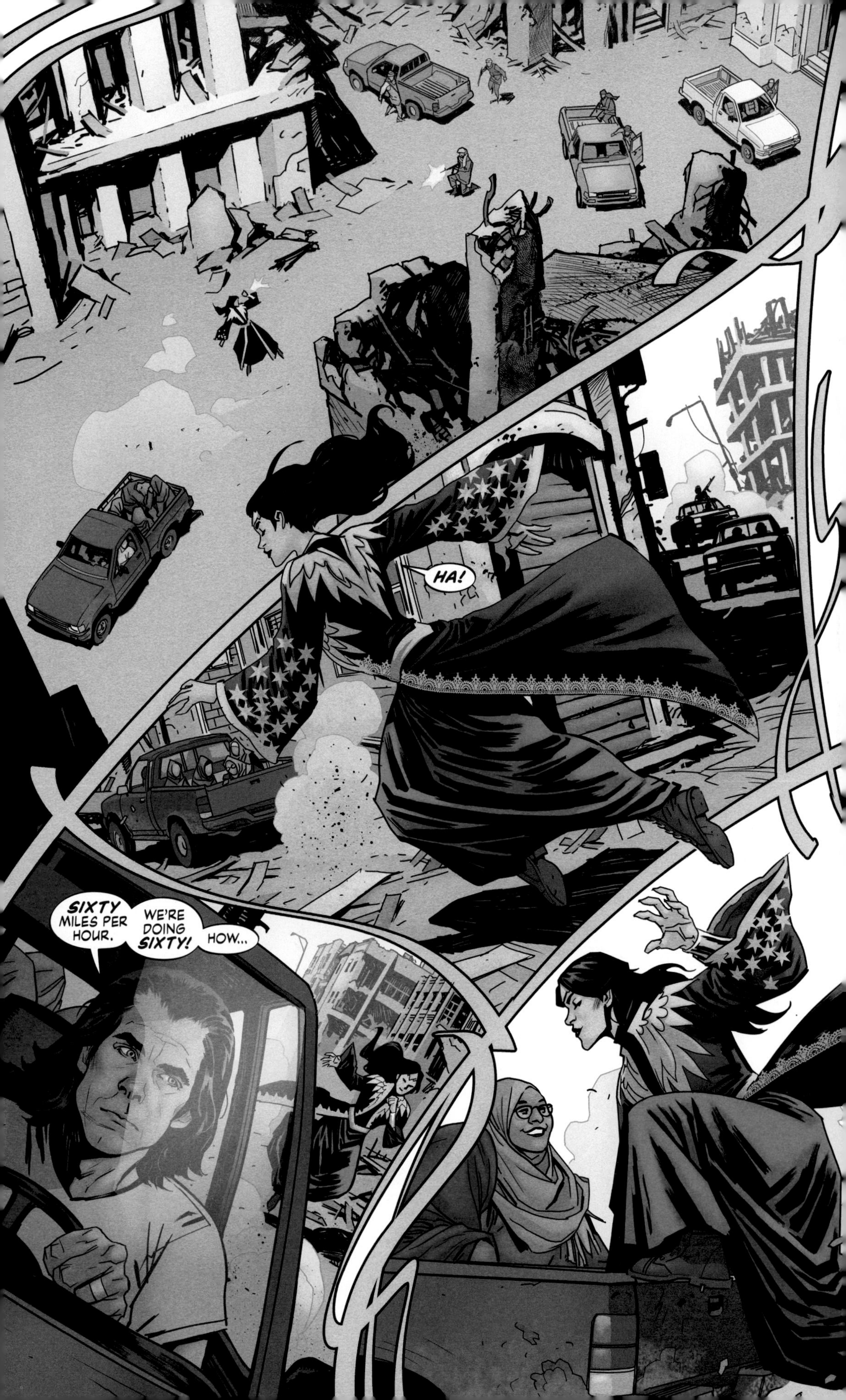
HA!
SIXTY MILES PER HOUR.
WE'RE DOING SIXTY!
HOW...

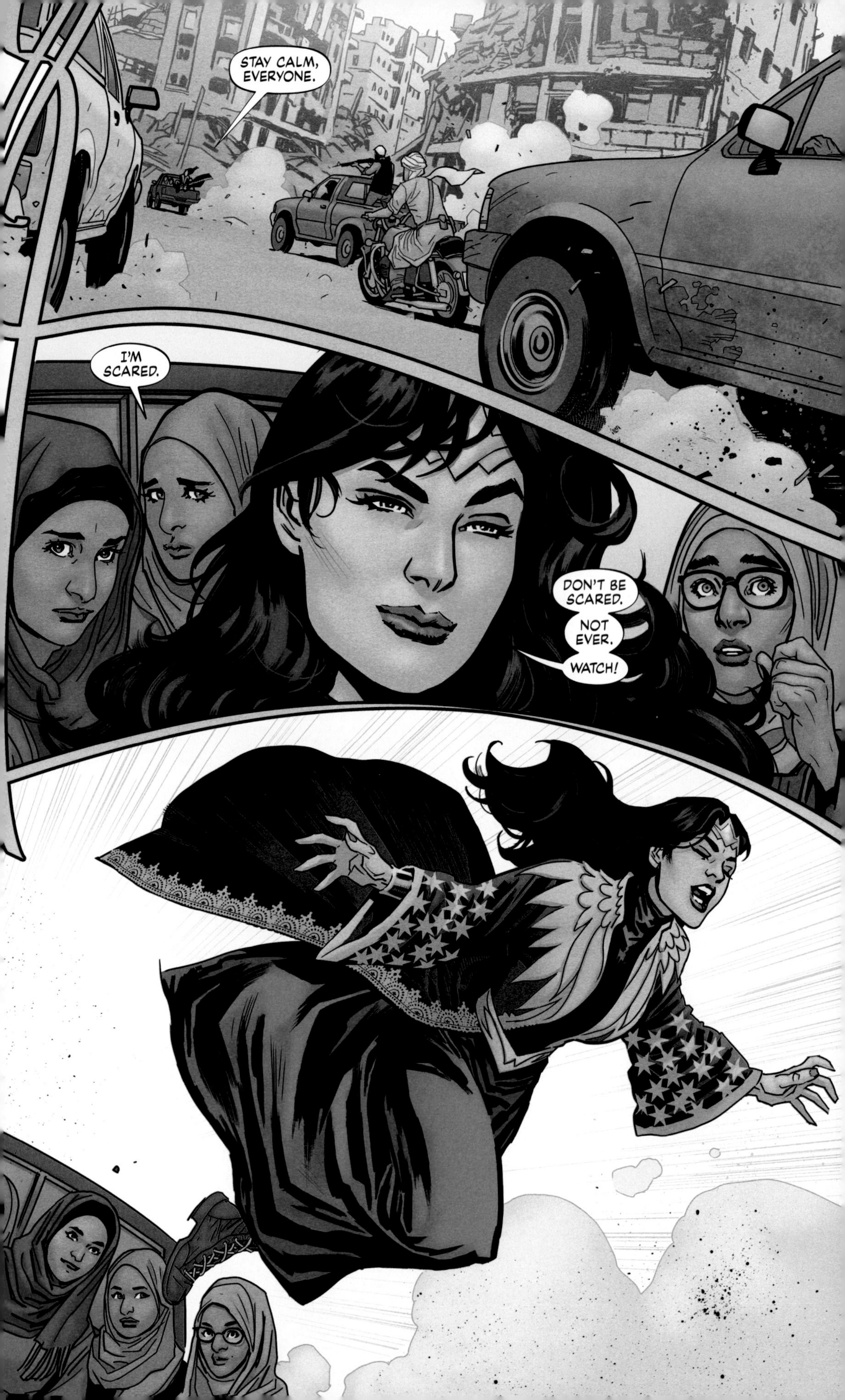
STAY CALM, EVERYONE.
I'M SCARED.
DON'T BE SCARED.
NOT EVER.
WATCH!

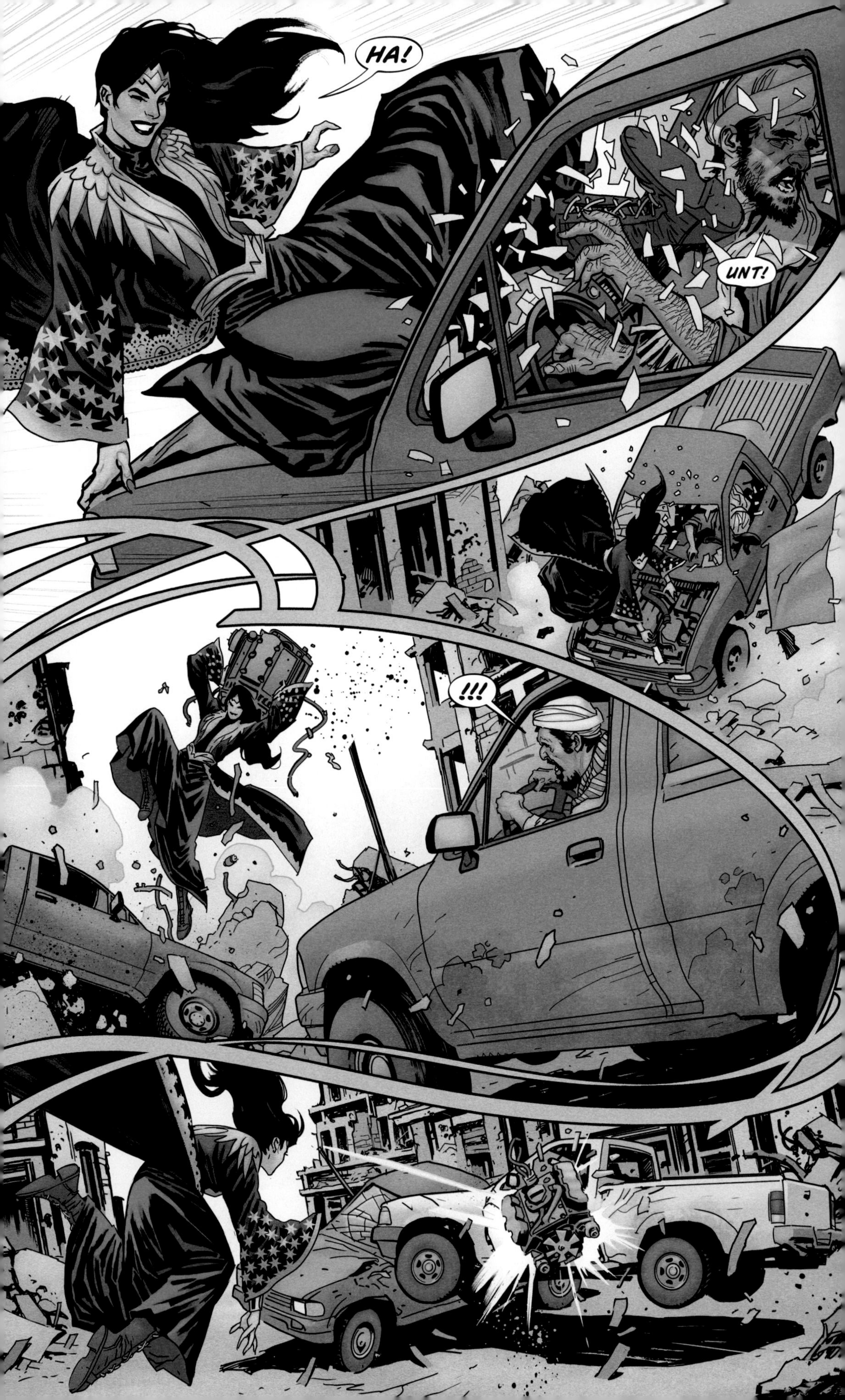
HA!
UNT!
!!!

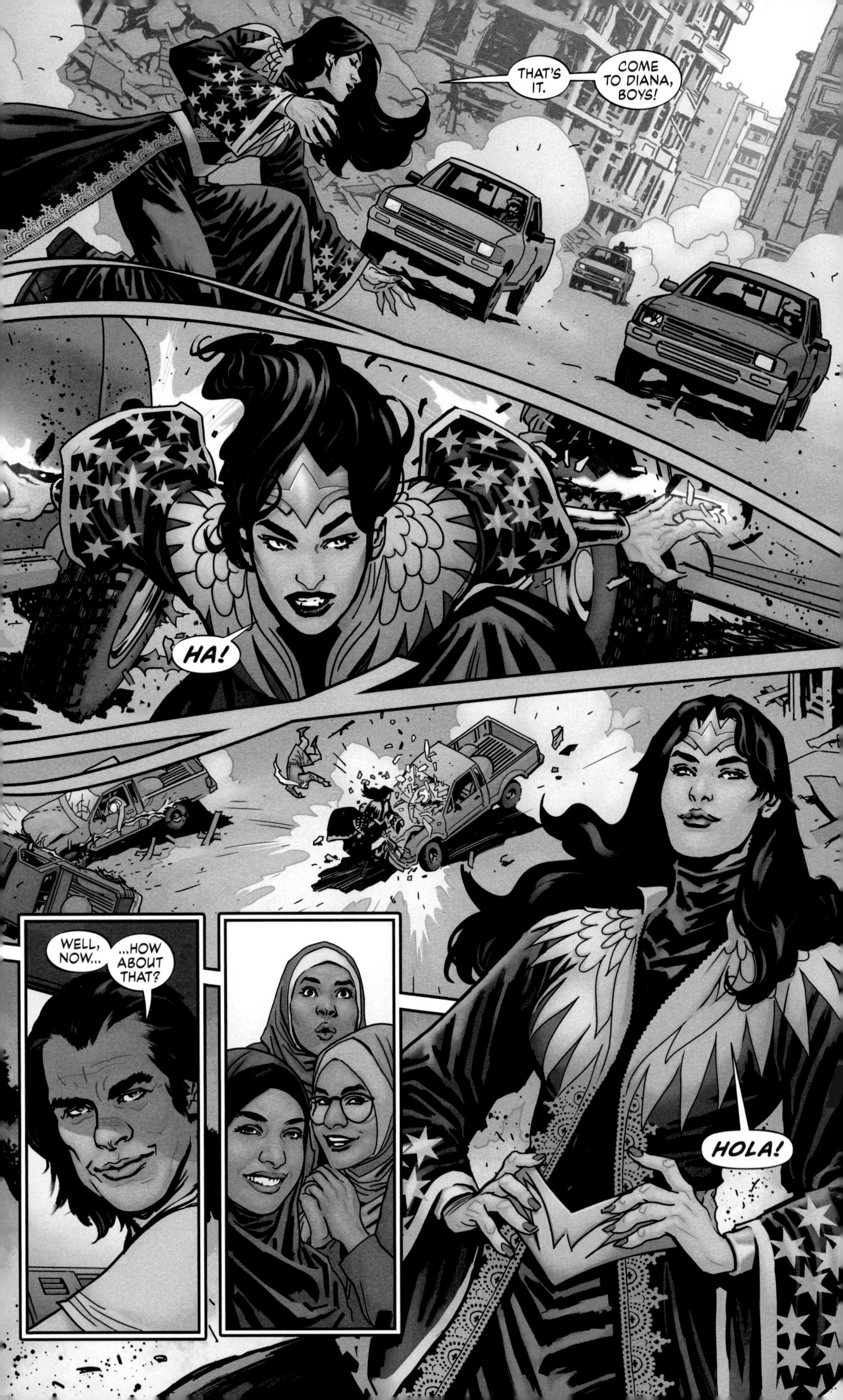
THAT'S IT.
COME TO DIANA, BOYS!
HA!
WELL, NOW...
...HOW ABOUT THAT?
HOLA!

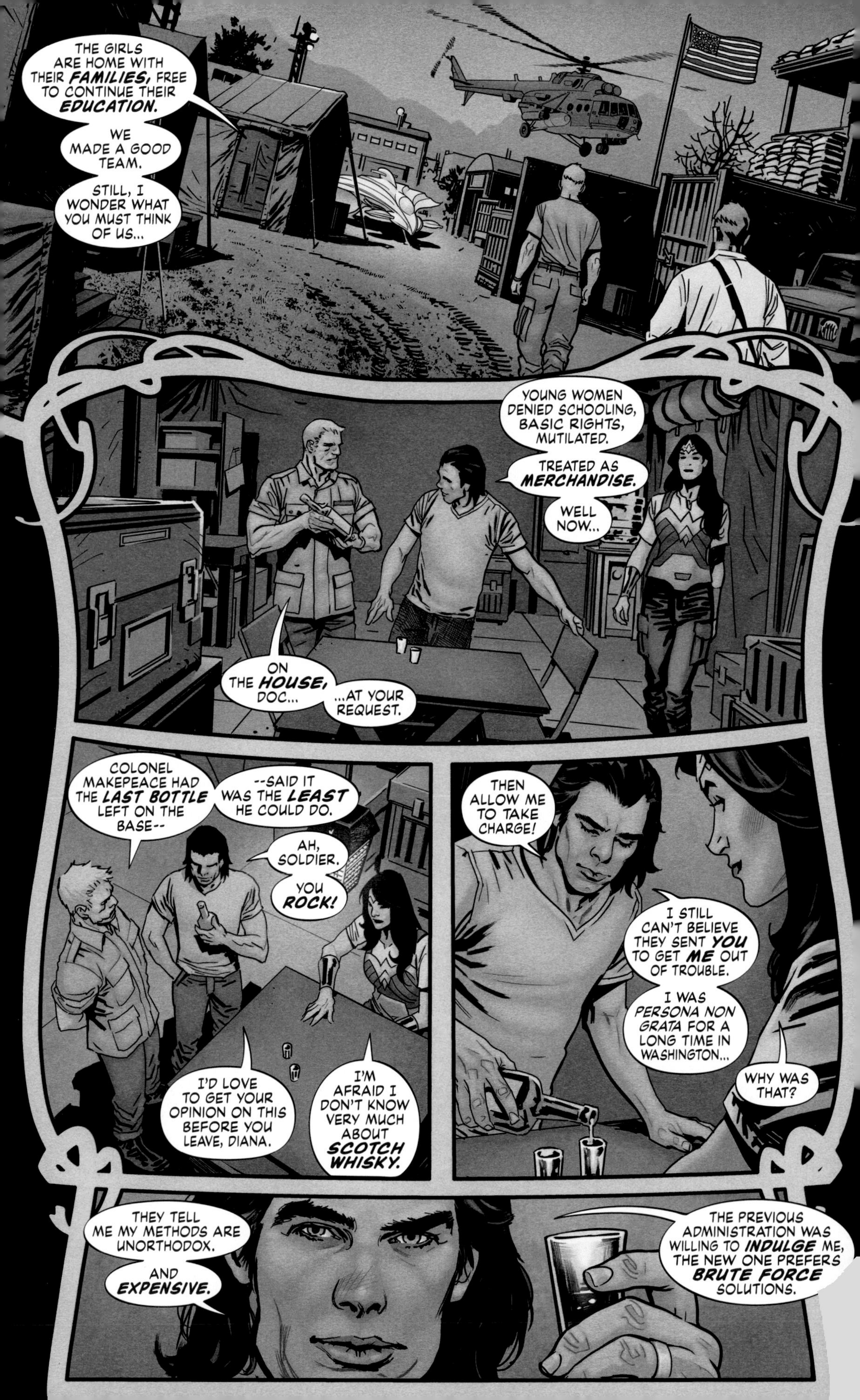
THE GIRLS ARE HOME WITH THEIR FAMILIES, FREE TO CONTINUE THEIR EDUCATION.
WE MADE A GOOD TEAM.
STILL, I WONDER WHAT YOU MUST THINK OF US...
YOUNG WOMEN DENIED SCHOOLING, BASIC RIGHTS, MUTILATED.
TREATED AS MERCHANDISE.
WELL NOW...
ON THE HOUSE, DOC...
...AT YOUR REQUEST.
COLONEL MAKEPEACE HAD THE LAST BOTTLE LEFT ON THE BASE--
--SAID IT WAS THE LEAST HE COULD DO.
AH, SOLDIER.
YOU ROCK!
I'D LOVE TO GET YOUR OPINION ON THIS BEFORE YOU LEAVE, DIANA.
I'M AFRAID I DON'T KNOW VERY MUCH ABOUT SCOTCH WHISKY.
THEN ALLOW ME TO TAKE CHARGE!
I STILL CAN'T BELIEVE THEY SENT YOU TO GET ME OUT OF TROUBLE.
I WAS PERSONA NON GRATA FOR A LONG TIME IN WASHINGTON...
WHY WAS THAT?
THEY TELL ME MY METHODS ARE UNORTHODOX.
AND EXPENSIVE.
THE PREVIOUS ADMINISTRATION WAS WILLING TO INDULGE ME, THE NEW ONE PREFERS BRUTE FORCE SOLUTIONS.

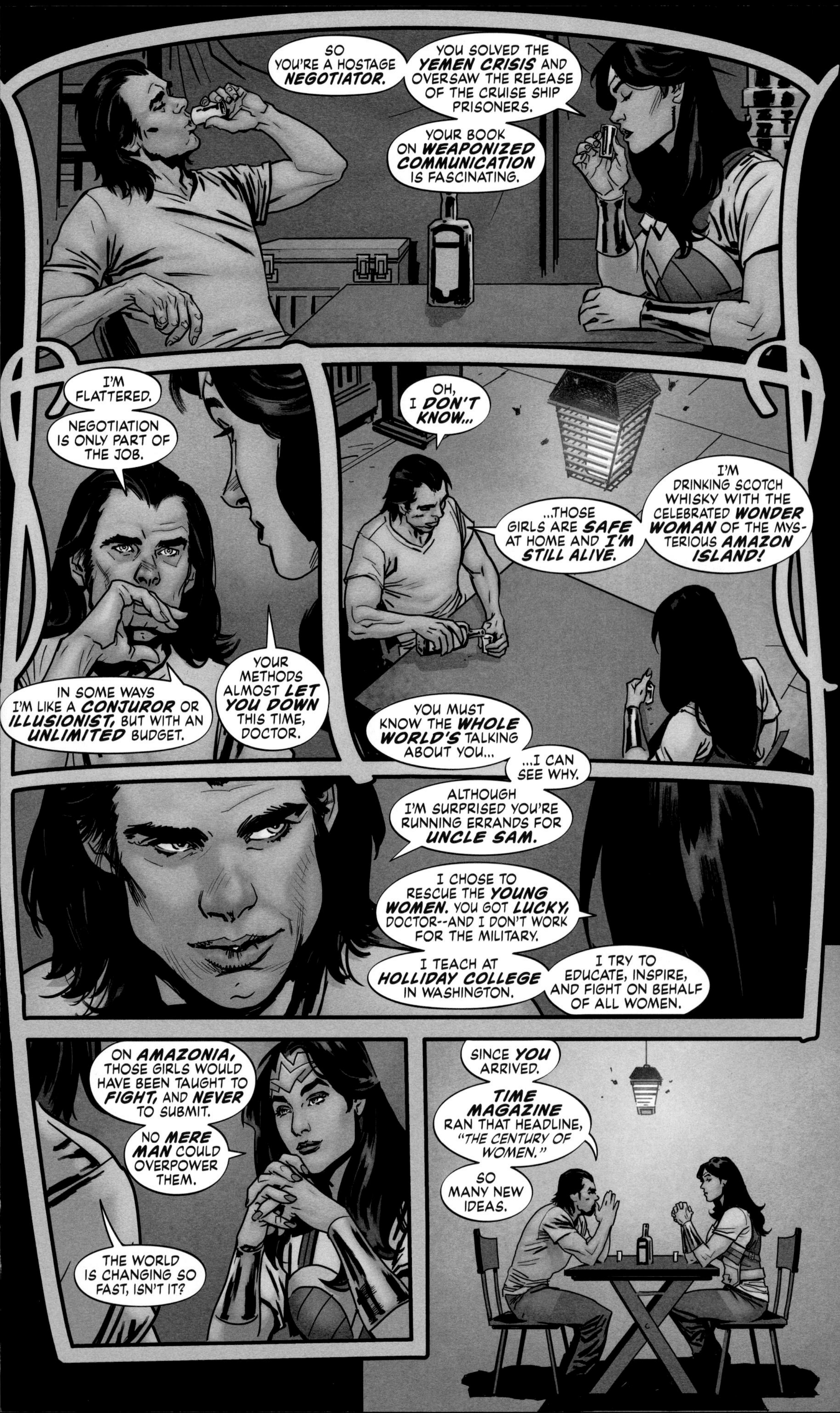

SO YOU'RE A HOSTAGE NEGOTIATOR.
YOU SOLVED THE YEMEN CRISIS AND OVERSAW THE RELEASE OF THE CRUISE SHIP PRISONERS.
YOUR BOOK ON WEAPONIZED COMMUNICATION IS FASCINATING.
I'M FLATTERED.
NEGOTIATION IS ONLY PART OF THE JOB.
IN SOME WAYS I'M LIKE A CONJUROR OR ILLUSIONIST, BUT WITH AN UNLIMITED BUDGET.
YOUR METHODS ALMOST LET YOU DOWN THIS TIME, DOCTOR.
OH, I DON'T KNOW...
...THOSE GIRLS ARE SAFE AT HOME AND I'M STILL ALIVE.
I'M DRINKING SCOTCH WHISKY WITH THE CELEBRATED WONDER WOMAN OF THE MYS-TERIOUS AMAZON ISLAND!
YOU MUST KNOW THE WHOLE WORLD'S TALKING ABOUT YOU...
...I CAN SEE WHY.
ALTHOUGH I'M SURPRISED YOU'RE RUNNING ERRANDS FOR UNCLE SAM.
I CHOSE TO RESCUE THE YOUNG WOMEN. YOU GOT LUCKY, DOCTOR--AND I DON'T WORK FOR THE MILITARY.
I TEACH AT HOLLIDAY COLLEGE IN WASHINGTON.
I TRY TO EDUCATE, INSPIRE, AND FIGHT ON BEHALF OF ALL WOMEN.
ON AMAZONIA, THOSE GIRLS WOULD HAVE BEEN TAUGHT TO FIGHT, AND NEVER TO SUBMIT.
NO MERE MAN COULD OVERPOWER THEM.
THE WORLD IS CHANGING SO FAST, ISN'T IT?
SINCE YOU ARRIVED.
TIME MAGAZINE RAN THAT HEADLINE, "THE CENTURY OF WOMEN."
SO MANY NEW IDEAS.

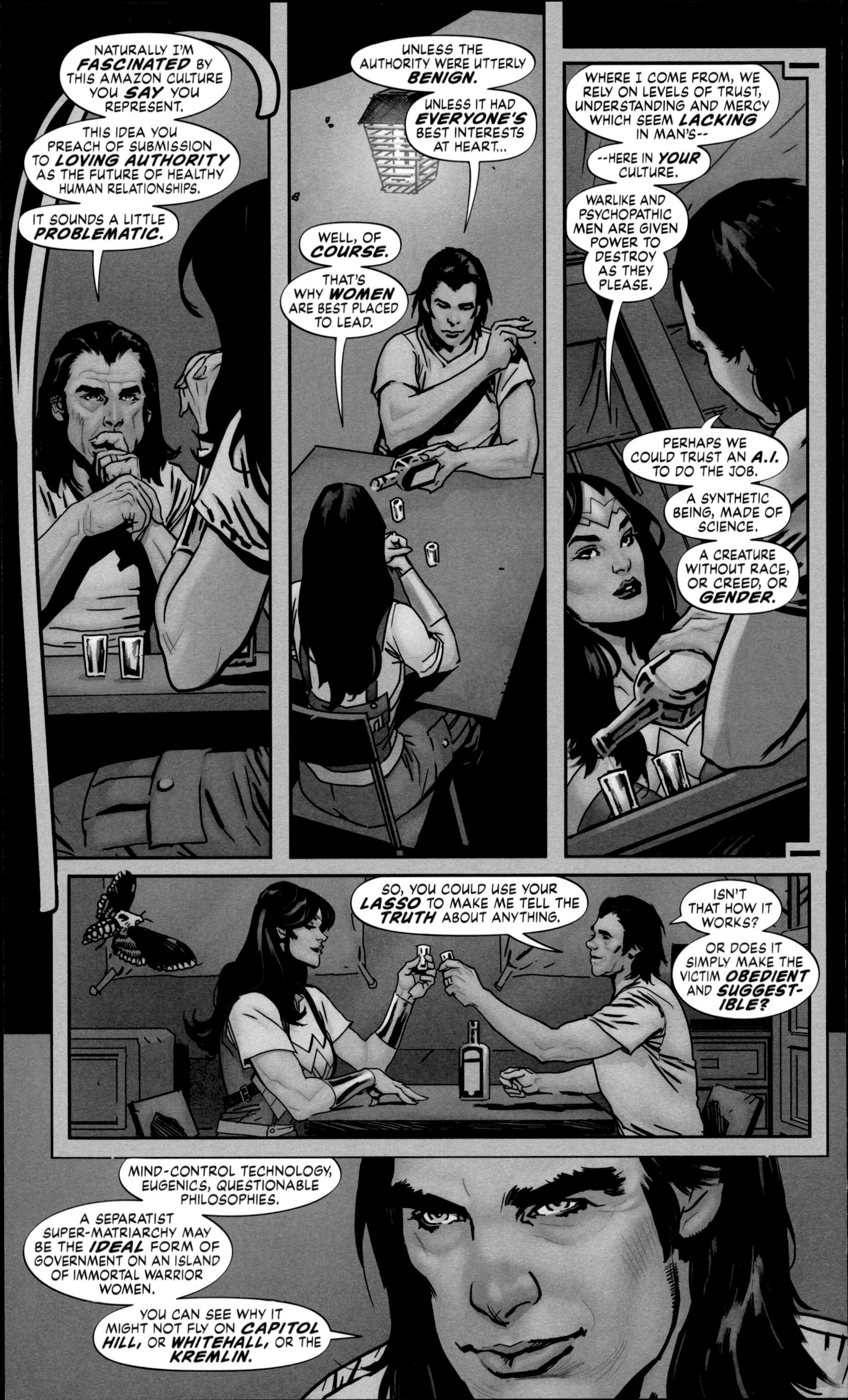
NATURALLY I'M FASCINATED BY THIS AMAZON CULTURE YOU SAY YOU REPRESENT.
THIS IDEA YOU PREACH OF SUBMISSION TO LOVING AUTHORITY AS THE FUTURE OF HEALTHY HUMAN RELATIONSHIPS.
IT SOUNDS A LITTLE PROBLEMATIC.
UNLESS THE AUTHORITY WERE UTTERLY BENIGN.
UNLESS IT HAD EVERYONE'S BEST INTERESTS AT HEART...
WELL, OF COURSE.
THAT'S WHY WOMEN ARE BEST PLACED TO LEAD.
WHERE I COME FROM, WE RELY ON LEVELS OF TRUST, UNDERSTANDING AND MERCY WHICH SEEM LACKING IN MAN'S--
--HERE IN YOUR CULTURE.
WARLIKE AND PSYCHOPATHIC MEN ARE GIVEN POWER TO DESTROY AS THEY PLEASE.
PERHAPS WE COULD TRUST AN A.I. TO DO THE JOB.
A SYNTHETIC BEING, MADE OF SCIENCE.
A CREATURE WITHOUT RACE, OR CREED, OR GENDER.
SO, YOU COULD USE YOUR LASSO TO MAKE ME TELL THE TRUTH ABOUT ANYTHING.
ISN'T THAT HOW IT WORKS?
OR DOES IT SIMPLY MAKE THE VICTIM OBEDIENT AND SUGGEST-IBLE?
MIND-CONTROL TECHNOLOGY, EUGENICS, QUESTIONABLE PHILOSOPHIES.
A SEPARATIST SUPER-MATRIARCHY MAY BE THE IDEAL FORM OF GOVERNMENT ON AN ISLAND OF IMMORTAL WARRIOR WOMEN.
YOU CAN SEE WHY IT MIGHT NOT FLY ON CAPITOL HILL, OR WHITEHALL, OR THE KREMLIN.

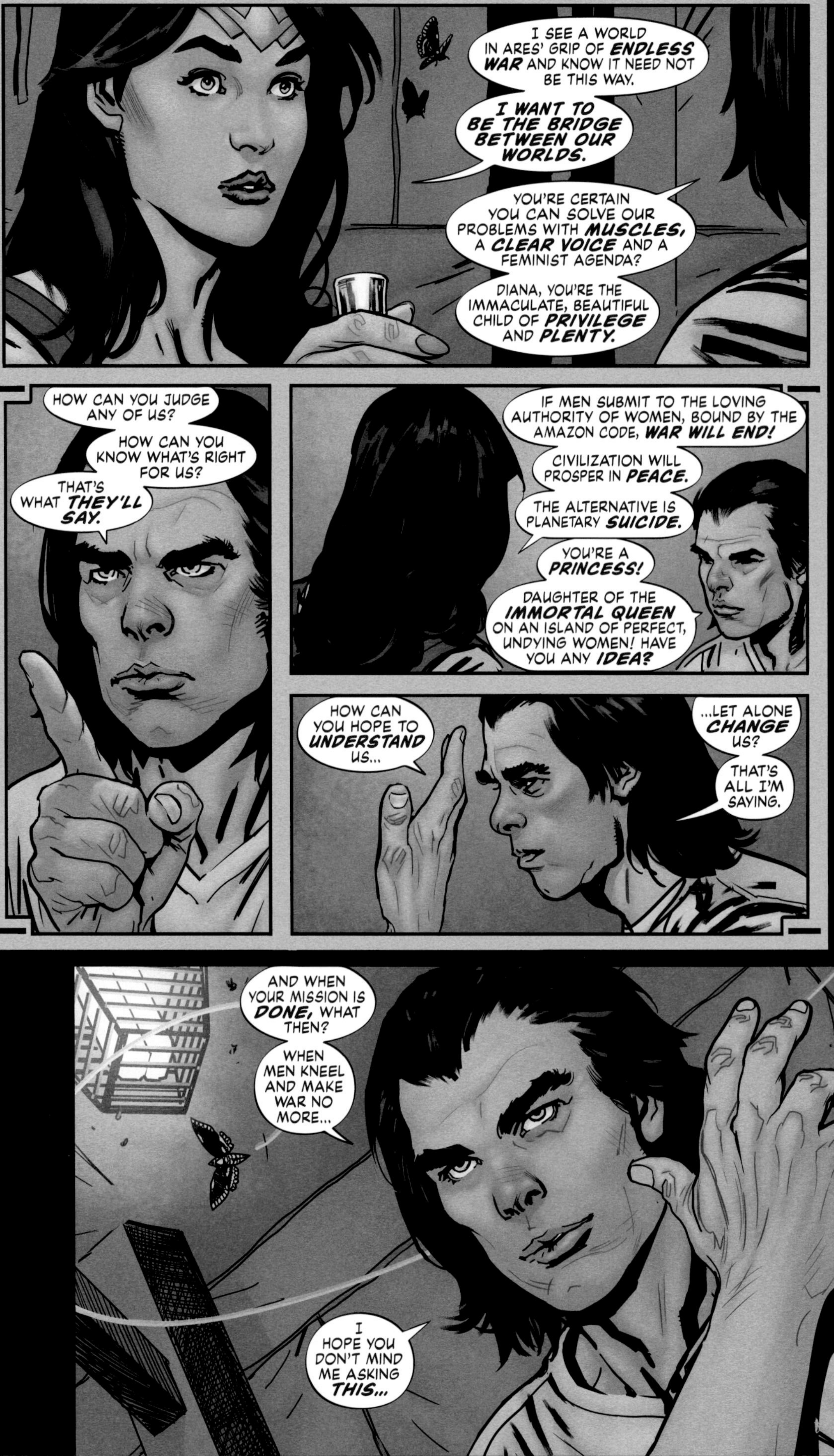
I SEE A WORLD IN ARES' GRIP OF ENDLESS WAR AND KNOW IT NEED NOT BE THIS WAY.
I WANT TO BE THE BRIDGE BETWEEN OUR WORLDS.
YOU'RE CERTAIN YOU CAN SOLVE OUR PROBLEMS WITH MUSCLES, A CLEAR VOICE AND A FEMINIST AGENDA?
DIANA, YOU'RE THE IMMACULATE, BEAUTIFUL CHILD OF PRIVILEGE AND PLENTY.
HOW CAN YOU JUDGE ANY OF US?
HOW CAN YOU KNOW WHAT'S RIGHT FOR US?
THAT'S WHAT THEY'LL SAY.
IF MEN SUBMIT TO THE LOVING AUTHORITY OF WOMEN, BOUND BY THE AMAZON CODE, WAR WILL END!
CIVILIZATION WILL PROSPER IN PEACE.
THE ALTERNATIVE IS PLANETARY SUICIDE.
YOU'RE A PRINCESS!
DAUGHTER OF THE IMMORTAL QUEEN ON AN ISLAND OF PERFECT, UNDYING WOMEN! HAVE YOU ANY IDEA?
HOW CAN YOU HOPE TO UNDERSTAND US...
...LET ALONE CHANGE US?
THAT'S ALL I'M SAYING.
AND WHEN YOUR MISSION IS DONE, WHAT THEN?
WHEN MEN KNEEL AND MAKE WAR NO MORE...
I HOPE YOU DON'T MIND ME ASKING THIS...

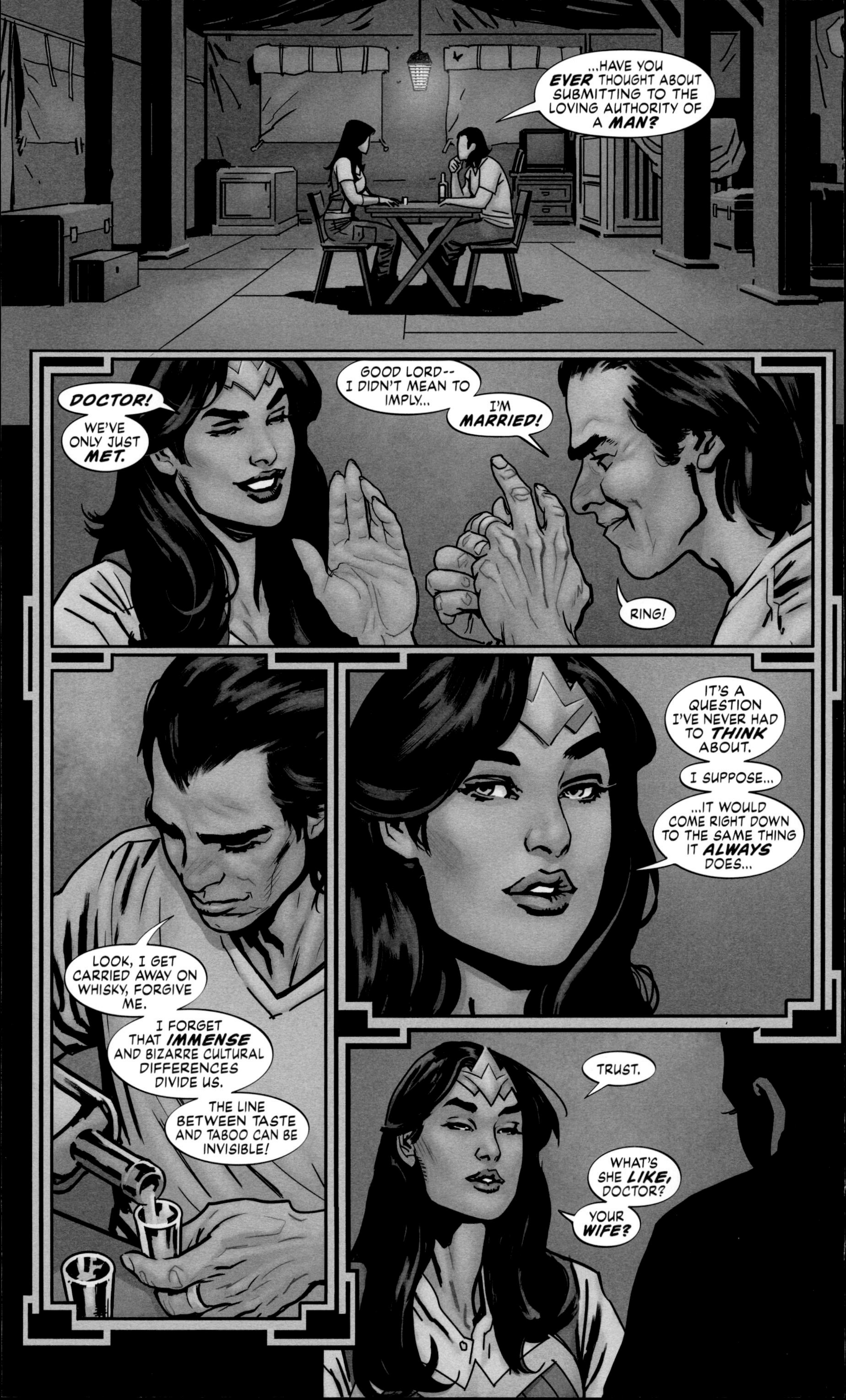
...HAVE YOU EVER THOUGHT ABOUT SUBMITTING TO THE LOVING AUTHORITY OF A MAN?
DOCTOR!
WE'VE ONLY JUST MET.
GOOD LORD-- I DIDN'T MEAN TO IMPLY...
I'M MARRIED!
RING!
LOOK, I GET CARRIED AWAY ON WHISKY, FORGIVE ME.
I FORGET THAT IMMENSE AND BIZARRE CULTURAL DIFFERENCES DIVIDE US.
THE LINE BETWEEN TASTE AND TABOO CAN BE INVISIBLE!
IT'S A QUESTION I'VE NEVER HAD TO THINK ABOUT.
I SUPPOSE...
...IT WOULD COME RIGHT DOWN TO THE SAME THING IT ALWAYS DOES...
TRUST.
WHAT'S SHE LIKE, DOCTOR?
YOUR WIFE?

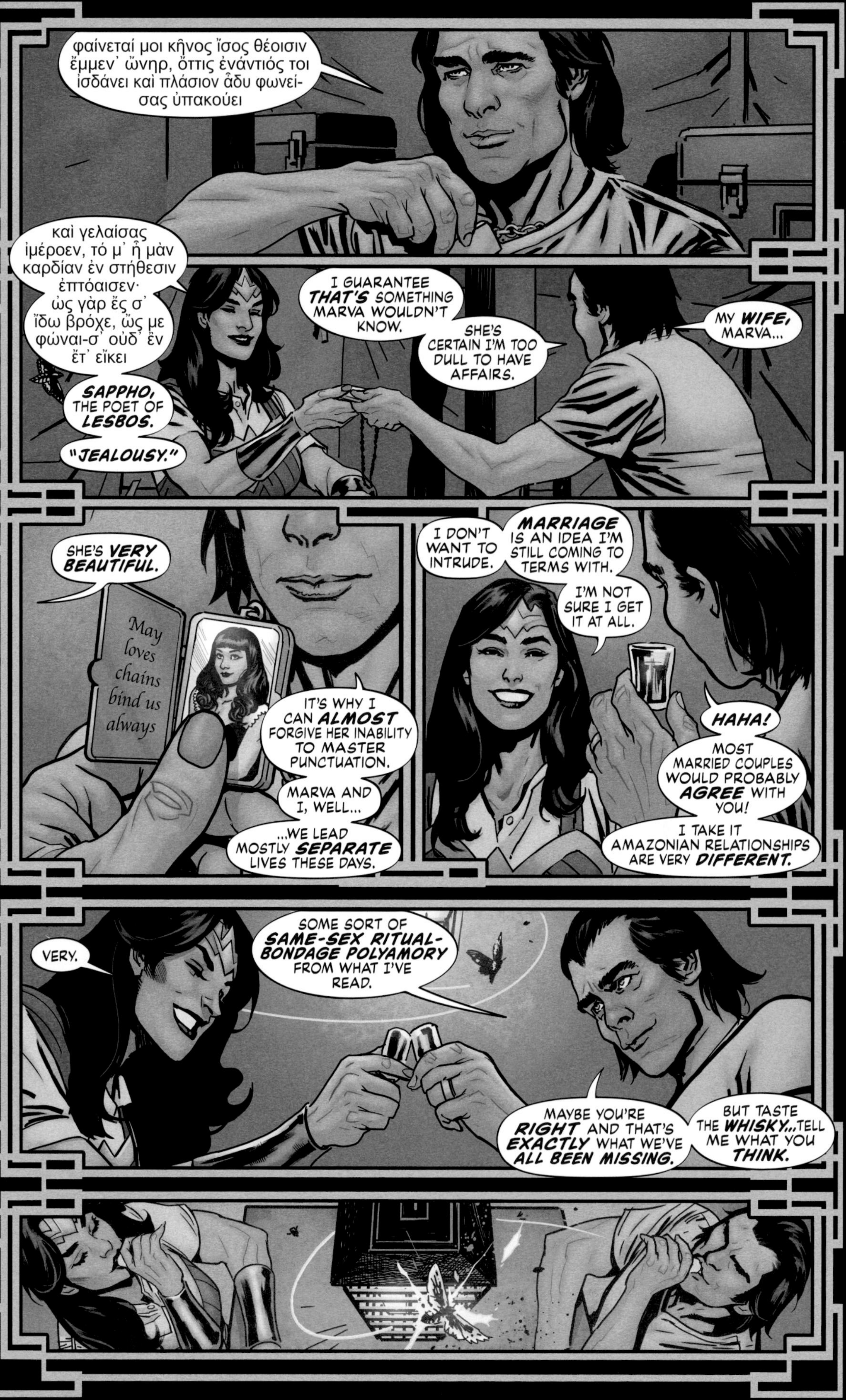
φαίνεταί μοι κῆνος ἴσος θέοισιν ἔμμεν᾽ ὤνηρ, ὄττις ἐνάντιός τοι ἰσδάνει καὶ πλάσιον ἆδυ φωνεί-σας ὐπακούει
καὶ γελαίσας ἰμέροεν, τό μ᾽ ἦ μὰν καρδίαν ἐν στήθεσιν ἐπτόαισεν· ὠς γὰρ ἔς σ᾽ ἴδω βρόχε, ὤς με φώναι-σ᾽ οὐδ᾽ ἒν ἔτ᾽ εἴκει
SAPPHO, THE POET OF LESBOS.
"JEALOUSY."
I GUARANTEE THAT'S SOMETHING MARVA WOULDN'T KNOW.
MY WIFE, MARVA...
SHE'S CERTAIN I'M TOO DULL TO HAVE AFFAIRS.
SHE'S VERY BEAUTIFUL.
May loves chains bind us always
IT'S WHY I CAN ALMOST FORGIVE HER INABILITY TO MASTER PUNCTUATION.
MARVA AND I, WELL...
...WE LEAD MOSTLY SEPARATE LIVES THESE DAYS.
I DON'T WANT TO INTRUDE.
MARRIAGE IS AN IDEA I'M STILL COMING TO TERMS WITH.
I'M NOT SURE I GET IT AT ALL.
HAHA!
MOST MARRIED COUPLES WOULD PROBABLY AGREE WITH YOU!
I TAKE IT AMAZONIAN RELATIONSHIPS ARE VERY DIFFERENT.
VERY.
SOME SORT OF SAME-SEX RITUAL-BONDAGE POLYAMORY FROM WHAT I'VE READ.
MAYBE YOU'RE RIGHT AND THAT'S EXACTLY WHAT WE'VE ALL BEEN MISSING.
BUT TASTE THE WHISKY...TELL ME WHAT YOU THINK.

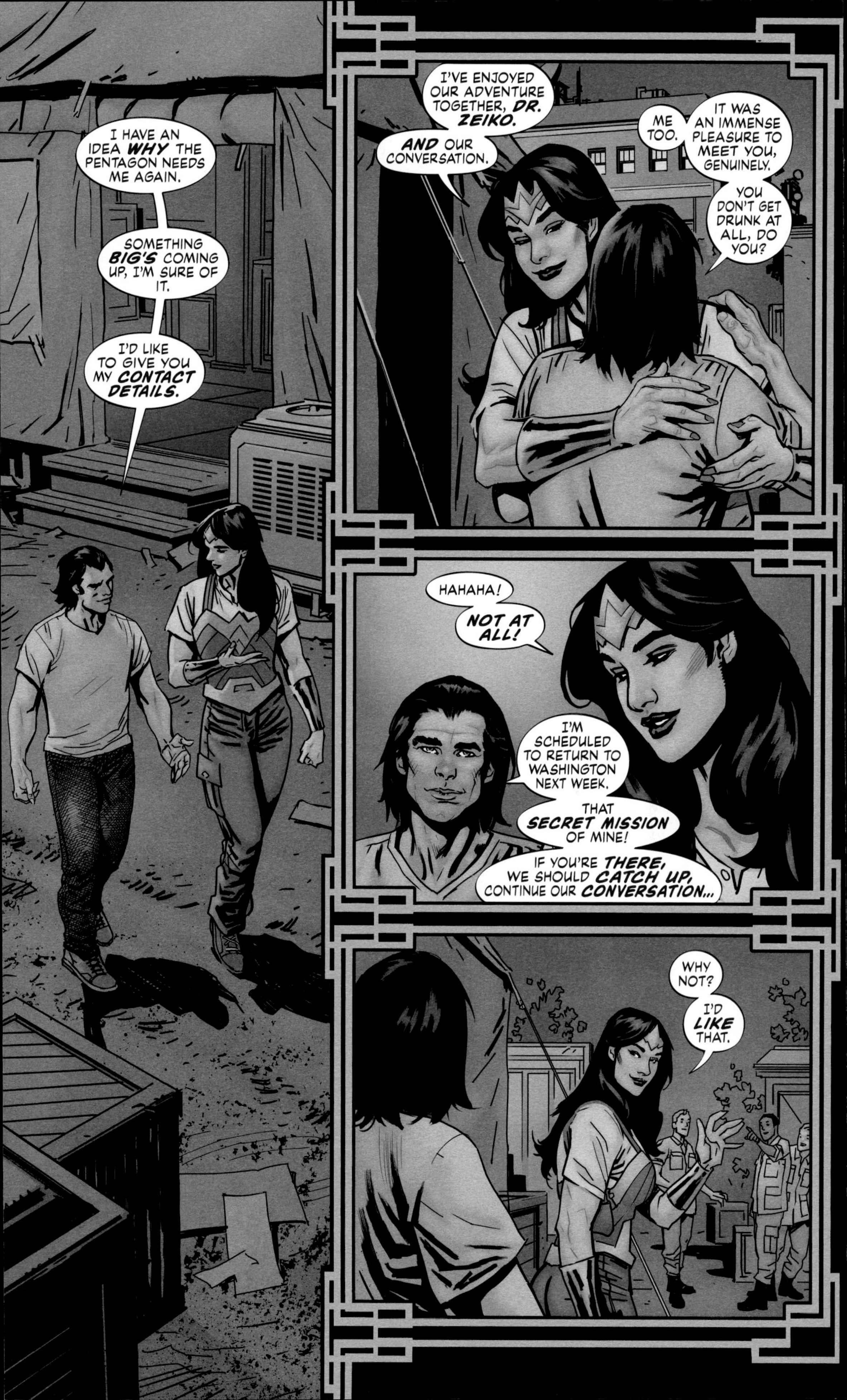
I HAVE AN IDEA WHY THE PENTAGON NEEDS ME AGAIN.
SOMETHING BIG'S COMING UP, I'M SURE OF IT.
I'D LIKE TO GIVE YOU MY CONTACT DETAILS.
I'VE ENJOYED OUR ADVENTURE TOGETHER, DR. ZEIKO.
AND OUR CONVERSATION.
ME TOO.
IT WAS AN IMMENSE PLEASURE TO MEET YOU, GENUINELY.
YOU DON'T GET DRUNK AT ALL, DO YOU?
HAHAHA! NOT AT ALL!
I'M SCHEDULED TO RETURN TO WASHINGTON NEXT WEEK.
THAT SECRET MISSION OF MINE!
IF YOU'RE THERE, WE SHOULD CATCH UP, CONTINUE OUR CONVERSATION...
WHY NOT?
I'D LIKE THAT.

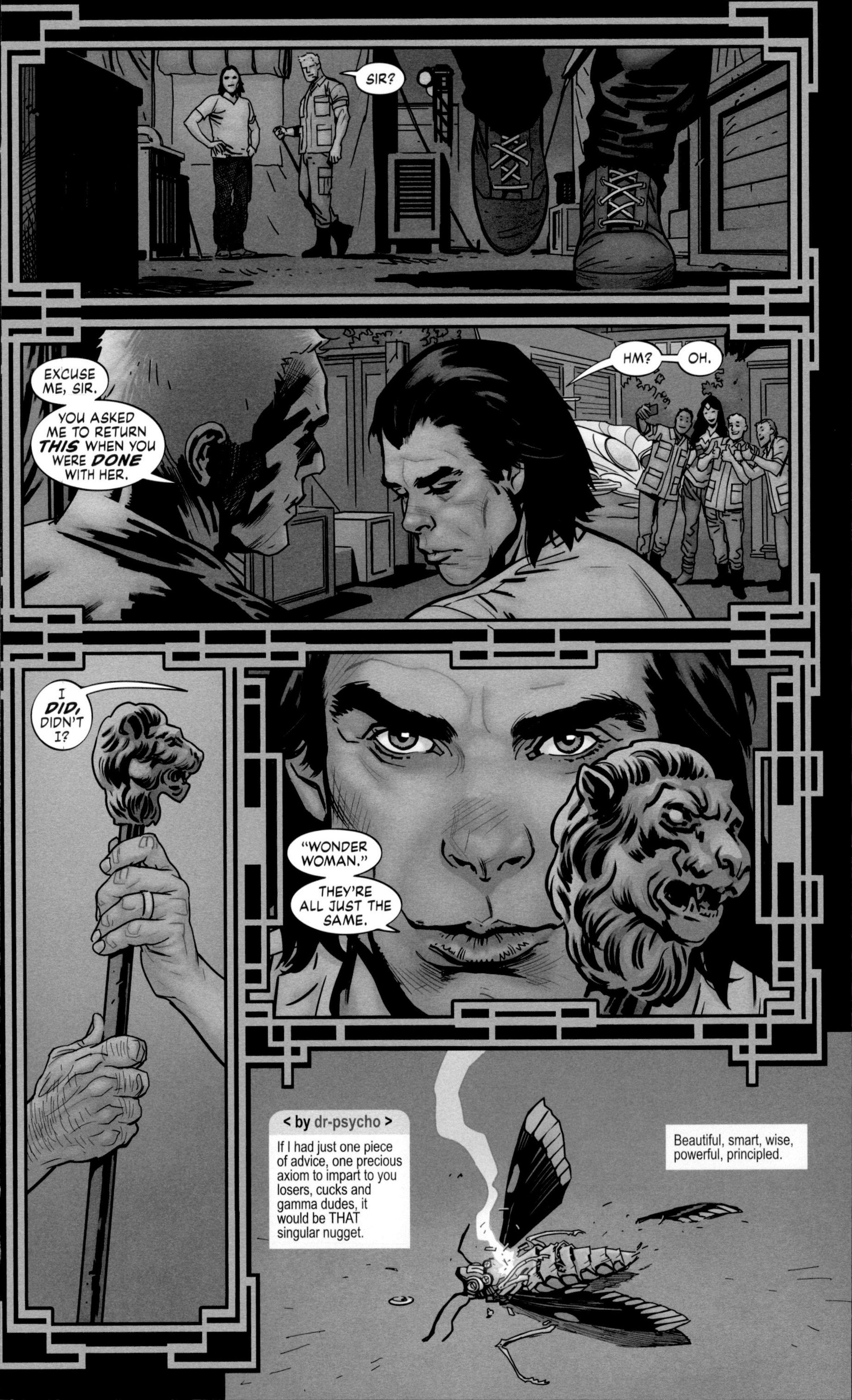
SIR?
EXCUSE ME, SIR.
YOU ASKED ME TO RETURN THIS WHEN YOU WERE DONE WITH HER.
HM?
OH.
I DID, DIDN'T I?
"WONDER WOMAN."
THEY'RE ALL JUST THE SAME.
< by dr-psycho >
If I had just one piece of advice, one precious axiom to impart to you losers, cucks and gamma dudes, it would be THAT singular nugget.
Beautiful, smart, wise, powerful, principled.

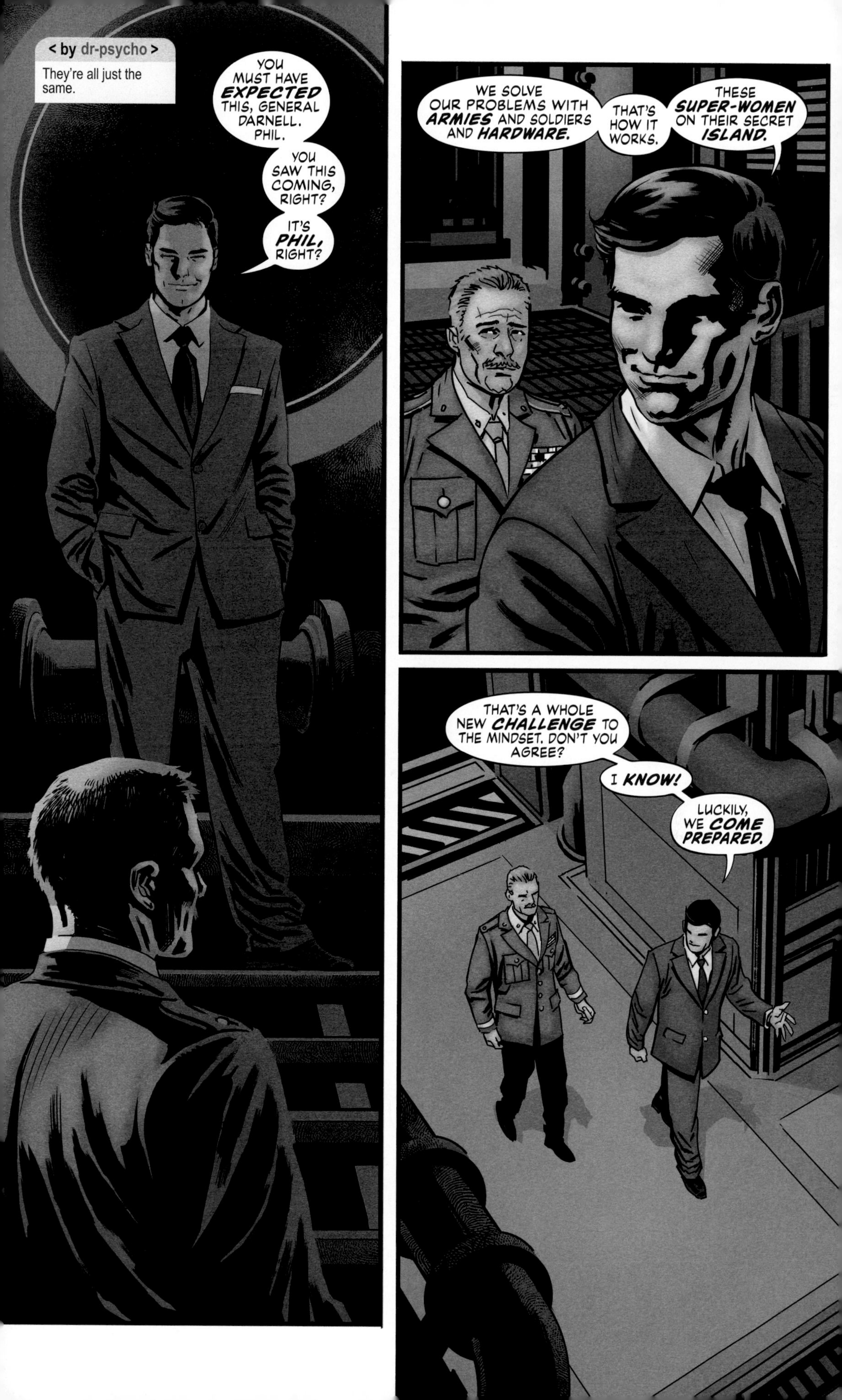
YOU MUST HAVE ***EXPECTED*** THIS, GENERAL DARNELL. PHIL.
YOU SAW THIS COMING, RIGHT?
IT'S ***PHIL,*** RIGHT?
WE SOLVE OUR PROBLEMS WITH ***ARMIES*** AND SOLDIERS AND ***HARDWARE.***
THAT'S HOW IT WORKS.
THESE ***SUPER-WOMEN*** ON THEIR SECRET ***ISLAND.***
THAT'S A WHOLE NEW ***CHALLENGE*** TO THE MINDSET. DON'T YOU AGREE?
I ***KNOW!***
LUCKILY, WE ***COME PREPARED.***

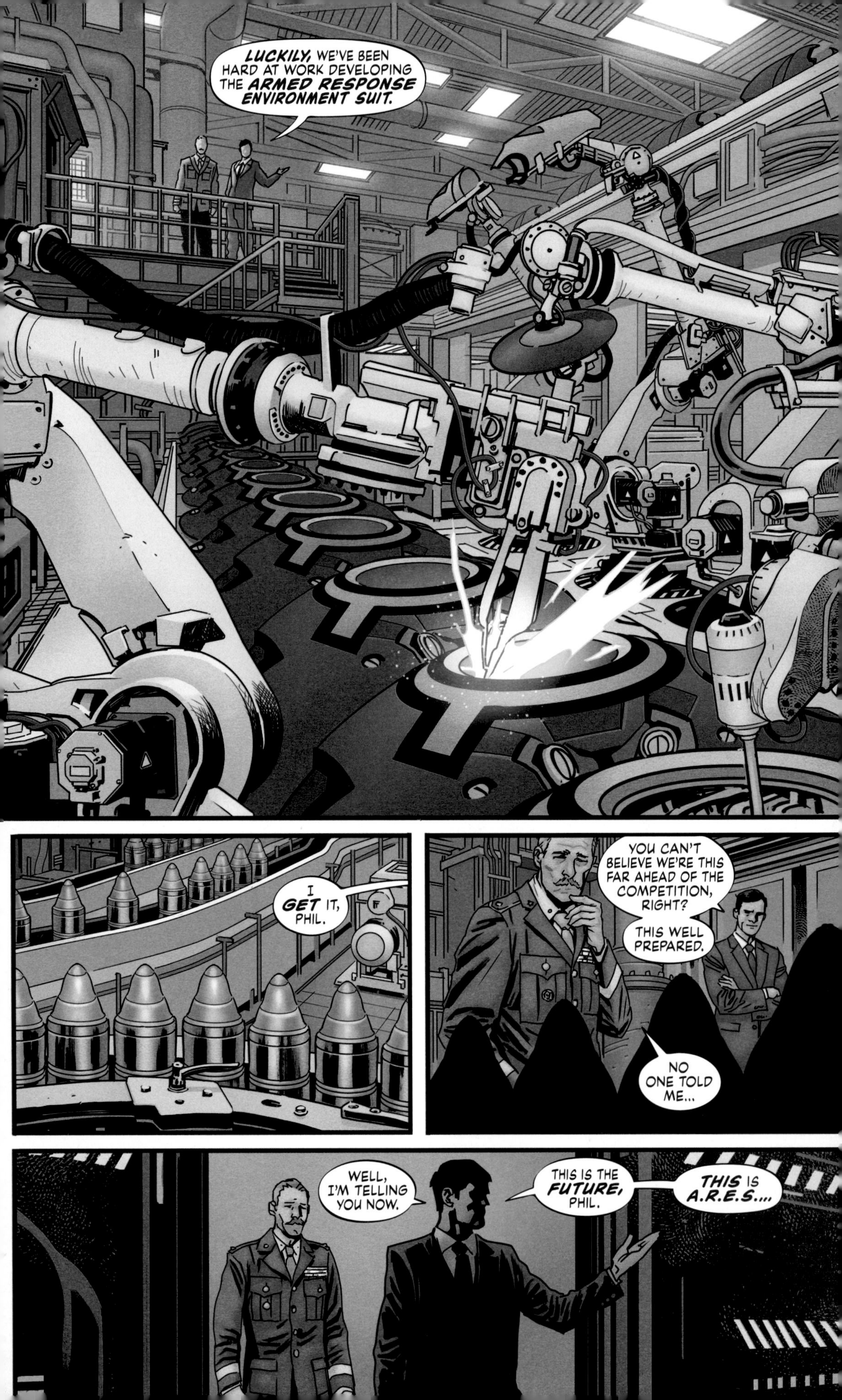
LUCKILY, WE'VE BEEN HARD AT WORK DEVELOPING THE ARMED RESPONSE ENVIRONMENT SUIT.
I GET IT, PHIL.
YOU CAN'T BELIEVE WE'RE THIS FAR AHEAD OF THE COMPETITION, RIGHT?
THIS WELL PREPARED.
NO ONE TOLD ME...
WELL, I'M TELLING YOU NOW.
THIS IS THE FUTURE, PHIL.
THIS IS A.R.E.S....

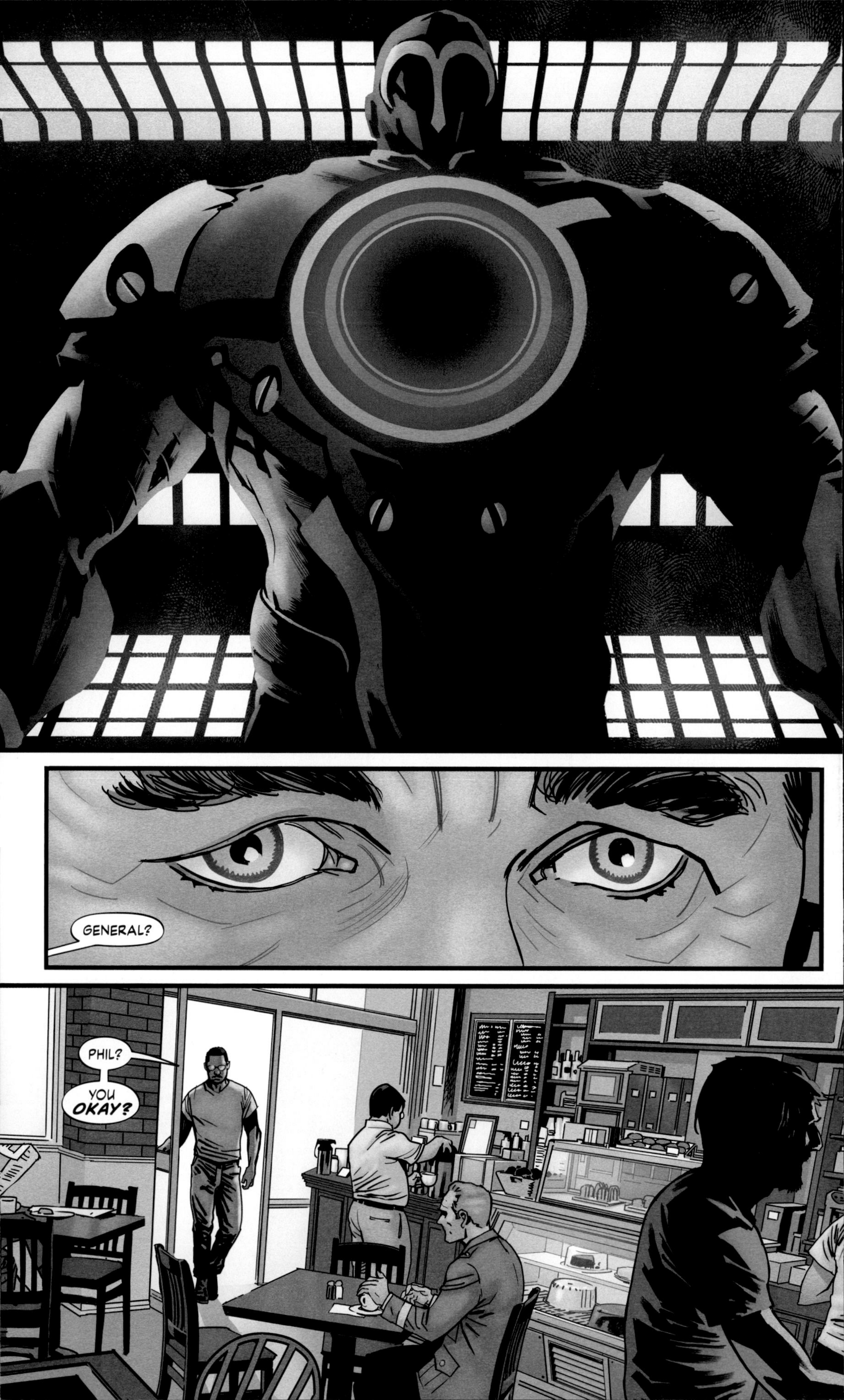
GENERAL?
PHIL?
YOU OKAY?

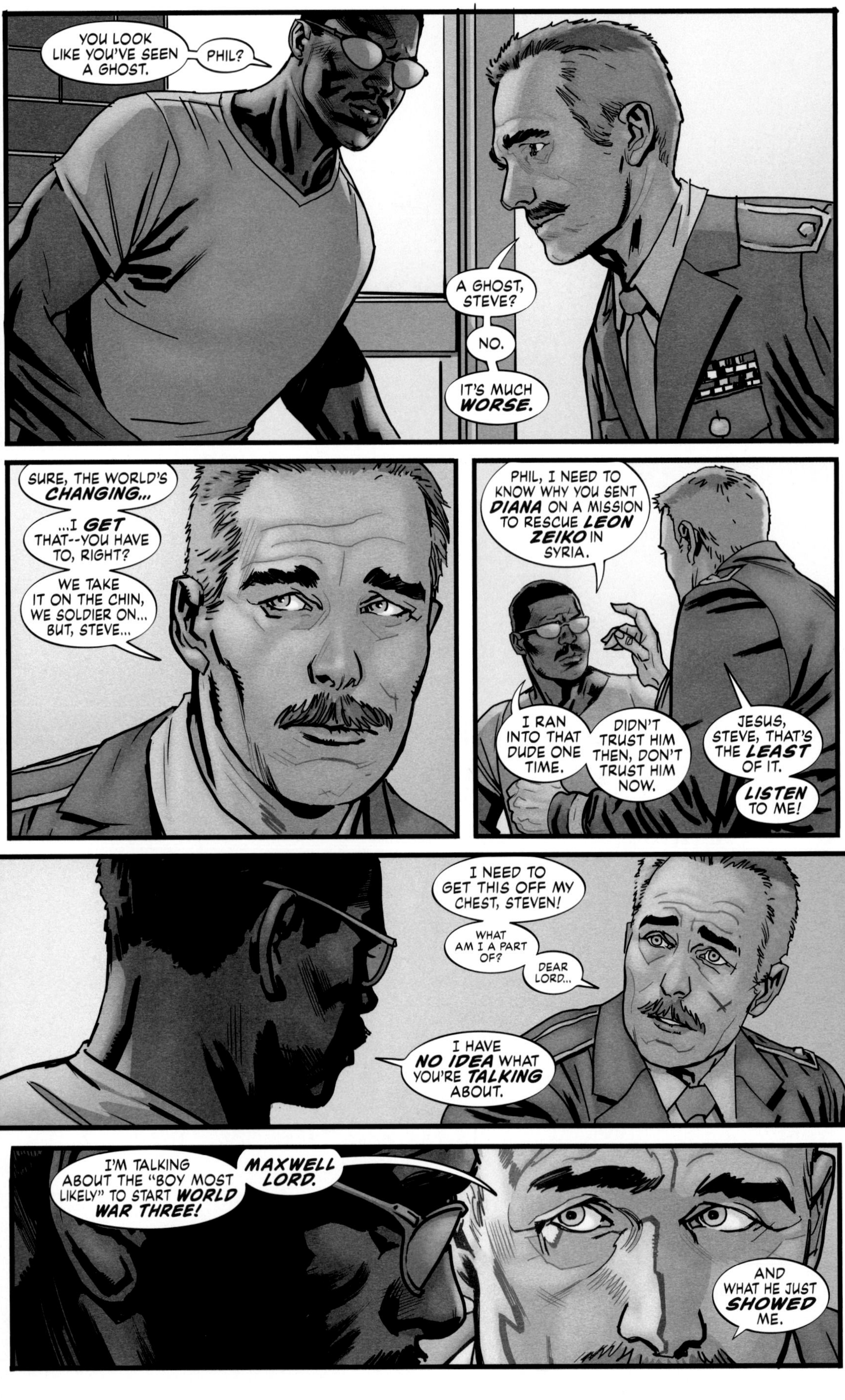
YOU LOOK LIKE YOU'VE SEEN A GHOST.
PHIL?
A GHOST, STEVE?
NO.
IT'S MUCH WORSE.
SURE, THE WORLD'S CHANGING...
...I GET THAT--YOU HAVE TO, RIGHT?
WE TAKE IT ON THE CHIN, WE SOLDIER ON... BUT, STEVE...
PHIL, I NEED TO KNOW WHY YOU SENT DIANA ON A MISSION TO RESCUE LEON ZEIKO IN SYRIA.
I RAN INTO THAT DUDE ONE TIME.
DIDN'T TRUST HIM THEN, DON'T TRUST HIM NOW.
JESUS, STEVE, THAT'S THE LEAST OF IT.
LISTEN TO ME!
I NEED TO GET THIS OFF MY CHEST, STEVEN!
WHAT AM I A PART OF?
DEAR LORD...
I HAVE NO IDEA WHAT YOU'RE TALKING ABOUT.
I'M TALKING ABOUT THE "BOY MOST LIKELY" TO START WORLD WAR THREE!
MAXWELL LORD.
AND WHAT HE JUST SHOWED ME.

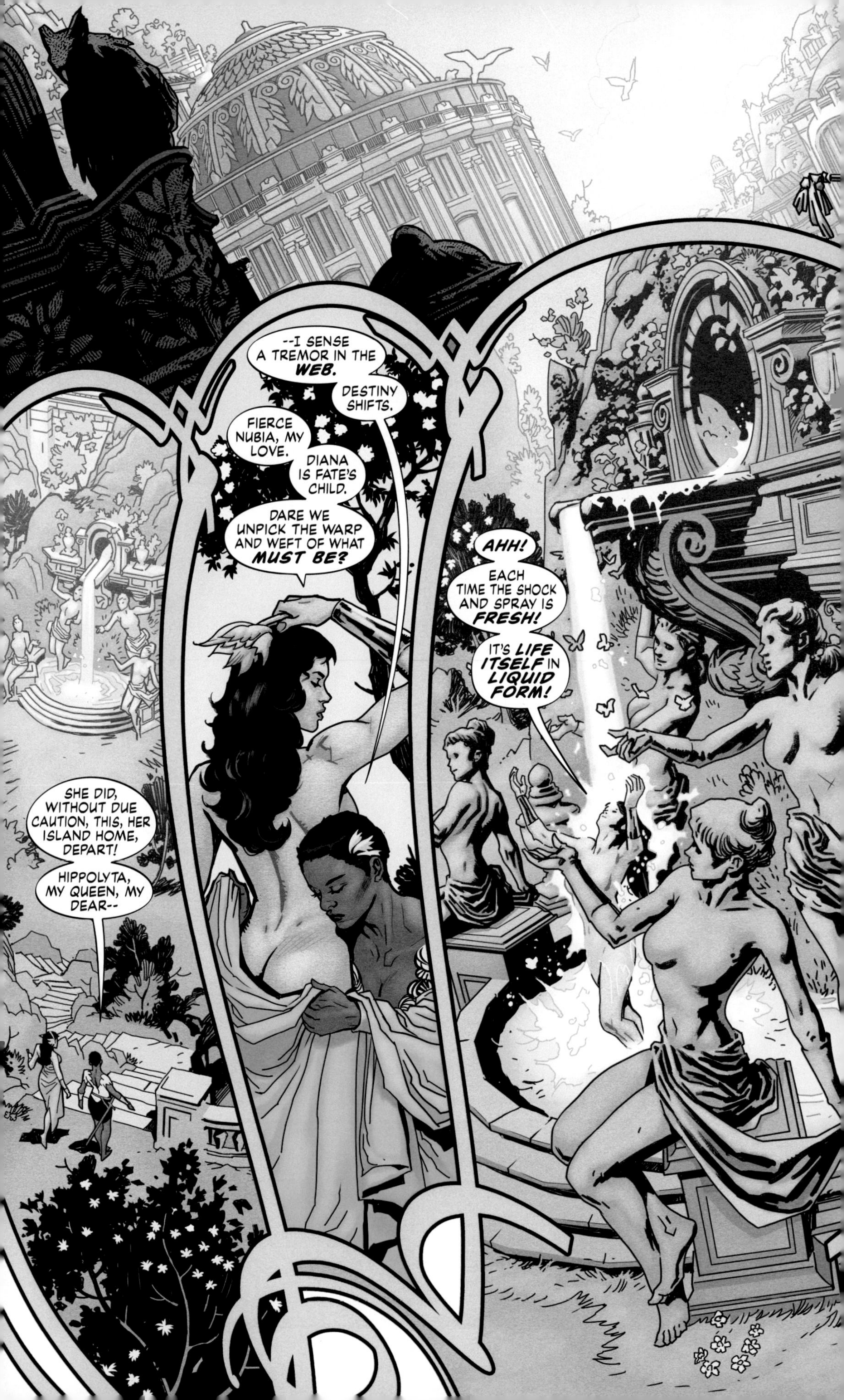

--I SENSE A TREMOR IN THE WEB.
DESTINY SHIFTS.
FIERCE NUBIA, MY LOVE.
DIANA IS FATE'S CHILD.
DARE WE UNPICK THE WARP AND WEFT OF WHAT MUST BE?
SHE DID, WITHOUT DUE CAUTION, THIS, HER ISLAND HOME, DEPART!
HIPPOLYTA, MY QUEEN, MY DEAR--
AHH!
EACH TIME THE SHOCK AND SPRAY IS FRESH!
IT'S LIFE ITSELF IN LIQUID FORM!

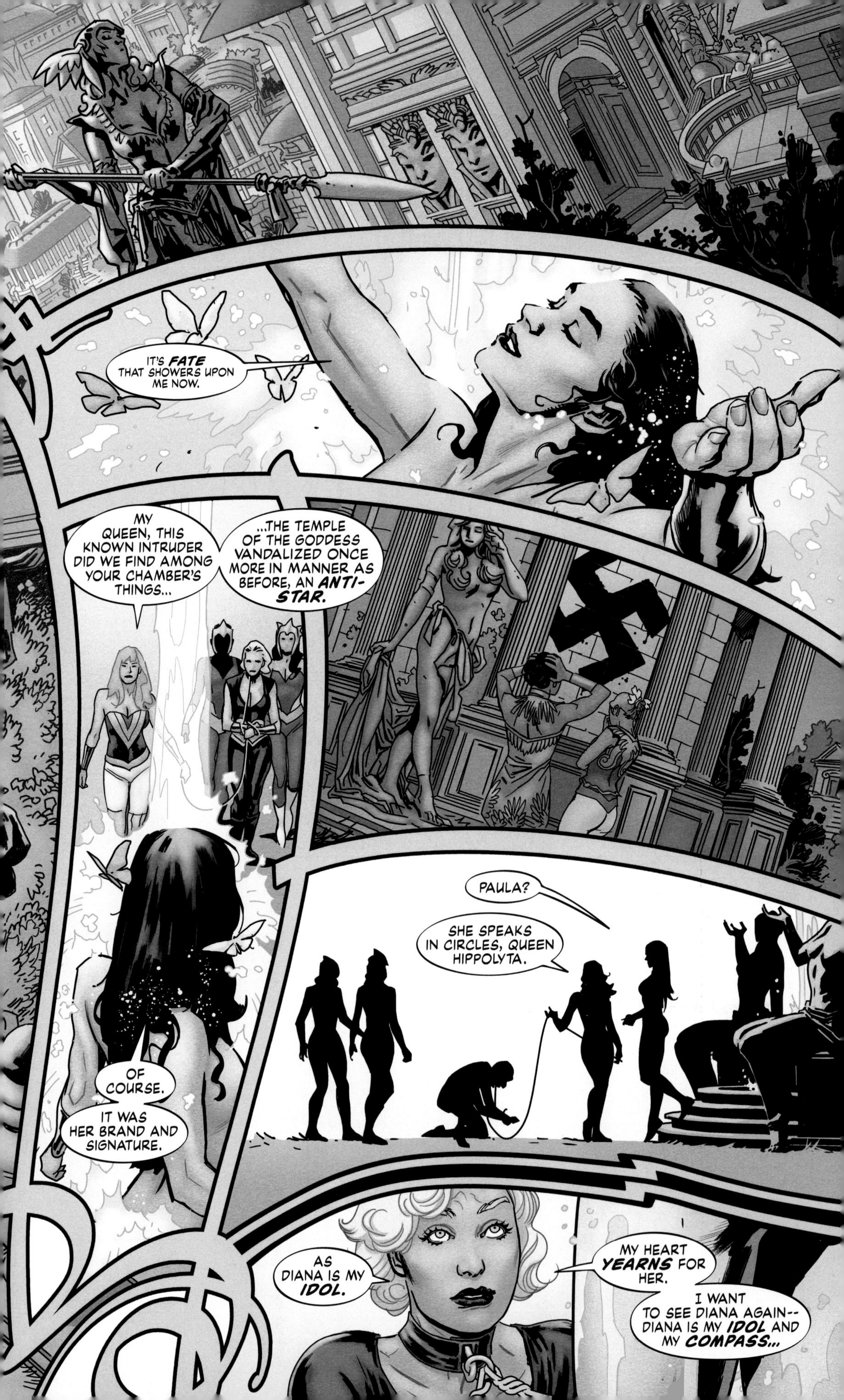
IT'S FATE THAT SHOWERS UPON ME NOW.
MY QUEEN, THIS KNOWN INTRUDER DID WE FIND AMONG YOUR CHAMBER'S THINGS...
...THE TEMPLE OF THE GODDESS VANDALIZED ONCE MORE IN MANNER AS BEFORE, AN ANTI-STAR.
OF COURSE.
IT WAS HER BRAND AND SIGNATURE.
PAULA?
SHE SPEAKS IN CIRCLES, QUEEN HIPPOLYTA.
AS DIANA IS MY IDOL.
MY HEART YEARNS FOR HER.
I WANT TO SEE DIANA AGAIN-- DIANA IS MY IDOL AND MY COMPASS...

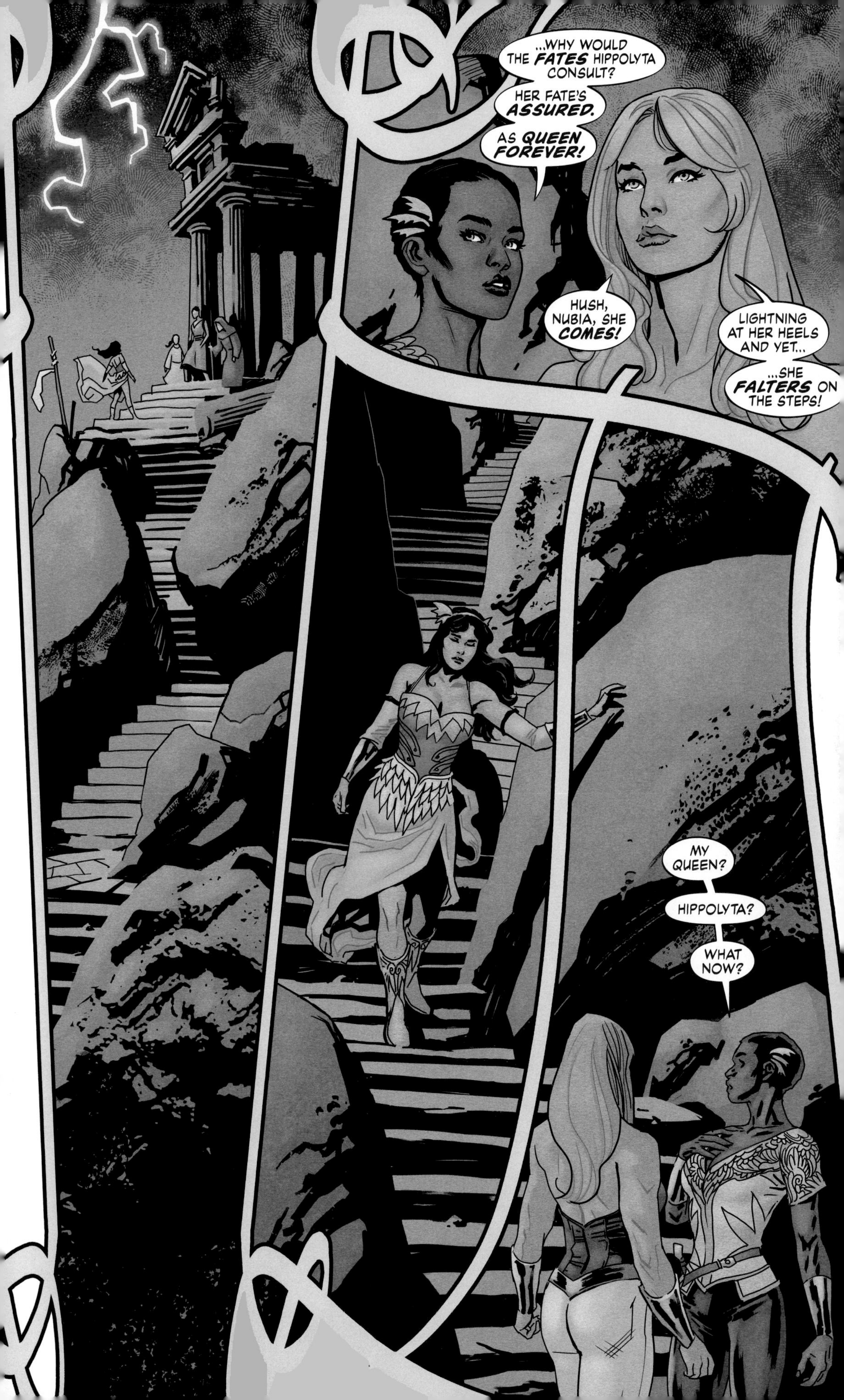
...WHY WOULD THE FATES HIPPOLYTA CONSULT?
HER FATE'S ASSURED.
AS QUEEN FOREVER!
HUSH, NUBIA, SHE COMES!
LIGHTNING AT HER HEELS AND YET...
...SHE FALTERS ON THE STEPS!
MY QUEEN?
HIPPOLYTA?
WHAT NOW?

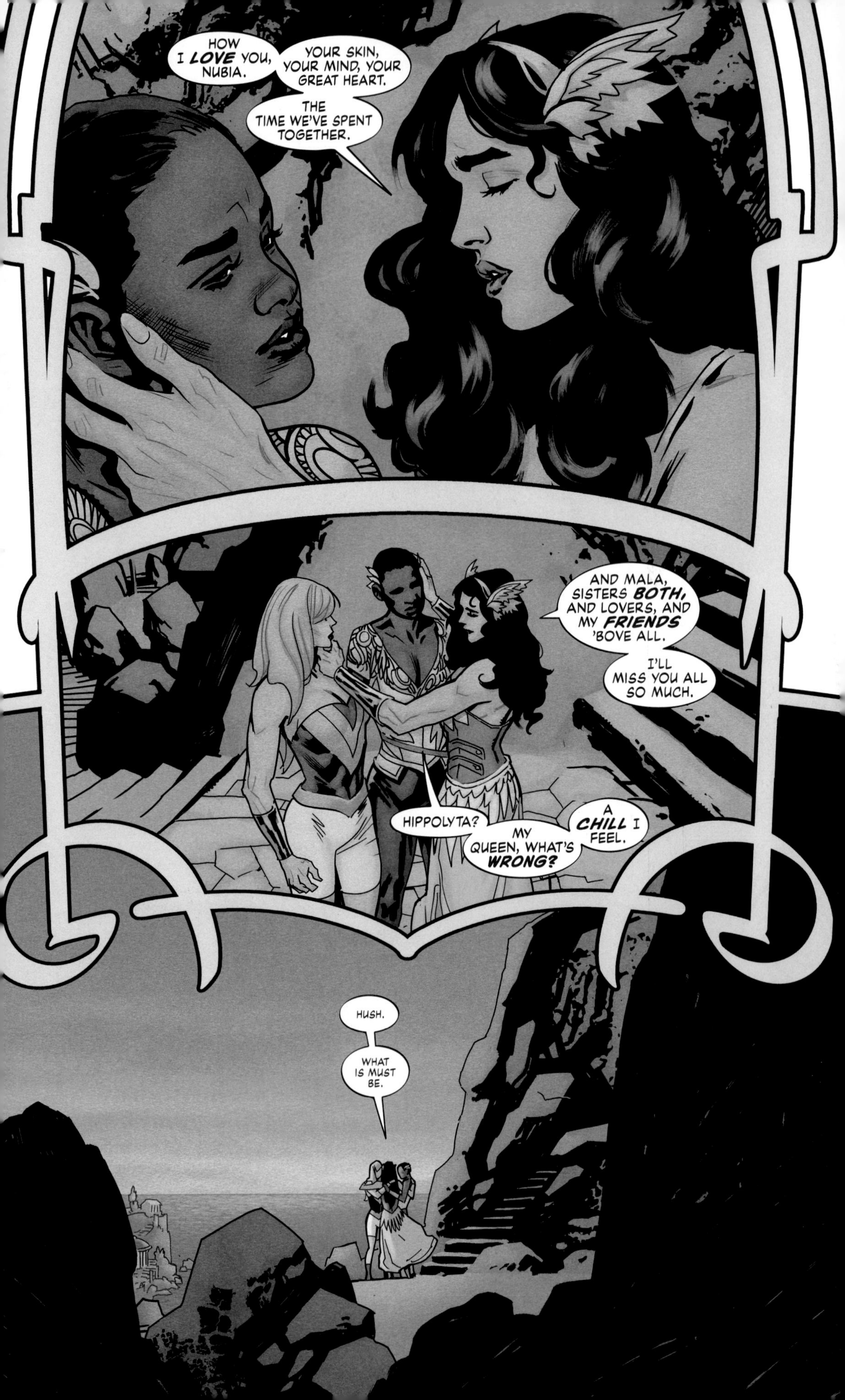
HOW I **LOVE** YOU, NUBIA.
YOUR SKIN, YOUR MIND, YOUR GREAT HEART.
THE TIME WE'VE SPENT TOGETHER.
AND MALA, SISTERS **BOTH,** AND LOVERS, AND MY **FRIENDS** 'BOVE ALL.
I'LL MISS YOU ALL SO MUCH.
HIPPOLYTA?
MY QUEEN, WHAT'S **WRONG?**
A **CHILL** I FEEL.
HUSH.
WHAT IS MUST BE.

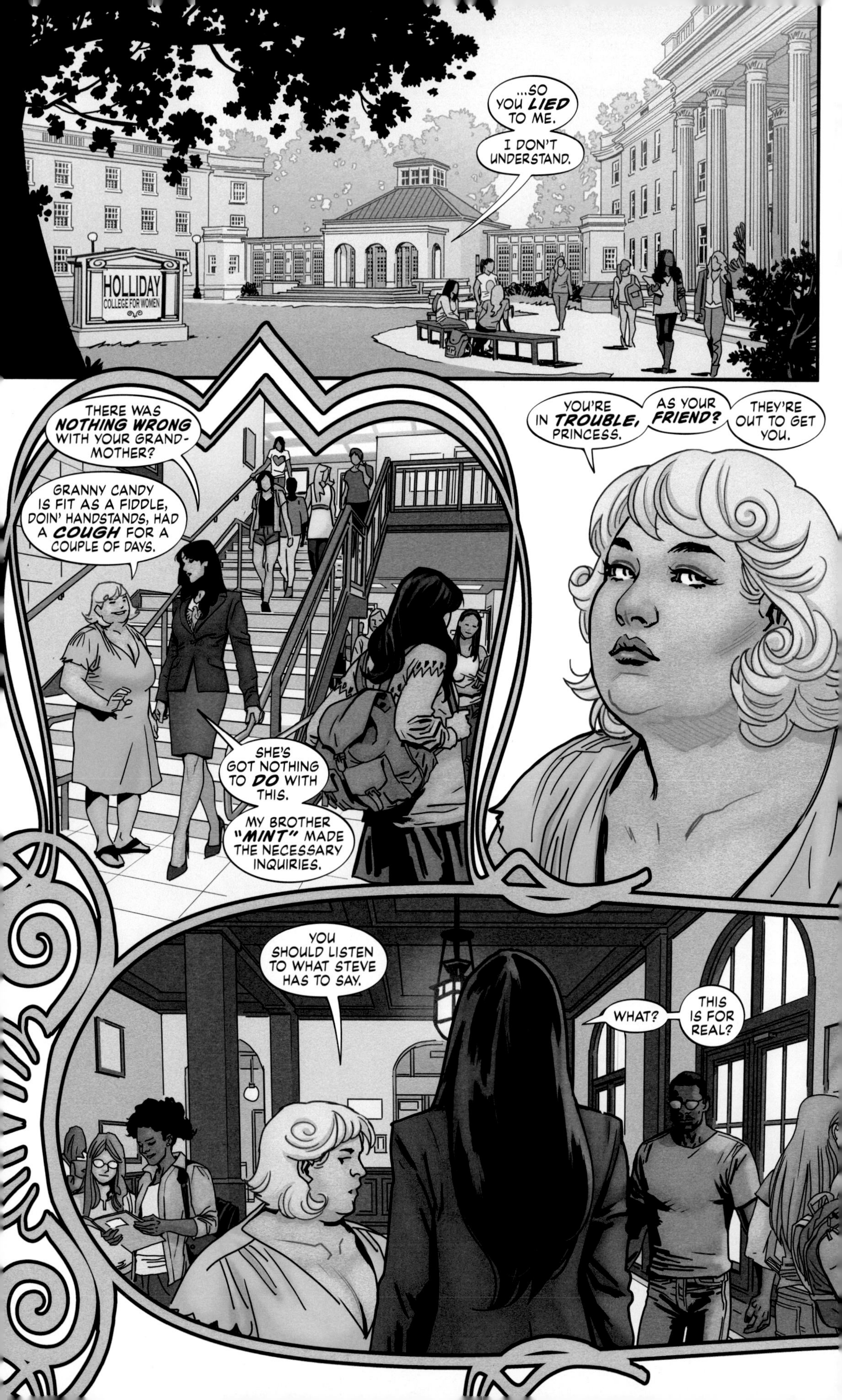
...SO YOU LIED TO ME.
I DON'T UNDERSTAND.
HOLLIDAY COLLEGE FOR WOMEN
THERE WAS NOTHING WRONG WITH YOUR GRAND-MOTHER?
GRANNY CANDY IS FIT AS A FIDDLE, DOIN' HANDSTANDS, HAD A COUGH FOR A COUPLE OF DAYS.
SHE'S GOT NOTHING TO DO WITH THIS.
MY BROTHER "MINT" MADE THE NECESSARY INQUIRIES.
YOU'RE IN TROUBLE, PRINCESS.
AS YOUR FRIEND?
THEY'RE OUT TO GET YOU.
YOU SHOULD LISTEN TO WHAT STEVE HAS TO SAY.
WHAT?
THIS IS FOR REAL?

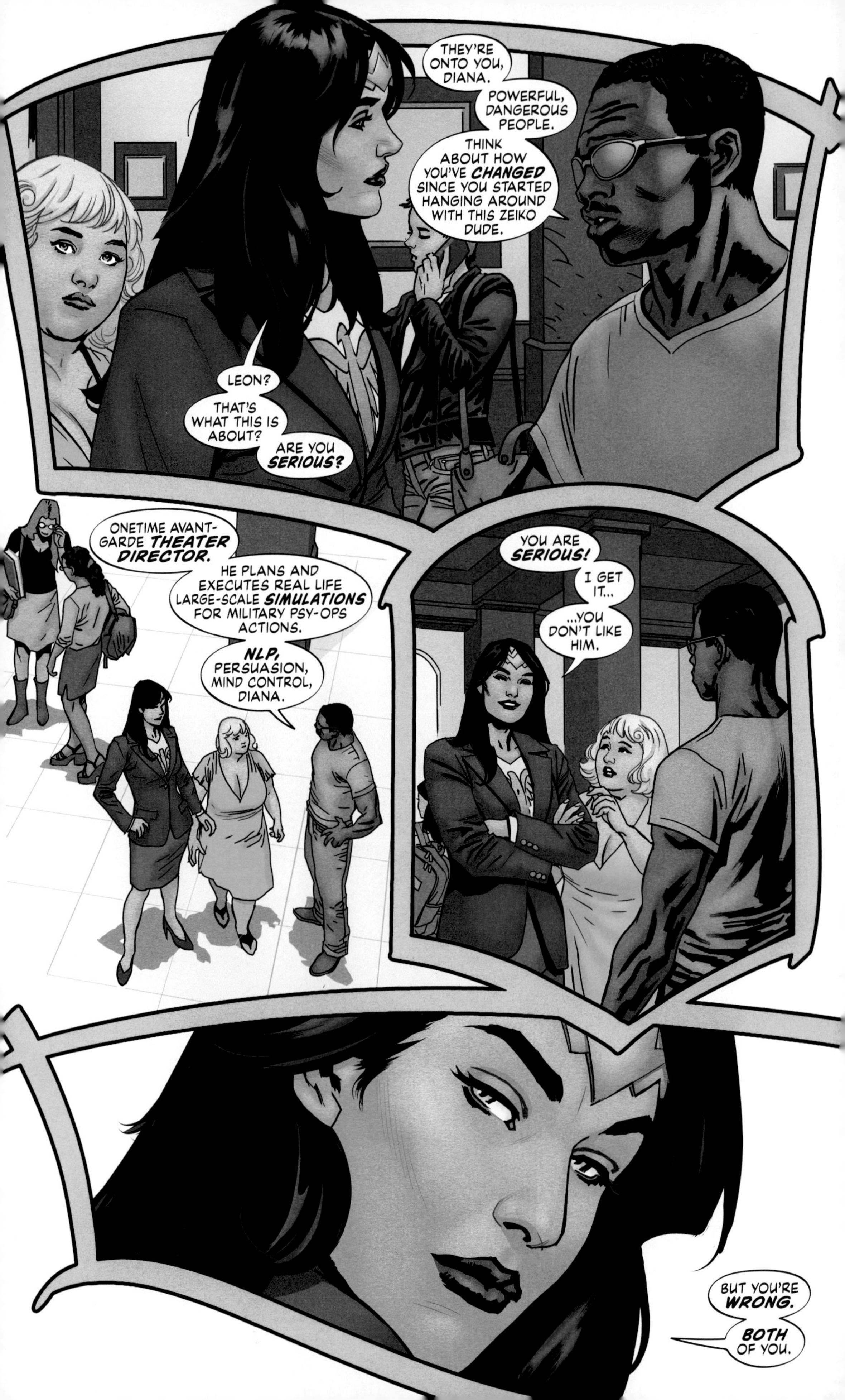
THEY'RE ONTO YOU, DIANA.
POWERFUL, DANGEROUS PEOPLE.
THINK ABOUT HOW YOU'VE CHANGED SINCE YOU STARTED HANGING AROUND WITH THIS ZEIKO DUDE.
LEON?
THAT'S WHAT THIS IS ABOUT?
ARE YOU SERIOUS?
ONETIME AVANT-GARDE THEATER DIRECTOR.
HE PLANS AND EXECUTES REAL LIFE LARGE-SCALE SIMULATIONS FOR MILITARY PSY-OPS ACTIONS.
NLP, PERSUASION, MIND CONTROL, DIANA.
YOU ARE SERIOUS!
I GET IT...
...YOU DON'T LIKE HIM.
BUT YOU'RE WRONG.
BOTH OF YOU.

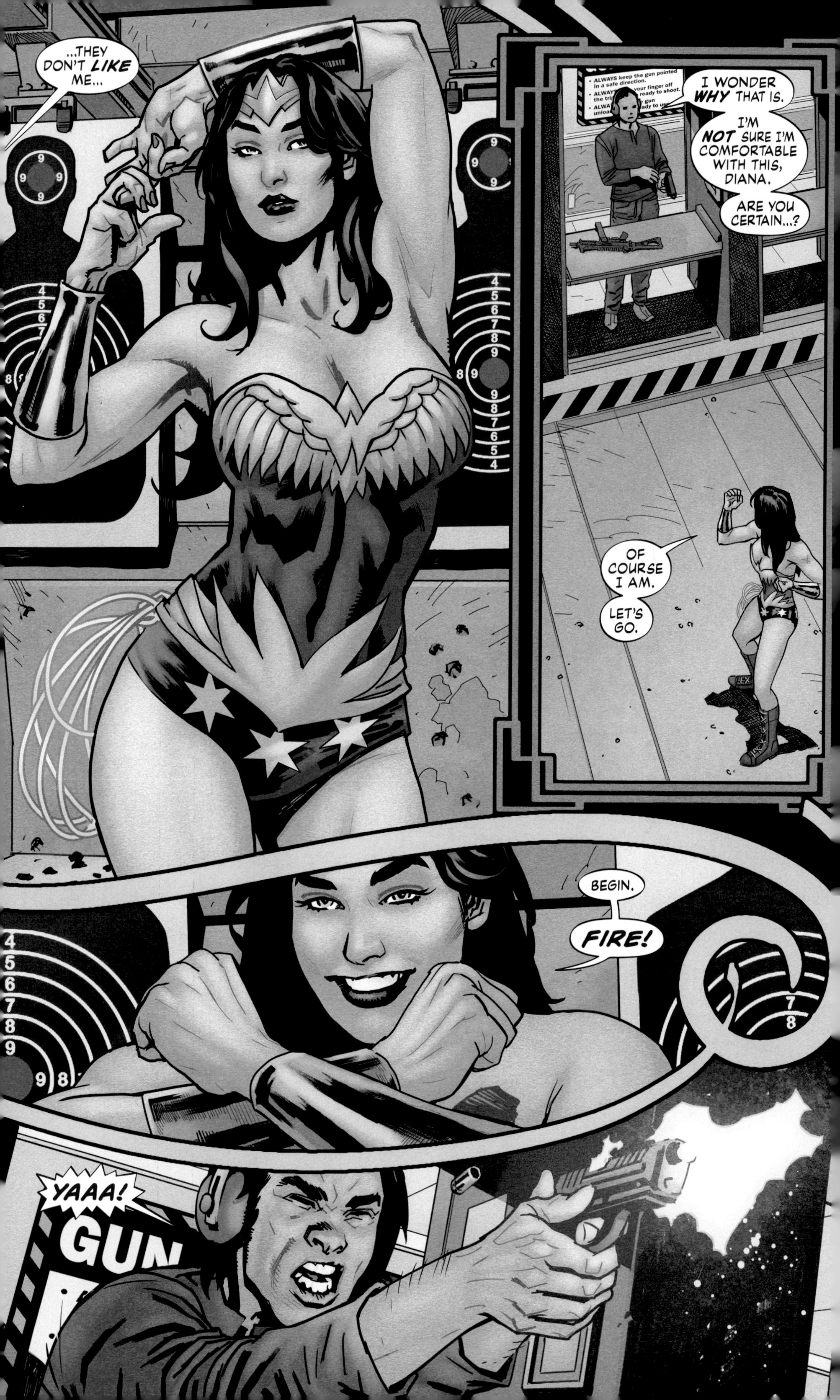
...THEY DON'T *LIKE* ME...
ALWAYS keep the gun pointed in a safe direction.
I WONDER *WHY* THAT IS.
I'M *NOT* SURE I'M COMFORTABLE WITH THIS, DIANA.
ARE YOU CERTAIN...?
OF COURSE I AM.
LET'S GO.
BEGIN.
FIRE!
YAAA!
GUN

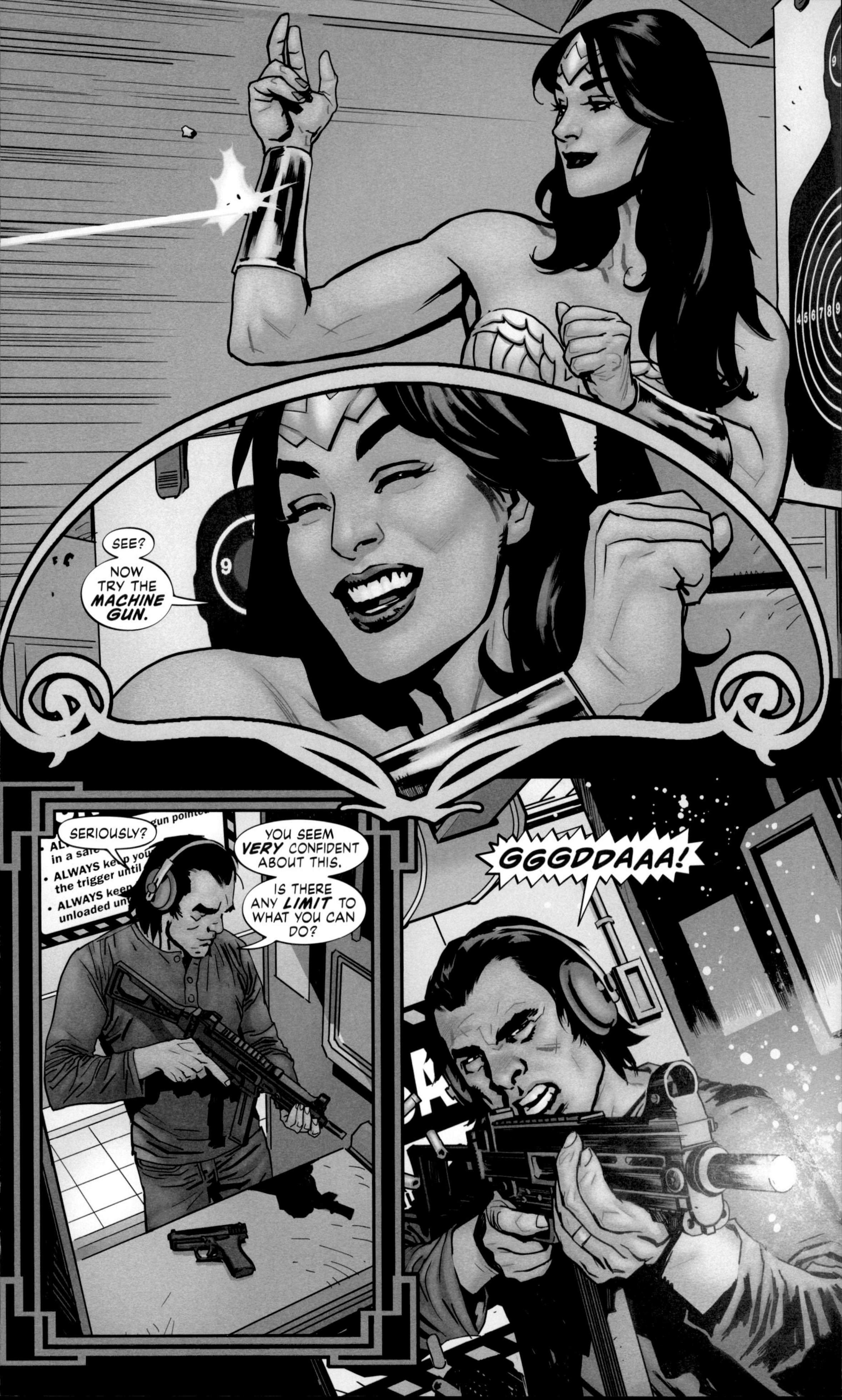
SEE? NOW TRY THE MACHINE GUN.
SERIOUSLY?
YOU SEEM VERY CONFIDENT ABOUT THIS.
IS THERE ANY LIMIT TO WHAT YOU CAN DO?
GGGDDAAA!

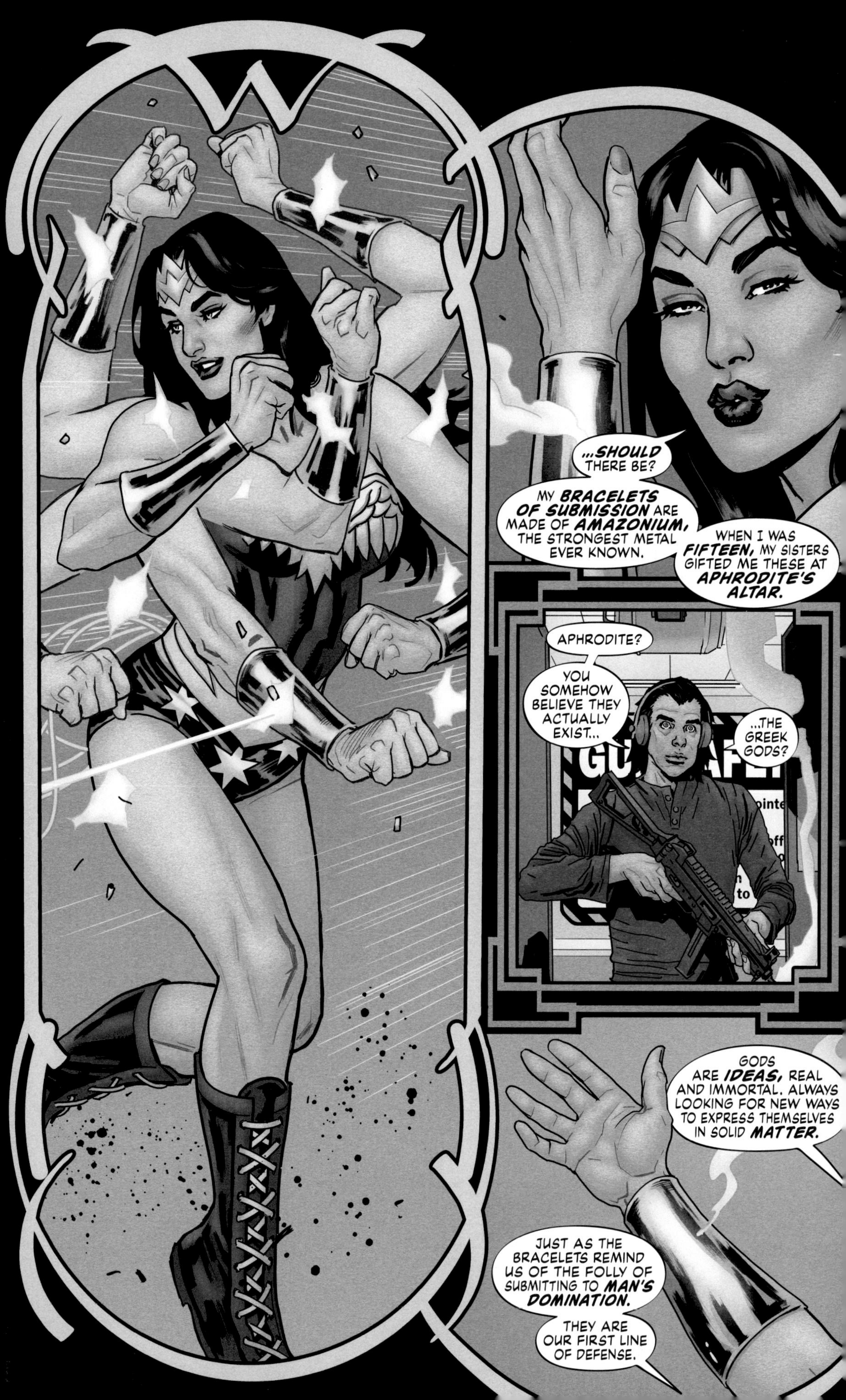
...SHOULD THERE BE?
MY BRACELETS OF SUBMISSION ARE MADE OF AMAZONIUM, THE STRONGEST METAL EVER KNOWN.
WHEN I WAS FIFTEEN, MY SISTERS GIFTED ME THESE AT APHRODITE'S ALTAR.
APHRODITE?
YOU SOMEHOW BELIEVE THEY ACTUALLY EXIST...
...THE GREEK GODS?
GODS ARE IDEAS, REAL AND IMMORTAL. ALWAYS LOOKING FOR NEW WAYS TO EXPRESS THEMSELVES IN SOLID MATTER.
JUST AS THE BRACELETS REMIND US OF THE FOLLY OF SUBMITTING TO MAN'S DOMINATION.
THEY ARE OUR FIRST LINE OF DEFENSE.

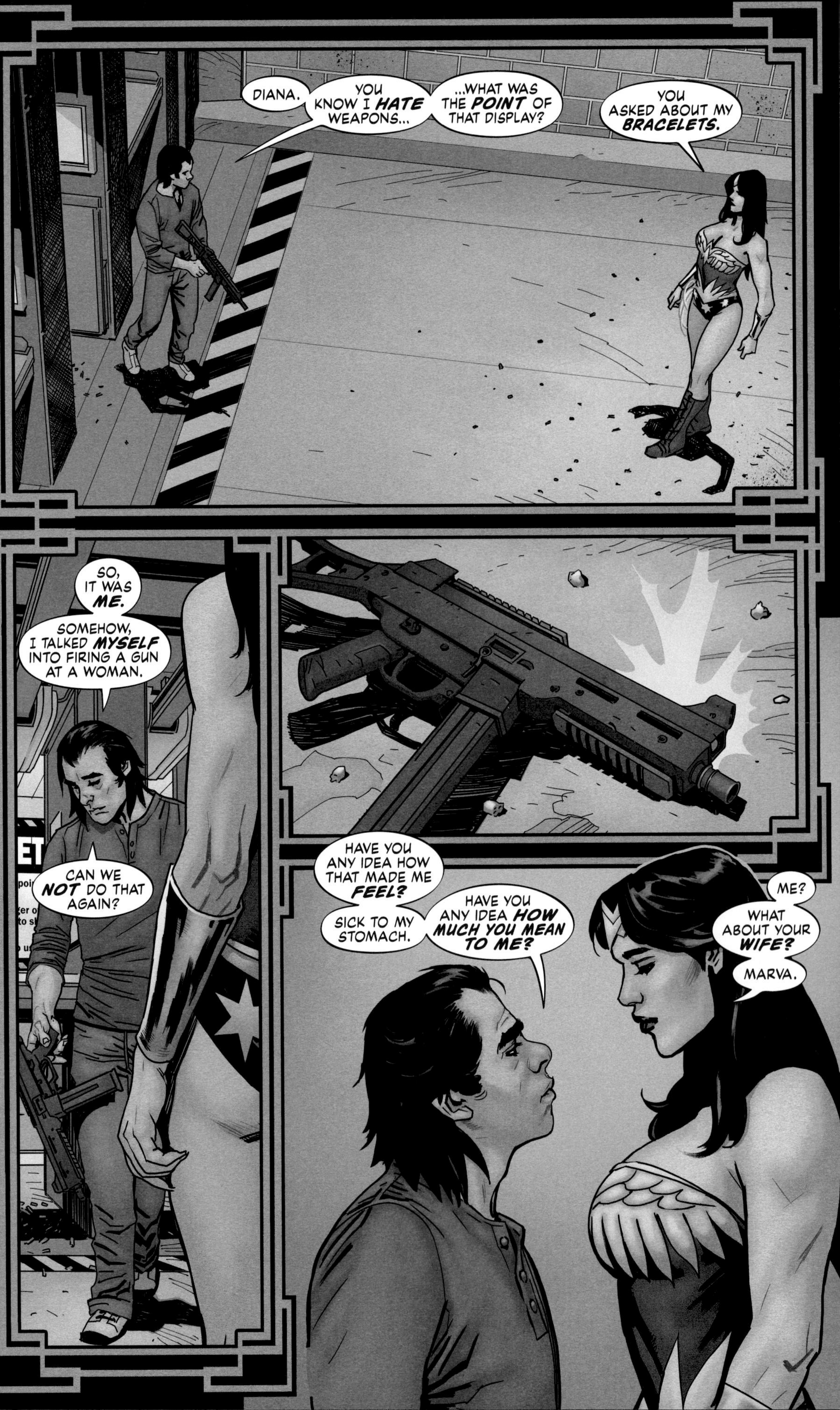

DIANA.
YOU KNOW I HATE WEAPONS...
...WHAT WAS THE POINT OF THAT DISPLAY?
YOU ASKED ABOUT MY BRACELETS.
SO, IT WAS ME.
SOMEHOW, I TALKED MYSELF INTO FIRING A GUN AT A WOMAN.
CAN WE NOT DO THAT AGAIN?
HAVE YOU ANY IDEA HOW THAT MADE ME FEEL?
SICK TO MY STOMACH.
HAVE YOU ANY IDEA HOW MUCH YOU MEAN TO ME?
ME?
WHAT ABOUT YOUR WIFE?
MARVA.

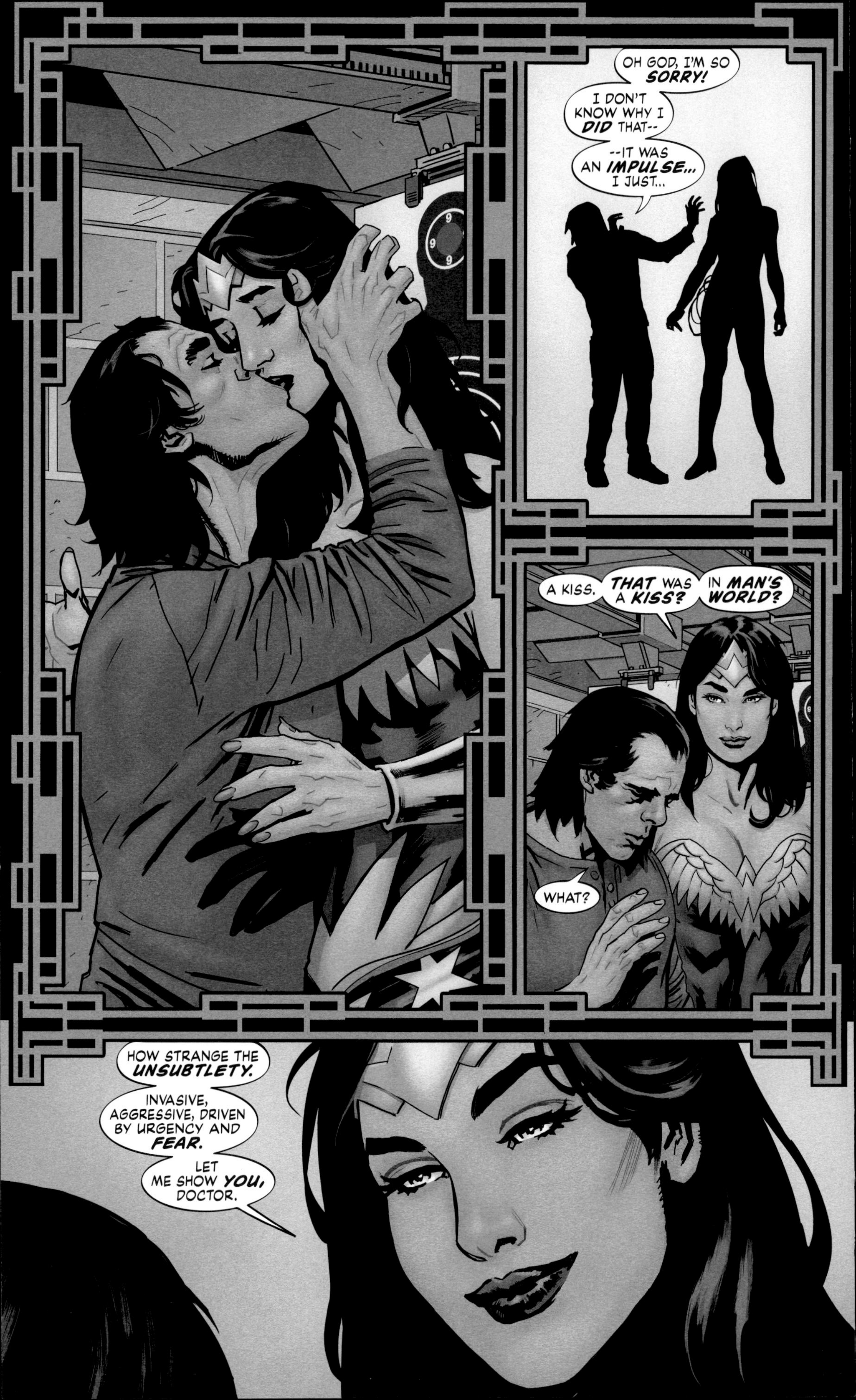
OH GOD, I'M SO SORRY!
I DON'T KNOW WHY I DID THAT--
--IT WAS AN IMPULSE... I JUST...
A KISS.
THAT WAS A KISS?
IN MAN'S WORLD?
WHAT?
HOW STRANGE THE UNSUBTLETY.
INVASIVE, AGGRESSIVE, DRIVEN BY URGENCY AND FEAR.
LET ME SHOW YOU, DOCTOR.

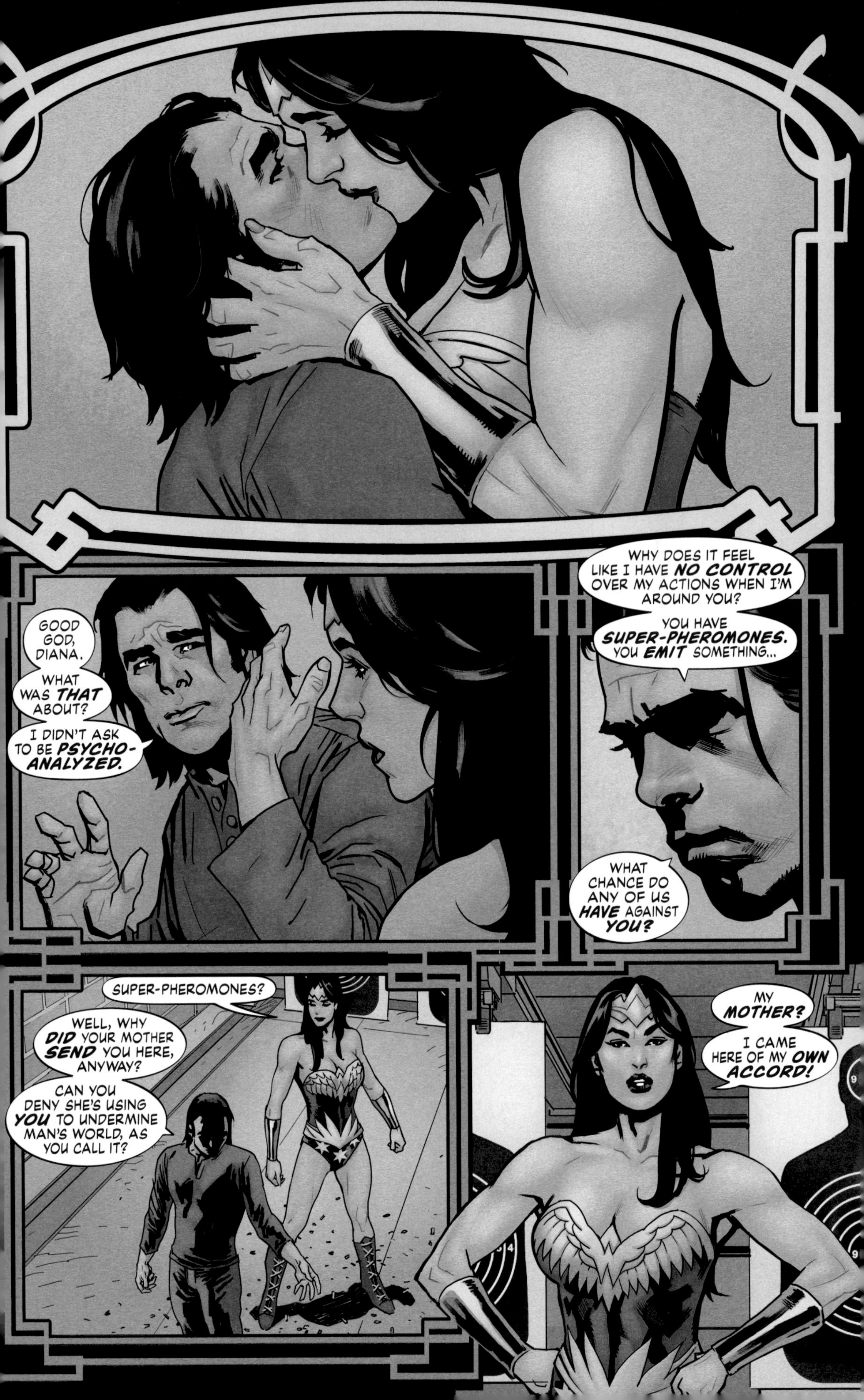
GOOD GOD, DIANA.
WHAT WAS THAT ABOUT?
I DIDN'T ASK TO BE PSYCHO-ANALYZED.
WHY DOES IT FEEL LIKE I HAVE NO CONTROL OVER MY ACTIONS WHEN I'M AROUND YOU?
YOU HAVE SUPER-PHEROMONES. YOU EMIT SOMETHING...
WHAT CHANCE DO ANY OF US HAVE AGAINST YOU?
SUPER-PHEROMONES?
WELL, WHY DID YOUR MOTHER SEND YOU HERE, ANYWAY?
CAN YOU DENY SHE'S USING YOU TO UNDERMINE MAN'S WORLD, AS YOU CALL IT?
MY MOTHER?
I CAME HERE OF MY OWN ACCORD!

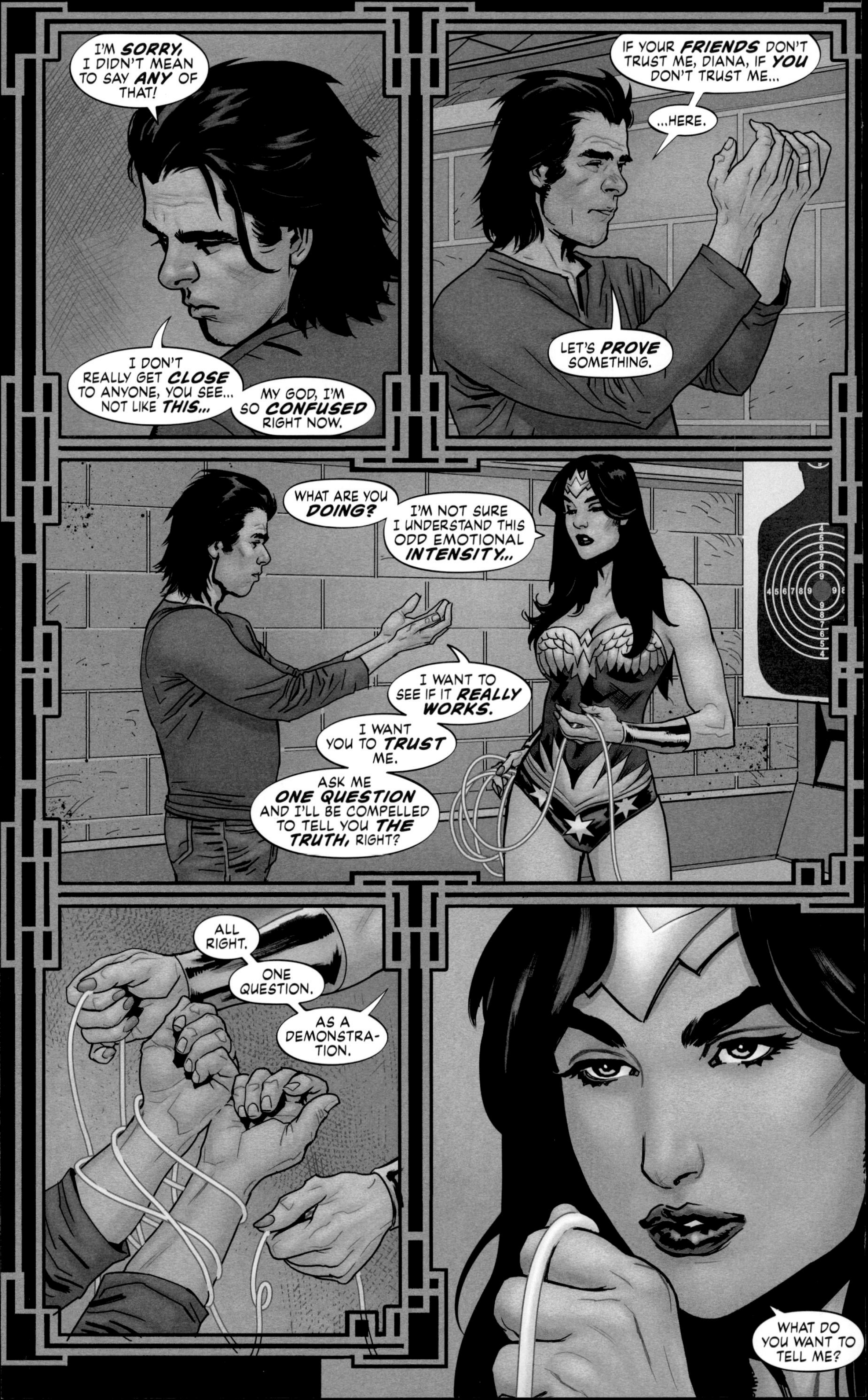
I'M SORRY, I DIDN'T MEAN TO SAY ANY OF THAT!
I DON'T REALLY GET CLOSE TO ANYONE, YOU SEE... NOT LIKE THIS...
MY GOD, I'M SO CONFUSED RIGHT NOW.
IF YOUR FRIENDS DON'T TRUST ME, DIANA, IF YOU DON'T TRUST ME...
...HERE.
LET'S PROVE SOMETHING.
WHAT ARE YOU DOING?
I'M NOT SURE I UNDERSTAND THIS ODD EMOTIONAL INTENSITY...
I WANT TO SEE IF IT REALLY WORKS.
I WANT YOU TO TRUST ME.
ASK ME ONE QUESTION AND I'LL BE COMPELLED TO TELL YOU THE TRUTH, RIGHT?
ALL RIGHT.
ONE QUESTION.
AS A DEMONSTRA-TION.
WHAT DO YOU WANT TO TELL ME?

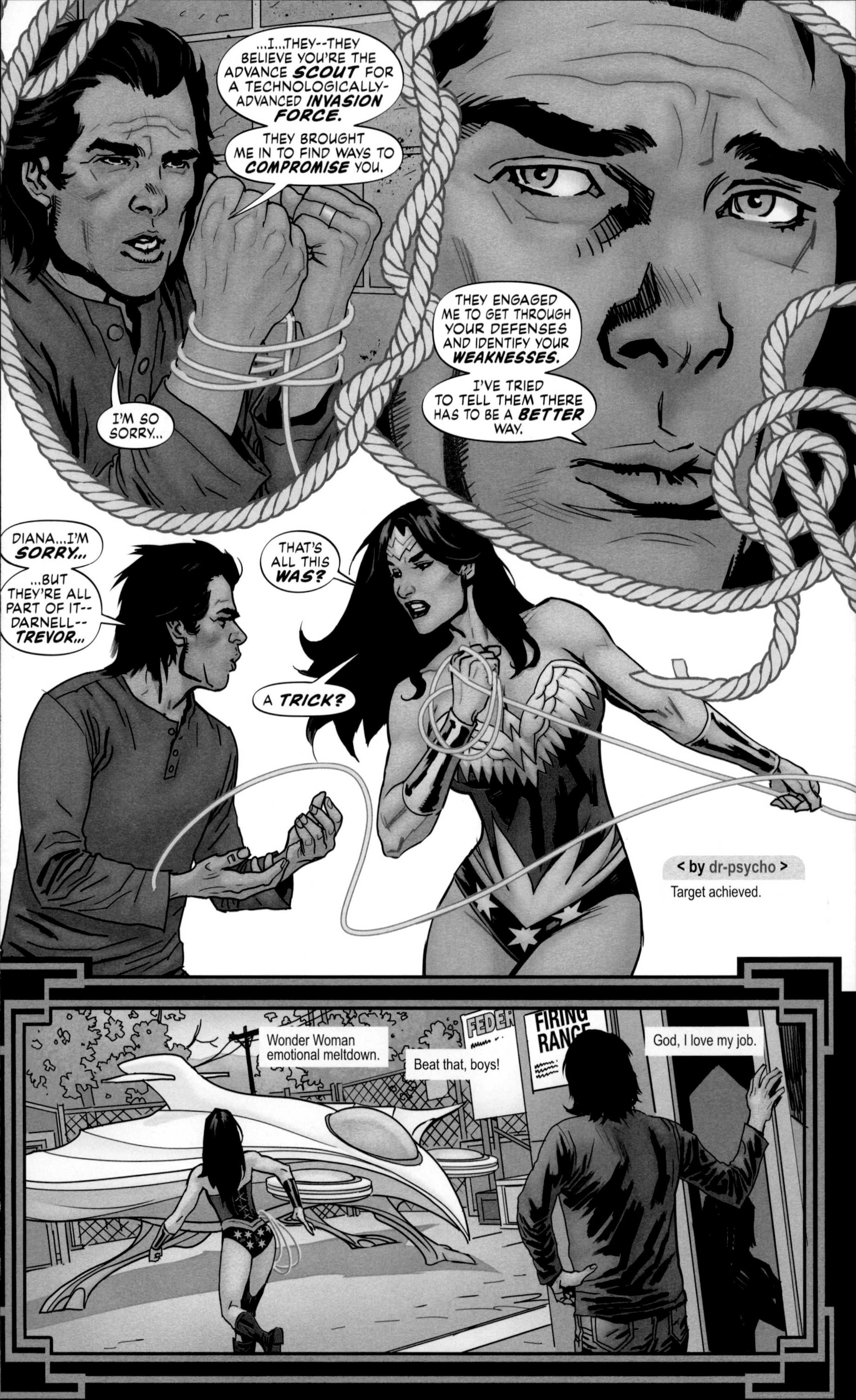
...I...THEY--THEY BELIEVE YOU'RE THE ADVANCE SCOUT FOR A TECHNOLOGICALLY-ADVANCED INVASION FORCE.
THEY BROUGHT ME IN TO FIND WAYS TO COMPROMISE YOU.
I'M SO SORRY...
THEY ENGAGED ME TO GET THROUGH YOUR DEFENSES AND IDENTIFY YOUR WEAKNESSES.
I'VE TRIED TO TELL THEM THERE HAS TO BE A BETTER WAY.
DIANA...I'M SORRY...
...BUT THEY'RE ALL PART OF IT--DARNELL--TREVOR...
THAT'S ALL THIS WAS?
A TRICK?
< by dr-psycho >
Target achieved.
Wonder Woman emotional meltdown.
Beat that, boys!
God, I love my job.
FIRING RANGE

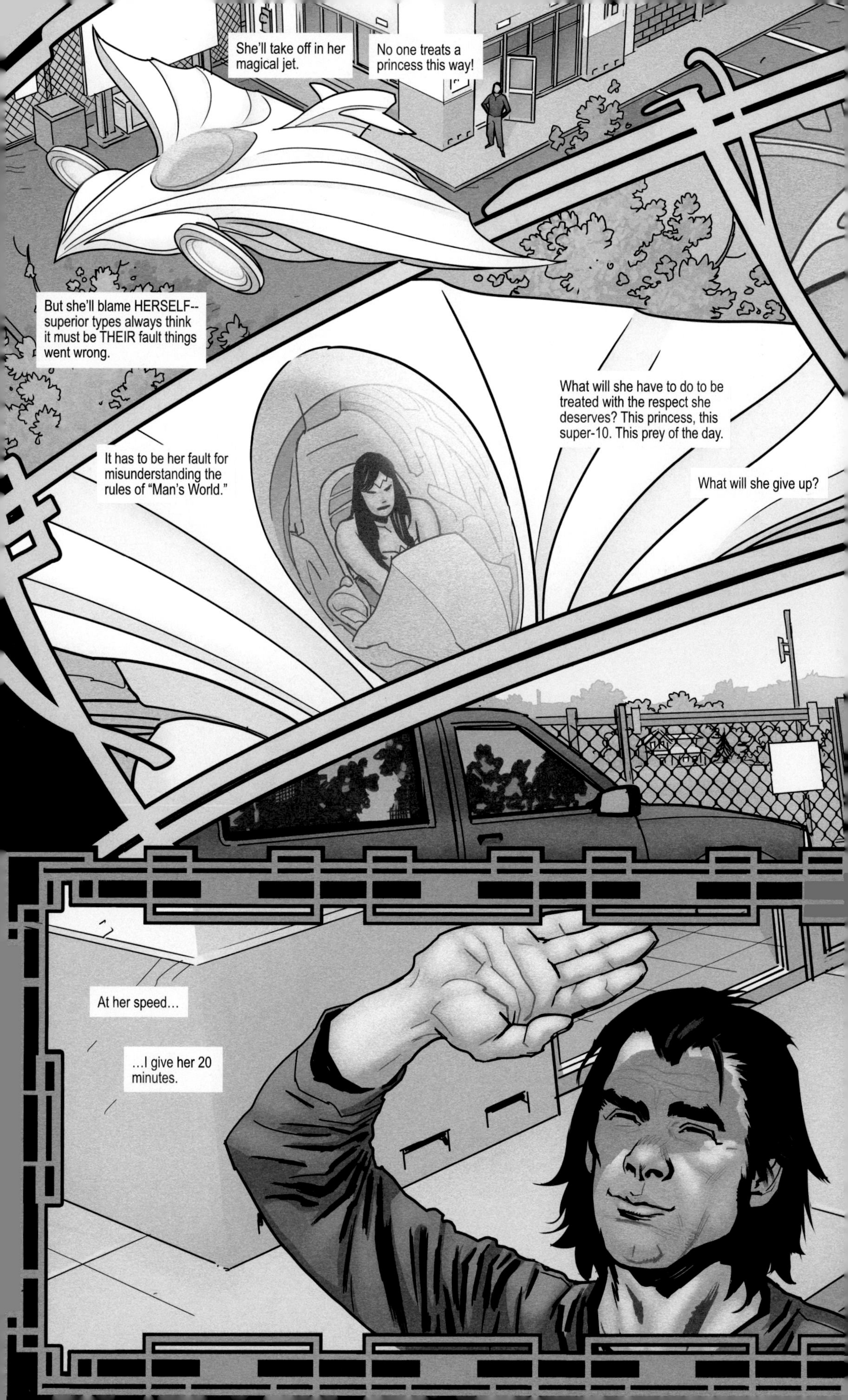
She'll take off in her magical jet.
No one treats a princess this way!
But she'll blame HERSELF-- superior types always think it must be THEIR fault things went wrong.
It has to be her fault for misunderstanding the rules of "Man's World."
What will she have to do to be treated with the respect she deserves? This princess, this super-10. This prey of the day.
What will she give up?
At her speed…
…I give her 20 minutes.

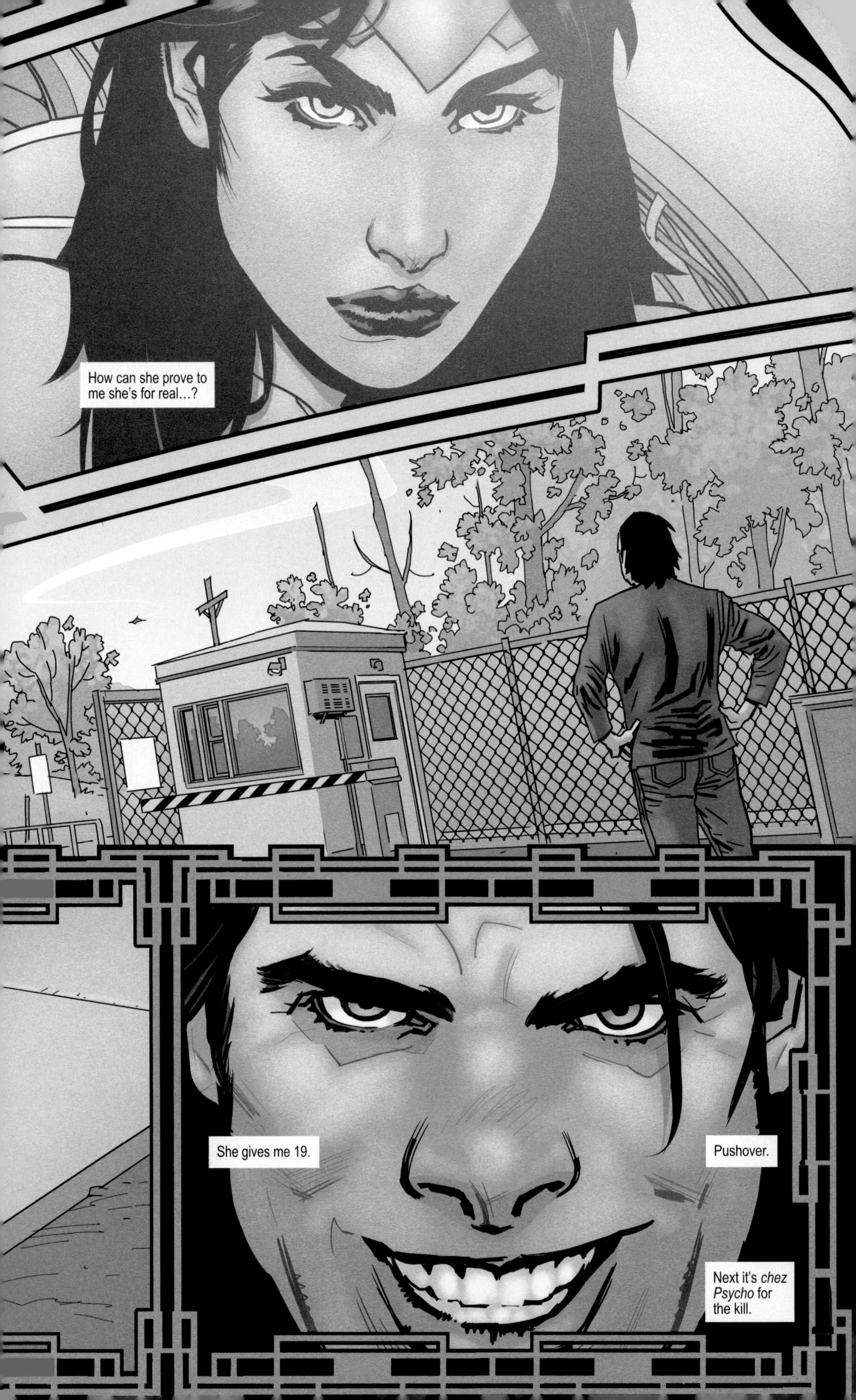
How can she prove to me she's for real…?
She gives me 19.
Pushover.
Next it's *chez Psycho* for the kill.

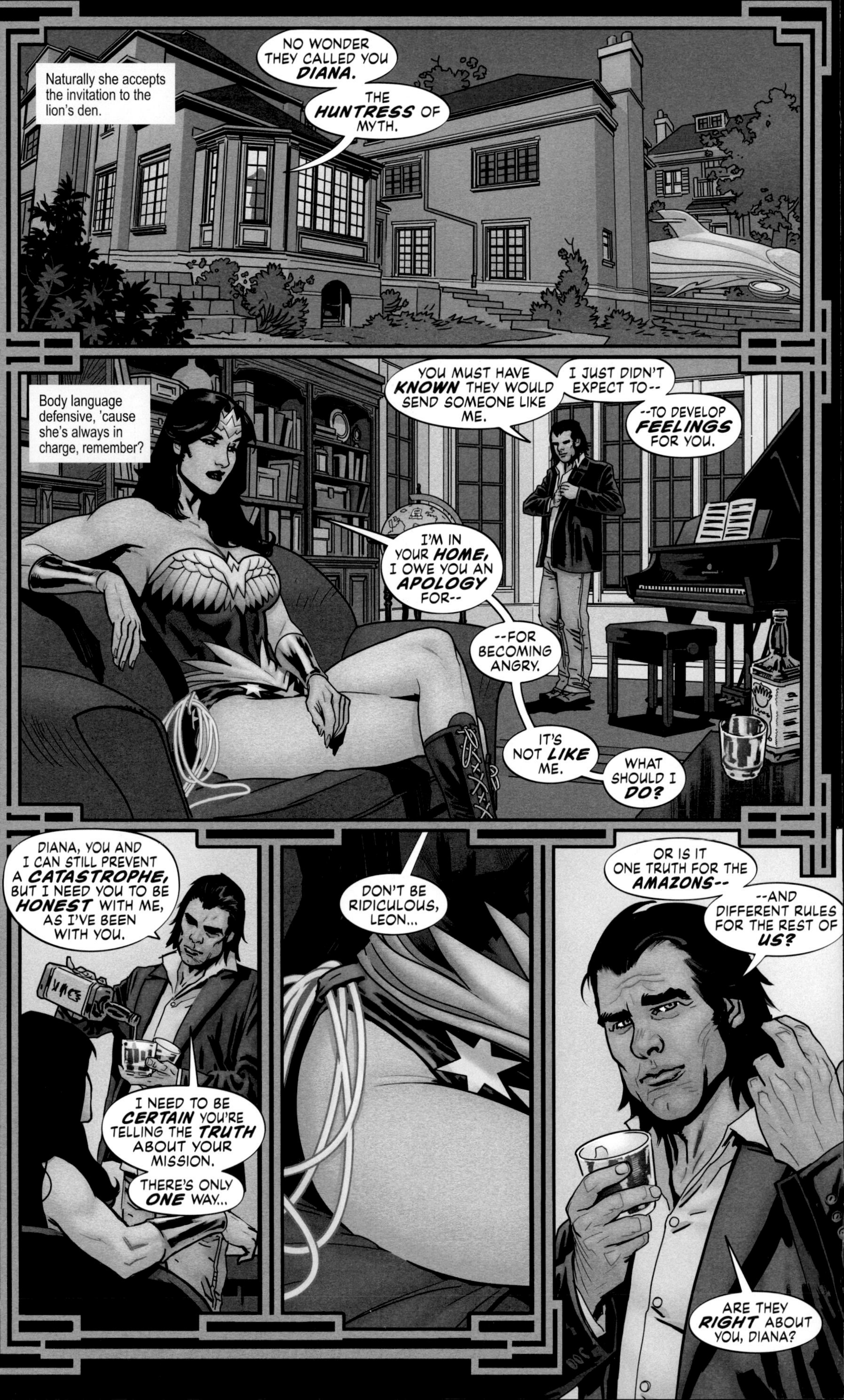
Naturally she accepts the invitation to the lion's den.
NO WONDER THEY CALLED YOU DIANA.
THE HUNTRESS OF MYTH.
Body language defensive, 'cause she's always in charge, remember?
YOU MUST HAVE KNOWN THEY WOULD SEND SOMEONE LIKE ME.
I JUST DIDN'T EXPECT TO--
--TO DEVELOP FEELINGS FOR YOU.
I'M IN YOUR HOME, I OWE YOU AN APOLOGY FOR--
--FOR BECOMING ANGRY.
IT'S NOT LIKE ME.
WHAT SHOULD I DO?
DIANA, YOU AND I CAN STILL PREVENT A CATASTROPHE, BUT I NEED YOU TO BE HONEST WITH ME, AS I'VE BEEN WITH YOU.
I NEED TO BE CERTAIN YOU'RE TELLING THE TRUTH ABOUT YOUR MISSION.
THERE'S ONLY ONE WAY...
DON'T BE RIDICULOUS, LEON...
OR IS IT ONE TRUTH FOR THE AMAZONS--
--AND DIFFERENT RULES FOR THE REST OF US?
ARE THEY RIGHT ABOUT YOU, DIANA?

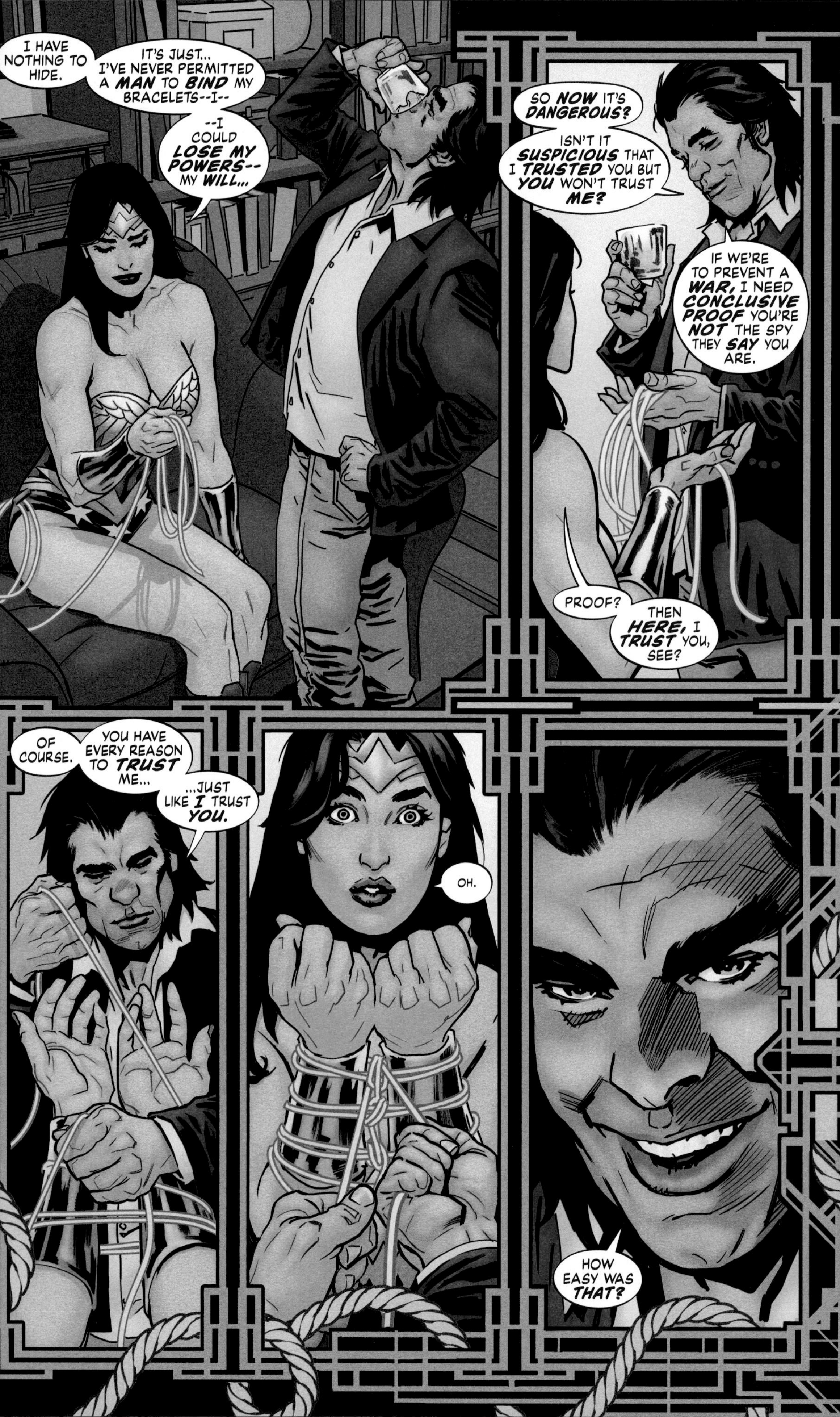
I HAVE NOTHING TO HIDE.
IT'S JUST... I'VE NEVER PERMITTED A MAN TO BIND MY BRACELETS--I--
--I COULD LOSE MY POWERS-- MY WILL...
SO NOW IT'S DANGEROUS?
ISN'T IT SUSPICIOUS THAT I TRUSTED YOU BUT YOU WON'T TRUST ME?
IF WE'RE TO PREVENT A WAR, I NEED CONCLUSIVE PROOF YOU'RE NOT THE SPY THEY SAY YOU ARE.
PROOF?
THEN HERE, I TRUST YOU, SEE?
OF COURSE.
YOU HAVE EVERY REASON TO TRUST ME...
...JUST LIKE I TRUST YOU.
OH.
HOW EASY WAS THAT?

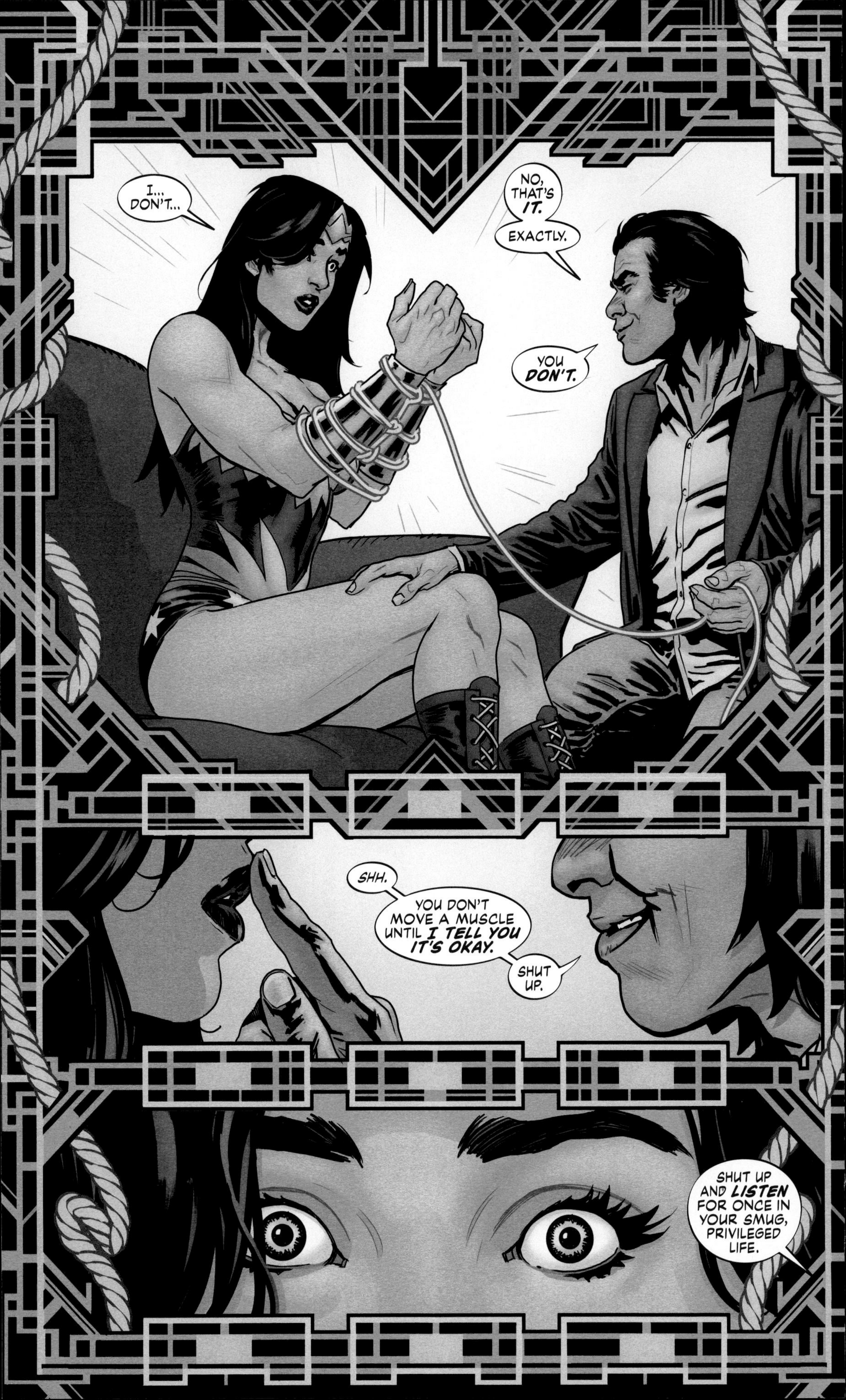

I... DON'T...
NO, THAT'S IT.
EXACTLY.
YOU DON'T.
SHH.
YOU DON'T MOVE A MUSCLE UNTIL I TELL YOU IT'S OKAY.
SHUT UP.
SHUT UP AND LISTEN FOR ONCE IN YOUR SMUG, PRIVILEGED LIFE.

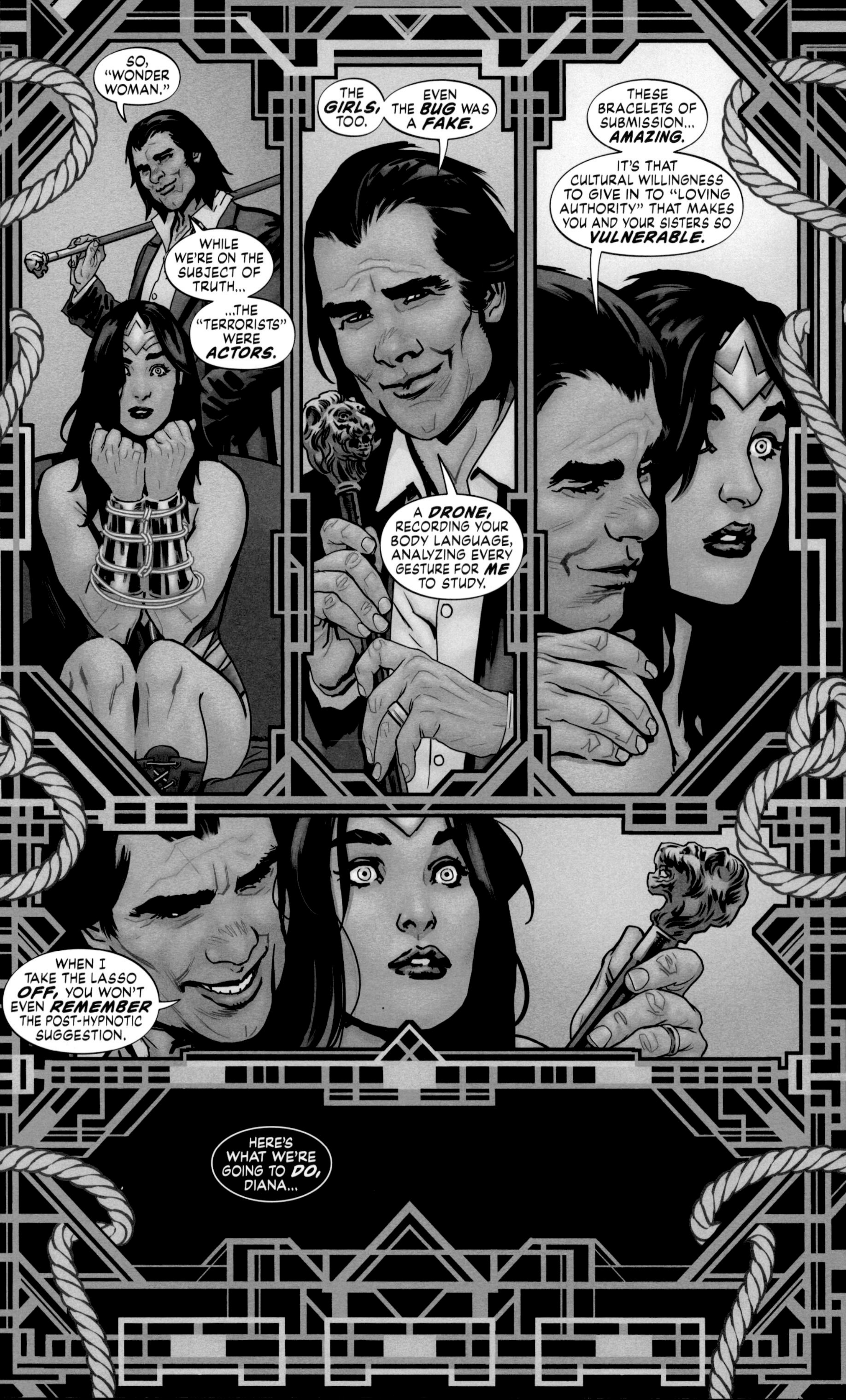
SO, "WONDER WOMAN."
WHILE WE'RE ON THE SUBJECT OF TRUTH...
...THE "TERRORISTS" WERE ACTORS.
THE GIRLS, TOO.
EVEN THE BUG WAS A FAKE.
A DRONE, RECORDING YOUR BODY LANGUAGE, ANALYZING EVERY GESTURE FOR ME TO STUDY.
THESE BRACELETS OF SUBMISSION... AMAZING.
IT'S THAT CULTURAL WILLINGNESS TO GIVE IN TO "LOVING AUTHORITY" THAT MAKES YOU AND YOUR SISTERS SO VULNERABLE.
WHEN I TAKE THE LASSO OFF, YOU WON'T EVEN REMEMBER THE POST-HYPNOTIC SUGGESTION.
HERE'S WHAT WE'RE GOING TO DO, DIANA...

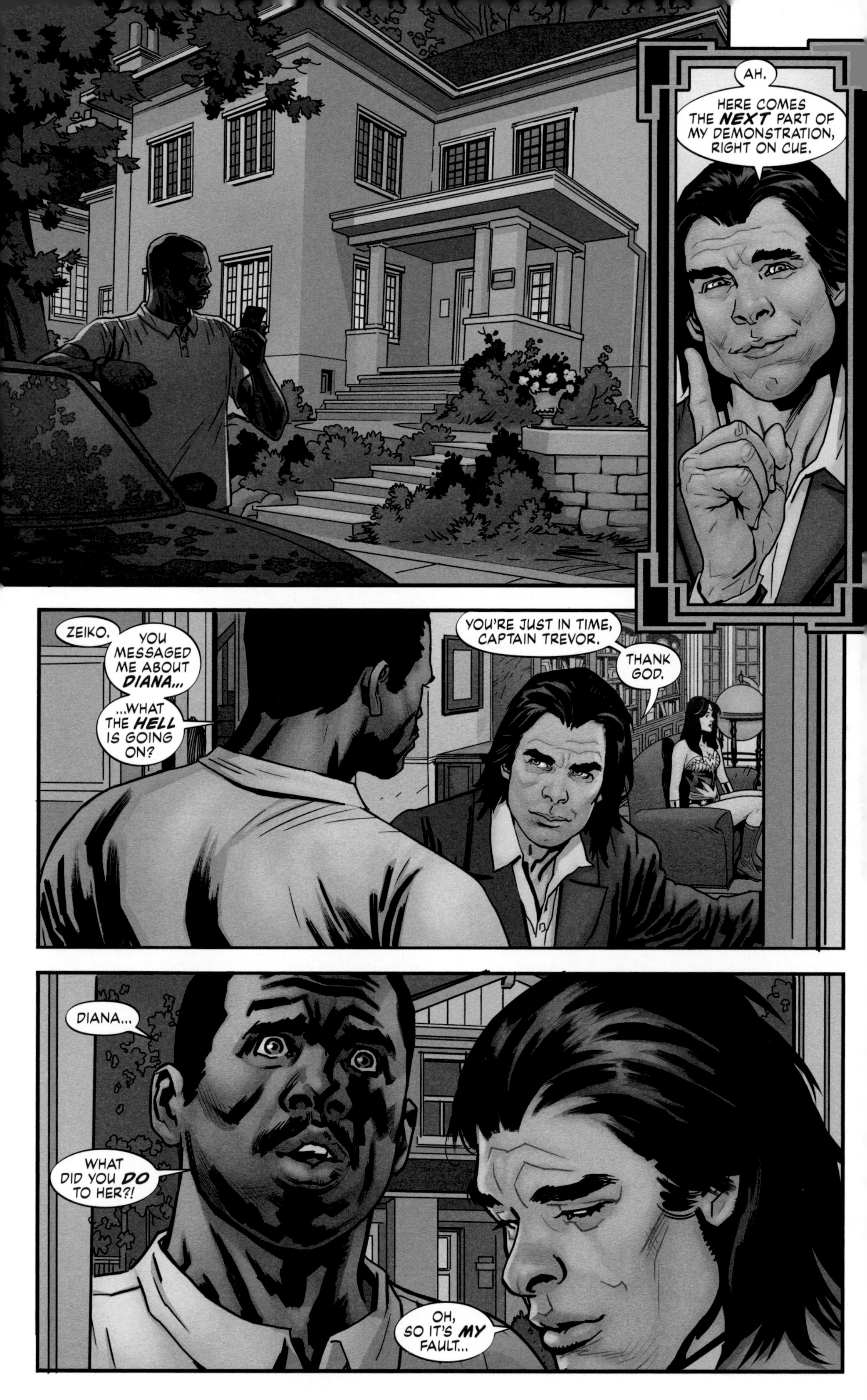
AH.
HERE COMES THE NEXT PART OF MY DEMONSTRATION, RIGHT ON CUE.
ZEIKO.
YOU MESSAGED ME ABOUT DIANA...
...WHAT THE HELL IS GOING ON?
YOU'RE JUST IN TIME, CAPTAIN TREVOR.
THANK GOD.
DIANA...
WHAT DID YOU DO TO HER?!
OH, SO IT'S MY FAULT...

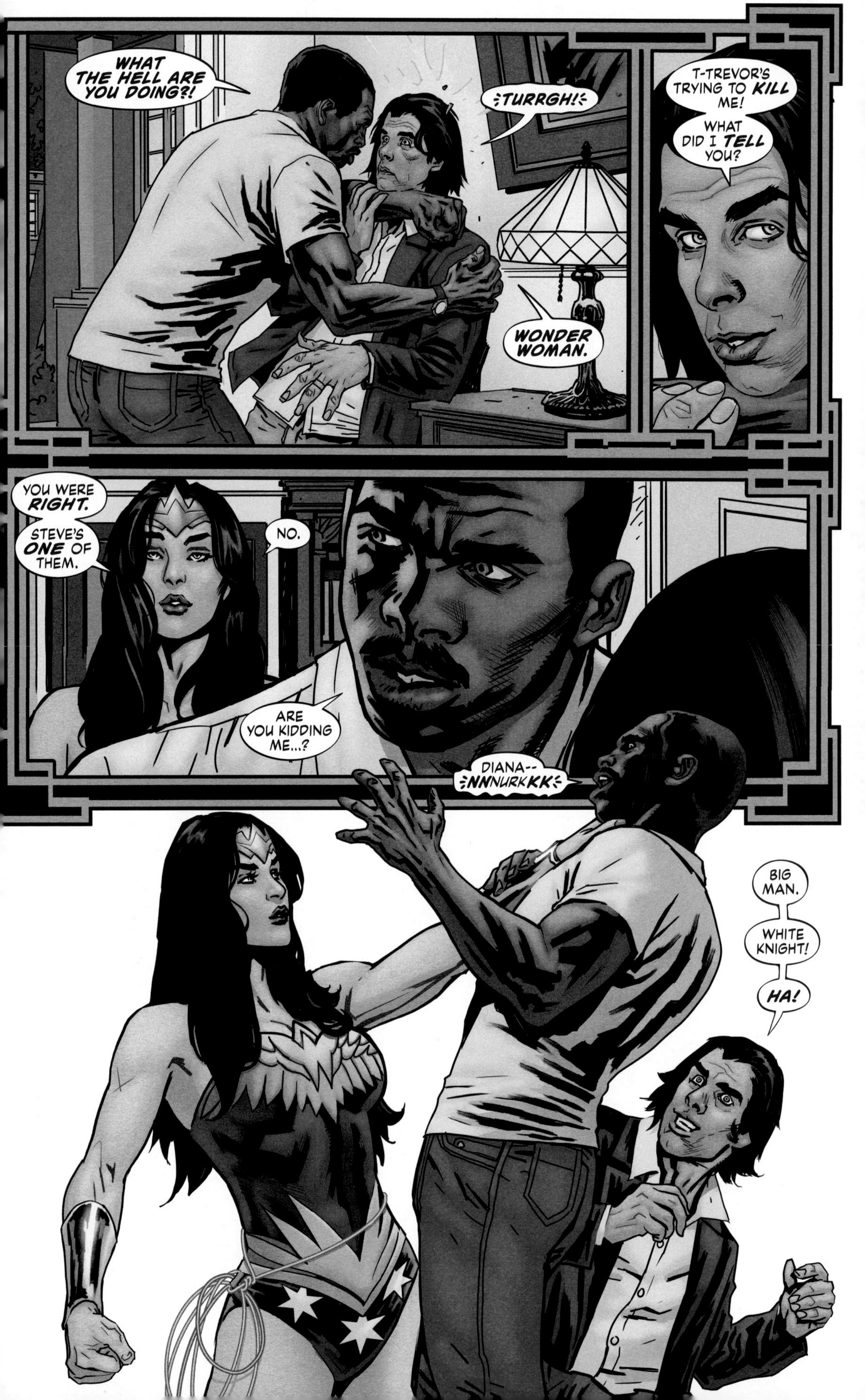
WHAT THE HELL ARE YOU DOING?!
TURRGH!
WONDER WOMAN.
T-TREVOR'S TRYING TO KILL ME!
WHAT DID I TELL YOU?
YOU WERE RIGHT.
STEVE'S ONE OF THEM.
NO.
ARE YOU KIDDING ME...?
DIANA--
NNNURKKK
BIG MAN.
WHITE KNIGHT!
HA!

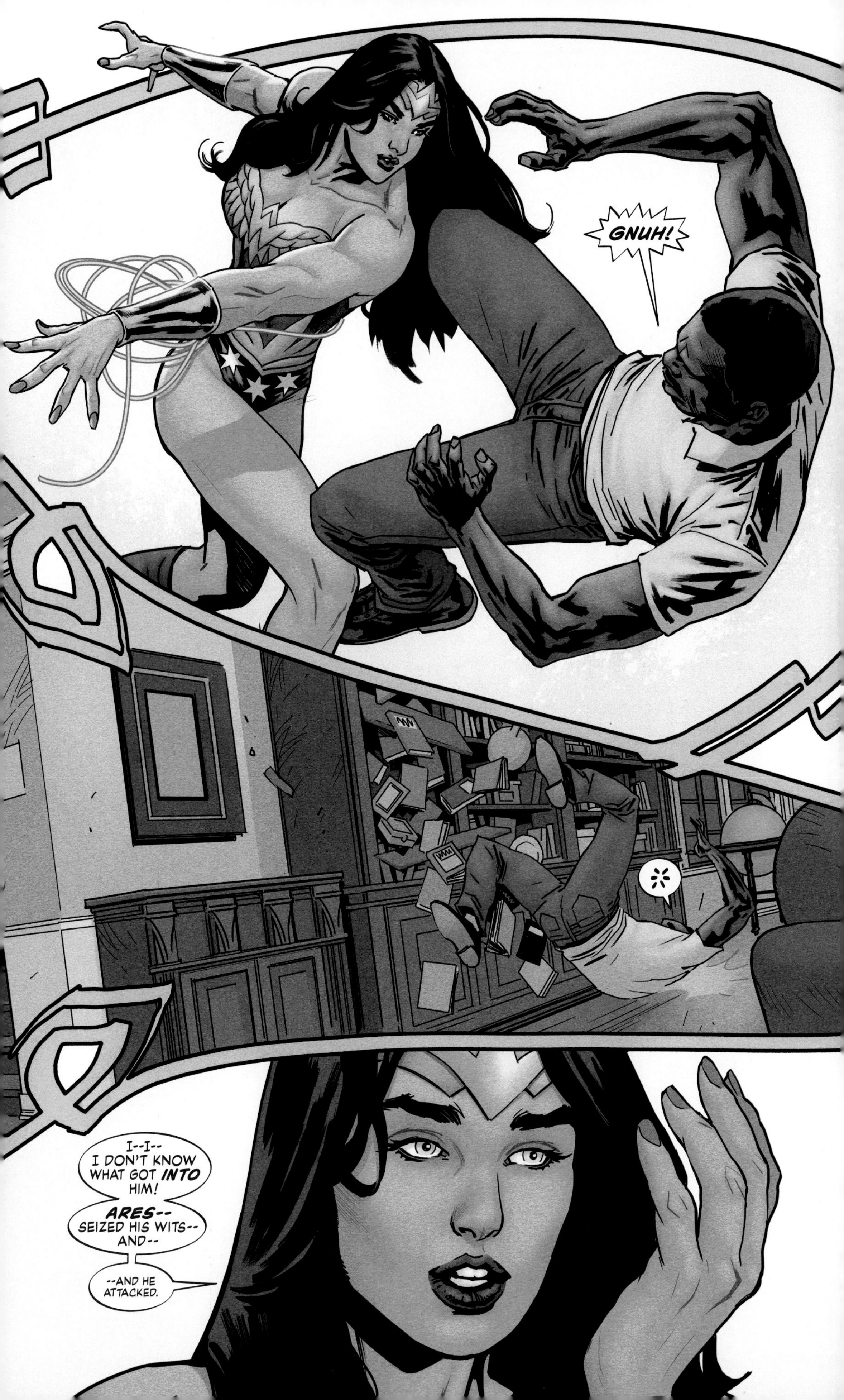
GNUH!
I--I--
I DON'T KNOW WHAT GOT INTO HIM!
ARES--
SEIZED HIS WITS--
AND--
--AND HE ATTACKED.

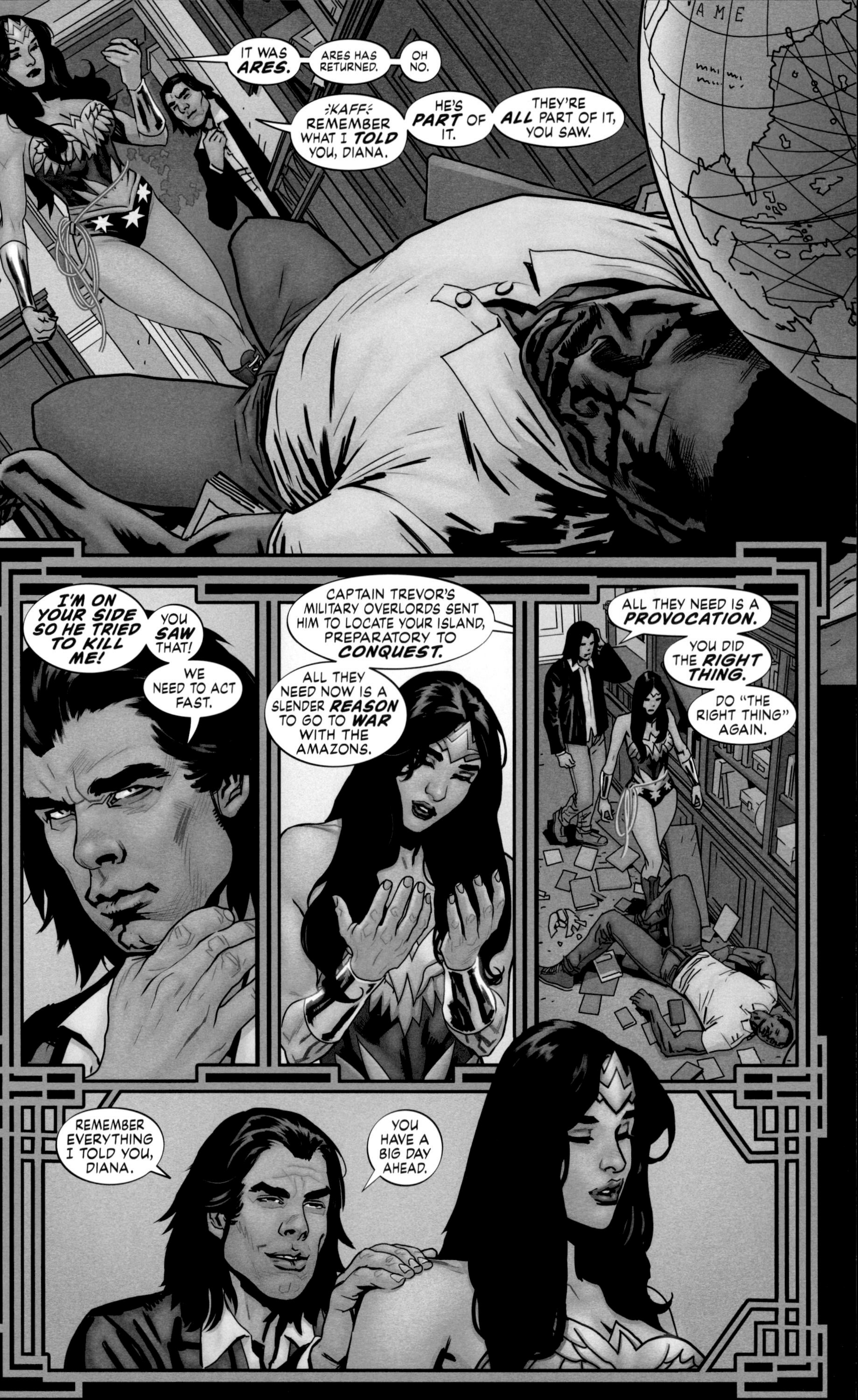
IT WAS ARES.
ARES HAS RETURNED.
OH NO.
KAFF REMEMBER WHAT I TOLD YOU, DIANA.
HE'S PART OF IT.
THEY'RE ALL PART OF IT, YOU SAW.
I'M ON YOUR SIDE SO HE TRIED TO KILL ME!
YOU SAW THAT!
WE NEED TO ACT FAST.
CAPTAIN TREVOR'S MILITARY OVERLORDS SENT HIM TO LOCATE YOUR ISLAND, PREPARATORY TO CONQUEST.
ALL THEY NEED NOW IS A SLENDER REASON TO GO TO WAR WITH THE AMAZONS.
ALL THEY NEED IS A PROVOCATION.
YOU DID THE RIGHT THING.
DO "THE RIGHT THING" AGAIN.
REMEMBER EVERYTHING I TOLD YOU, DIANA.
YOU HAVE A BIG DAY AHEAD.

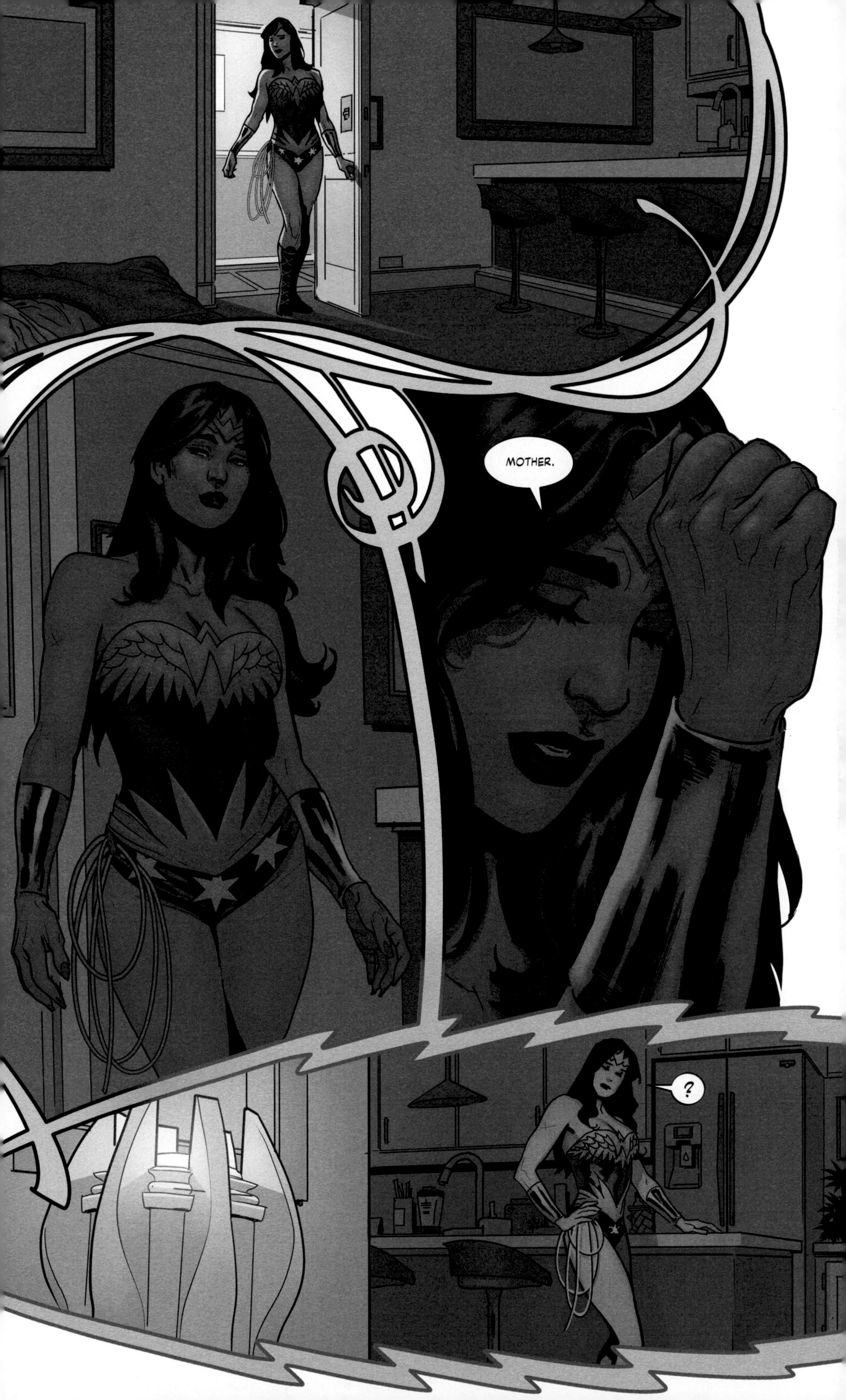
MOTHER.
?

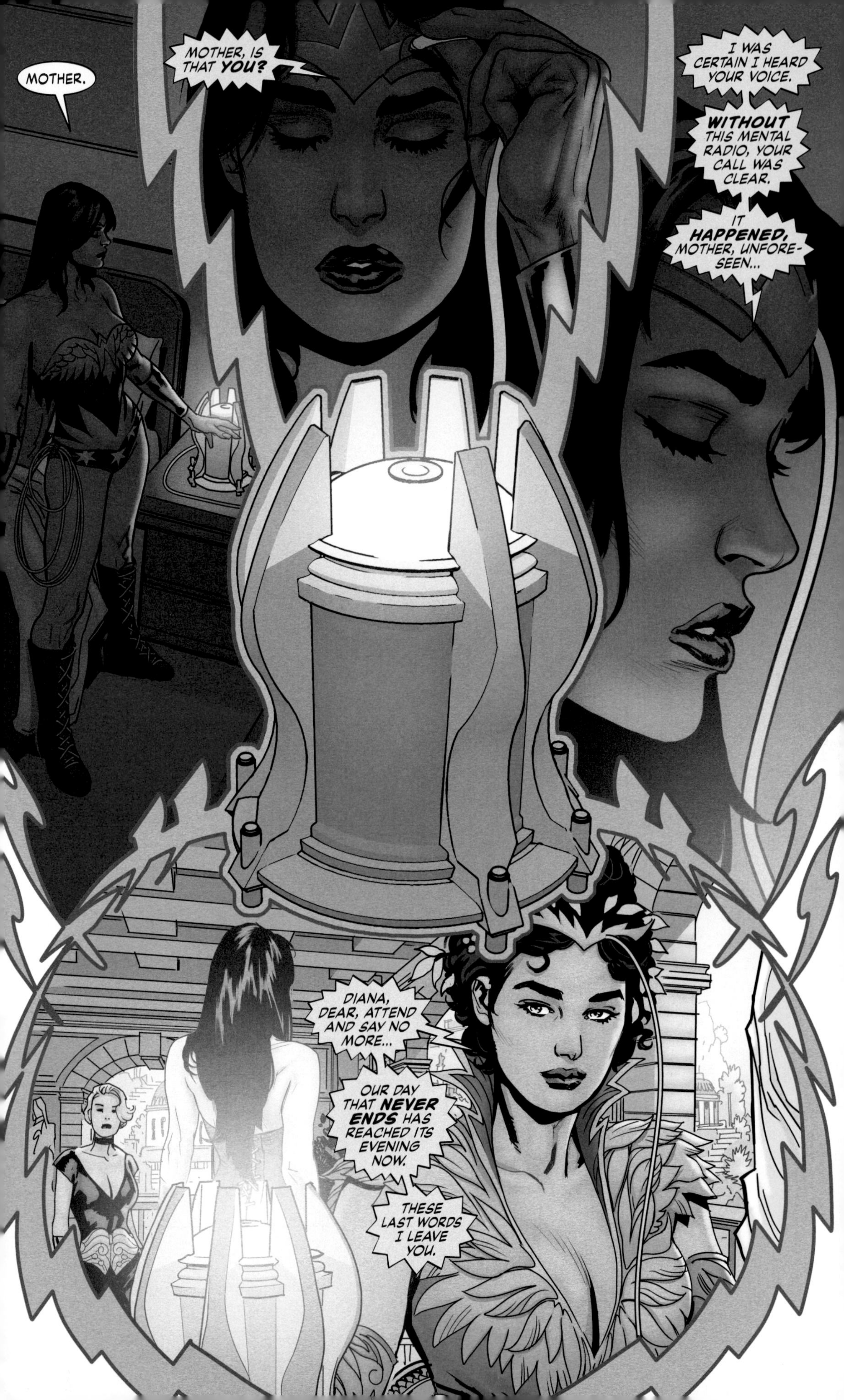
MOTHER.
MOTHER, IS THAT YOU?
I WAS CERTAIN I HEARD YOUR VOICE.
WITHOUT THIS MENTAL RADIO, YOUR CALL WAS CLEAR.
IT HAPPENED, MOTHER, UNFORE-SEEN...
DIANA, DEAR, ATTEND AND SAY NO MORE...
OUR DAY THAT NEVER ENDS HAS REACHED ITS EVENING NOW.
THESE LAST WORDS I LEAVE YOU.

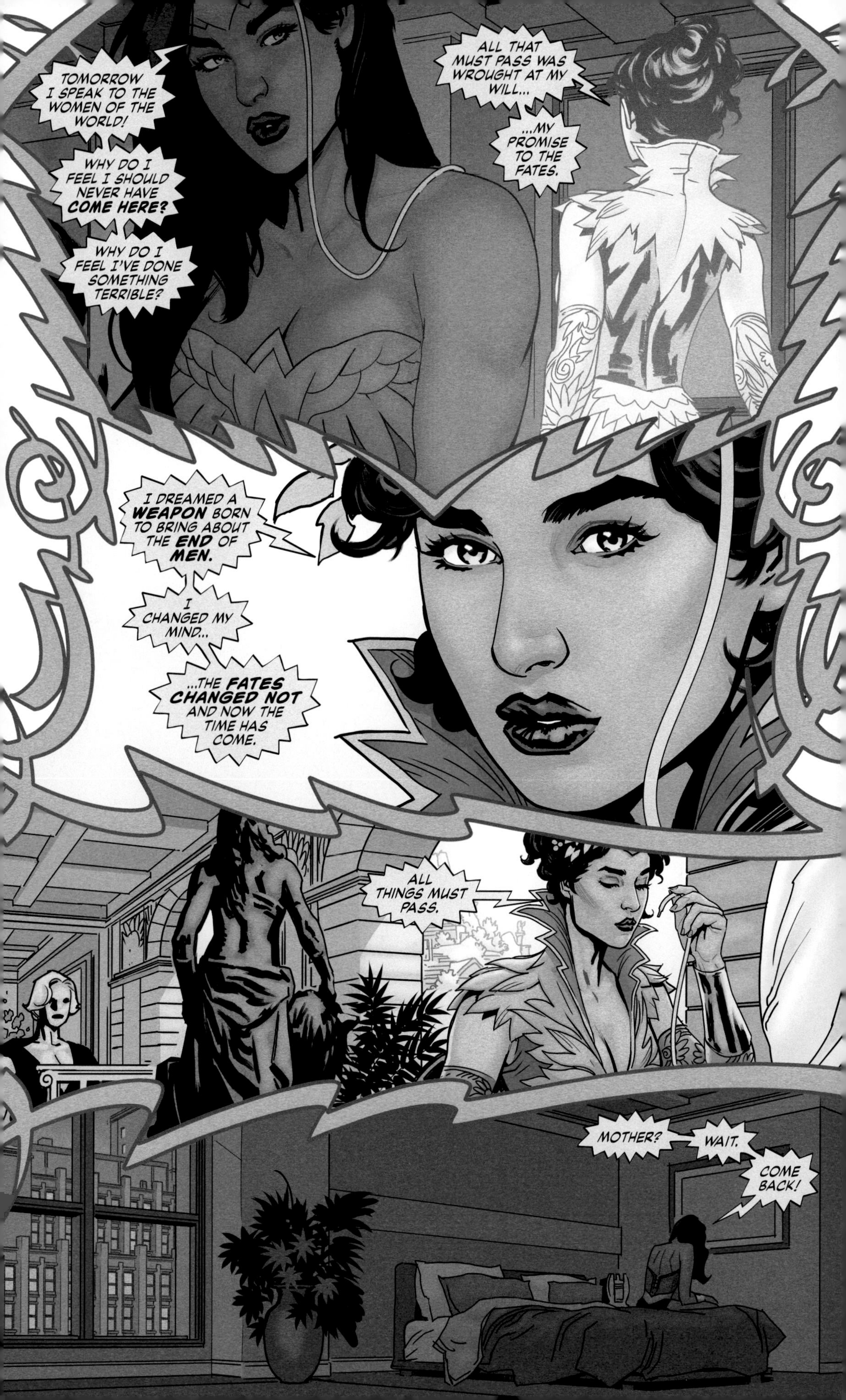
TOMORROW I SPEAK TO THE WOMEN OF THE WORLD!
WHY DO I FEEL I SHOULD NEVER HAVE **COME HERE?**
WHY DO I FEEL I'VE DONE SOMETHING TERRIBLE?
ALL THAT MUST PASS WAS WROUGHT AT MY WILL...
...MY PROMISE TO THE FATES.
I DREAMED A **WEAPON** BORN TO BRING ABOUT THE **END** OF **MEN.**
I CHANGED MY MIND...
...THE **FATES CHANGED NOT** AND NOW THE TIME HAS COME.
ALL THINGS MUST PASS.
MOTHER?
WAIT.
COME BACK!

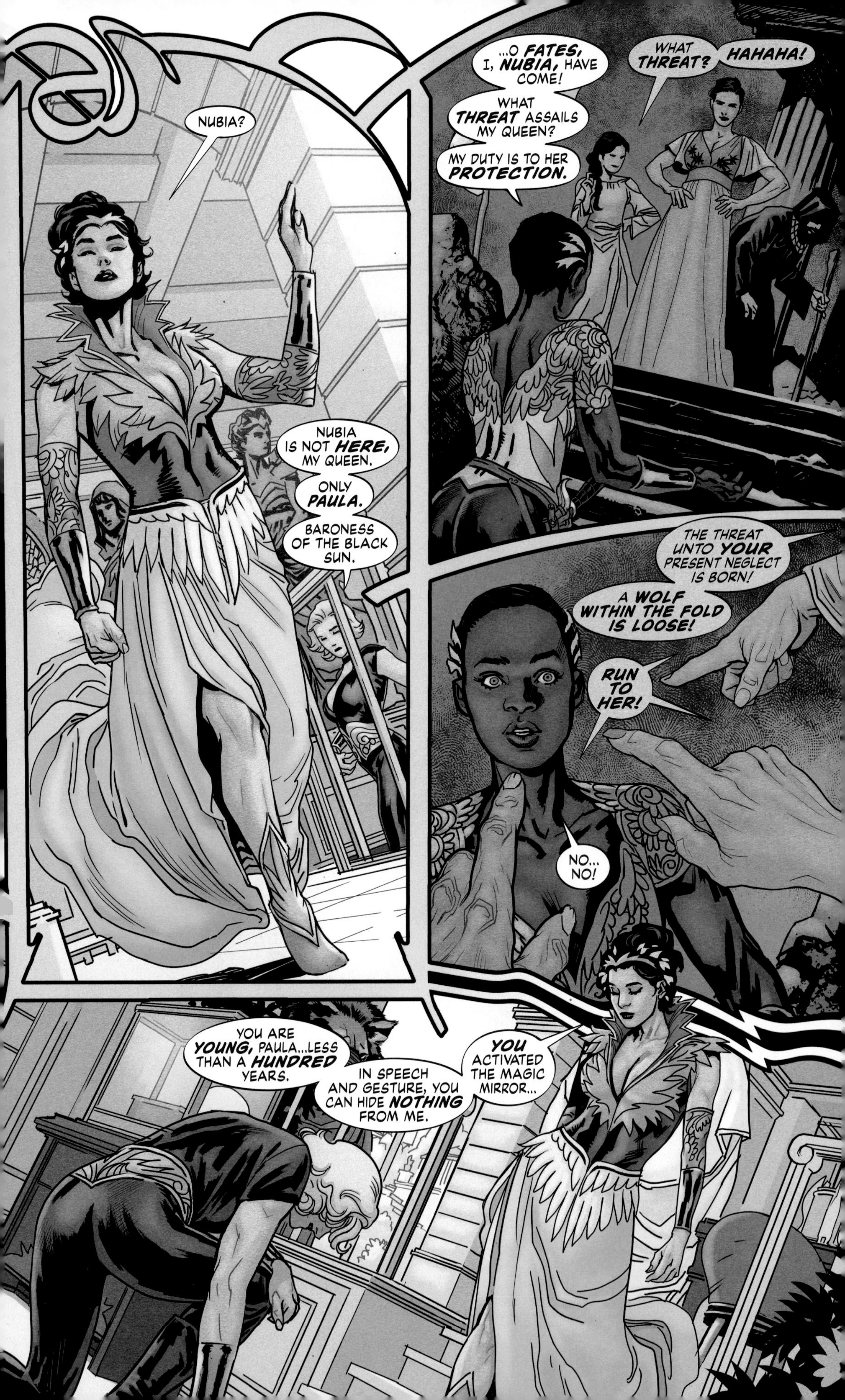
NUBIA?
NUBIA IS NOT HERE, MY QUEEN.
ONLY PAULA.
BARONESS OF THE BLACK SUN.
...O FATES, I, NUBIA, HAVE COME!
WHAT THREAT ASSAILS MY QUEEN?
MY DUTY IS TO HER PROTECTION.
WHAT THREAT?
HAHAHA!
THE THREAT UNTO YOUR PRESENT NEGLECT IS BORN!
A WOLF WITHIN THE FOLD IS LOOSE!
RUN TO HER!
NO... NO!
YOU ARE YOUNG, PAULA...LESS THAN A HUNDRED YEARS.
IN SPEECH AND GESTURE, YOU CAN HIDE NOTHING FROM ME.
YOU ACTIVATED THE MAGIC MIRROR...

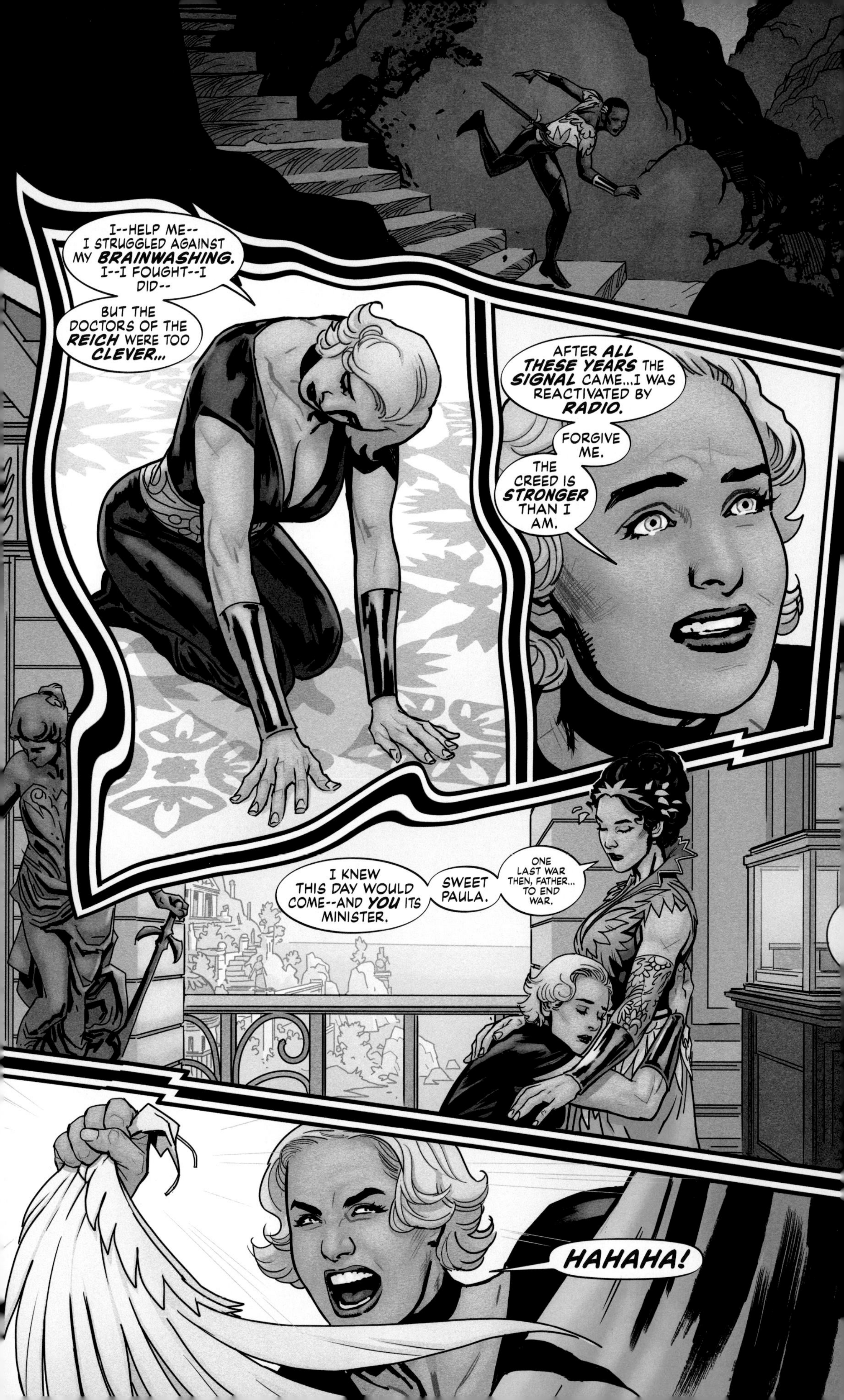
I--HELP ME--
I STRUGGLED AGAINST MY BRAINWASHING.
I--I FOUGHT--I DID--
BUT THE DOCTORS OF THE REICH WERE TOO CLEVER...
AFTER ALL THESE YEARS THE SIGNAL CAME...I WAS REACTIVATED BY RADIO.
FORGIVE ME.
THE CREED IS STRONGER THAN I AM.
I KNEW THIS DAY WOULD COME--AND YOU ITS MINISTER.
SWEET PAULA.
ONE LAST WAR THEN, FATHER... TO END WAR.
HAHAHA!

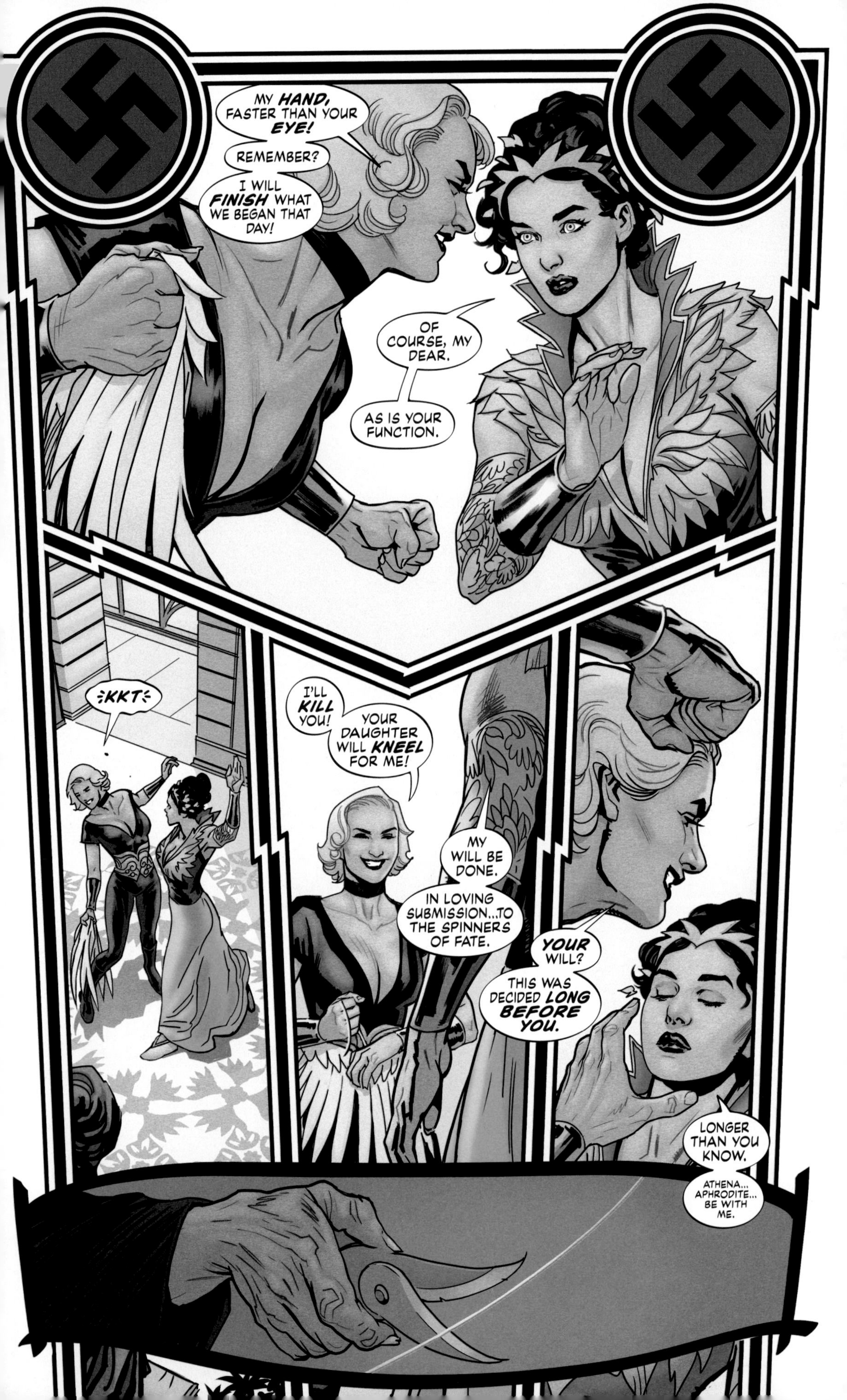

MY HAND, FASTER THAN YOUR EYE!
REMEMBER?
I WILL FINISH WHAT WE BEGAN THAT DAY!
OF COURSE, MY DEAR.
AS IS YOUR FUNCTION.
KKT
I'LL KILL YOU!
YOUR DAUGHTER WILL KNEEL FOR ME!
MY WILL BE DONE.
IN LOVING SUBMISSION...TO THE SPINNERS OF FATE.
YOUR WILL?
THIS WAS DECIDED LONG BEFORE YOU.
LONGER THAN YOU KNOW.
ATHENA... APHRODITE... BE WITH ME.

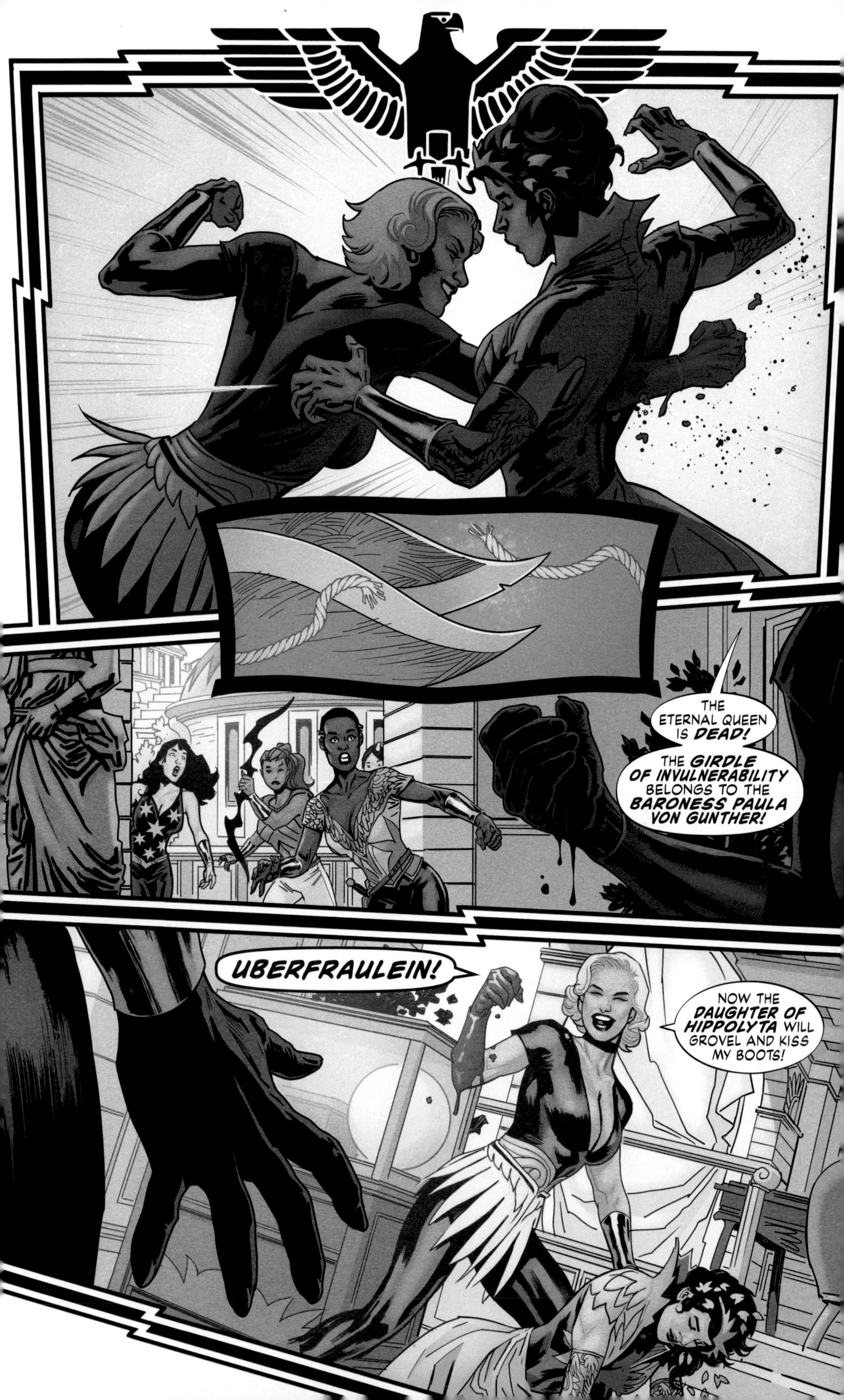
THE ETERNAL QUEEN IS DEAD!
THE GIRDLE OF INVULNERABILITY BELONGS TO THE BARONESS PAULA VON GUNTHER!
UBERFRAULEIN!
NOW THE DAUGHTER OF HIPPOLYTA WILL GROVEL AND KISS MY BOOTS!

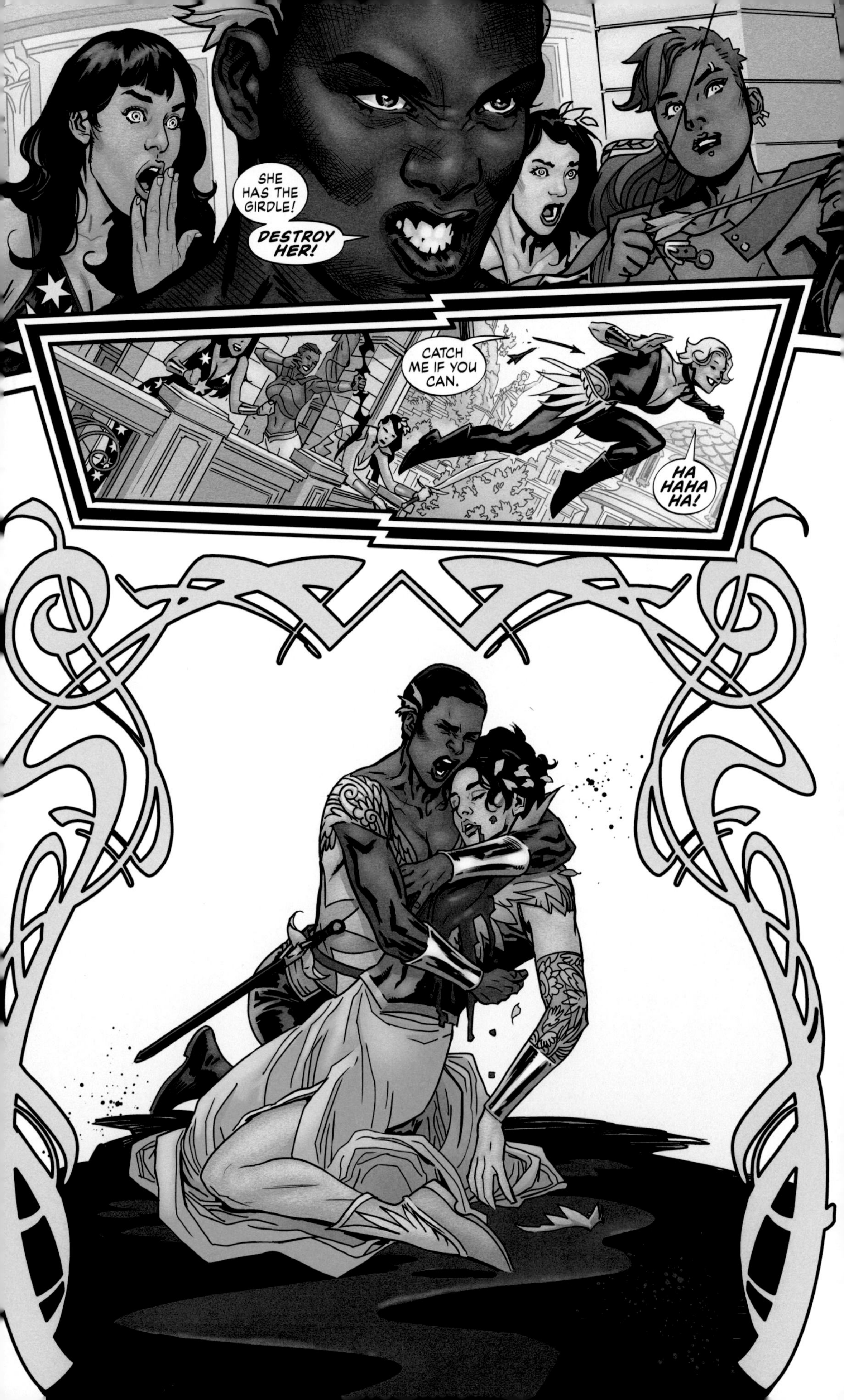

SHE HAS THE GIRDLE!
DESTROY HER!
CATCH ME IF YOU CAN.
HA HAHAHA HA!

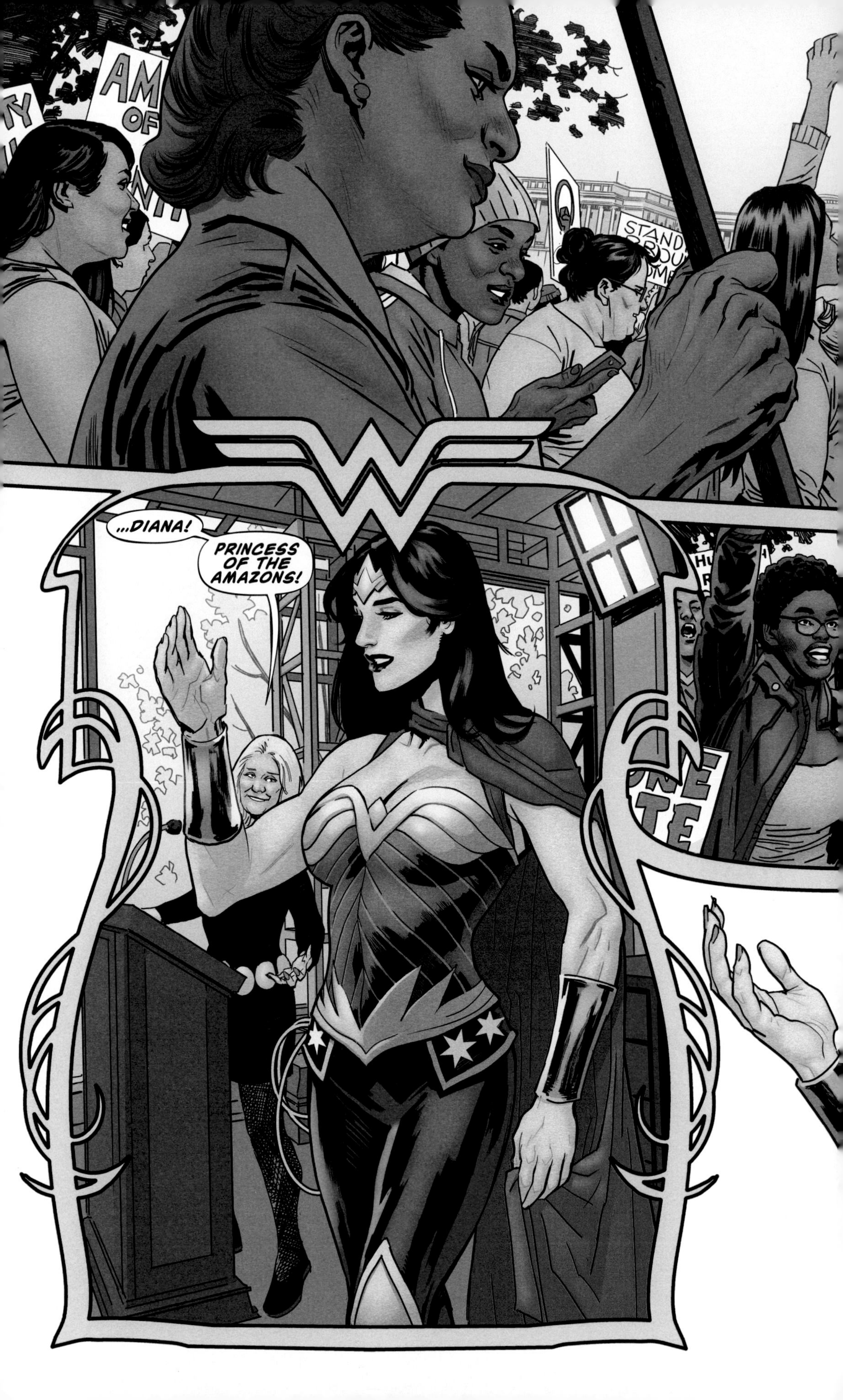
...DIANA!
PRINCESS OF THE AMAZONS!

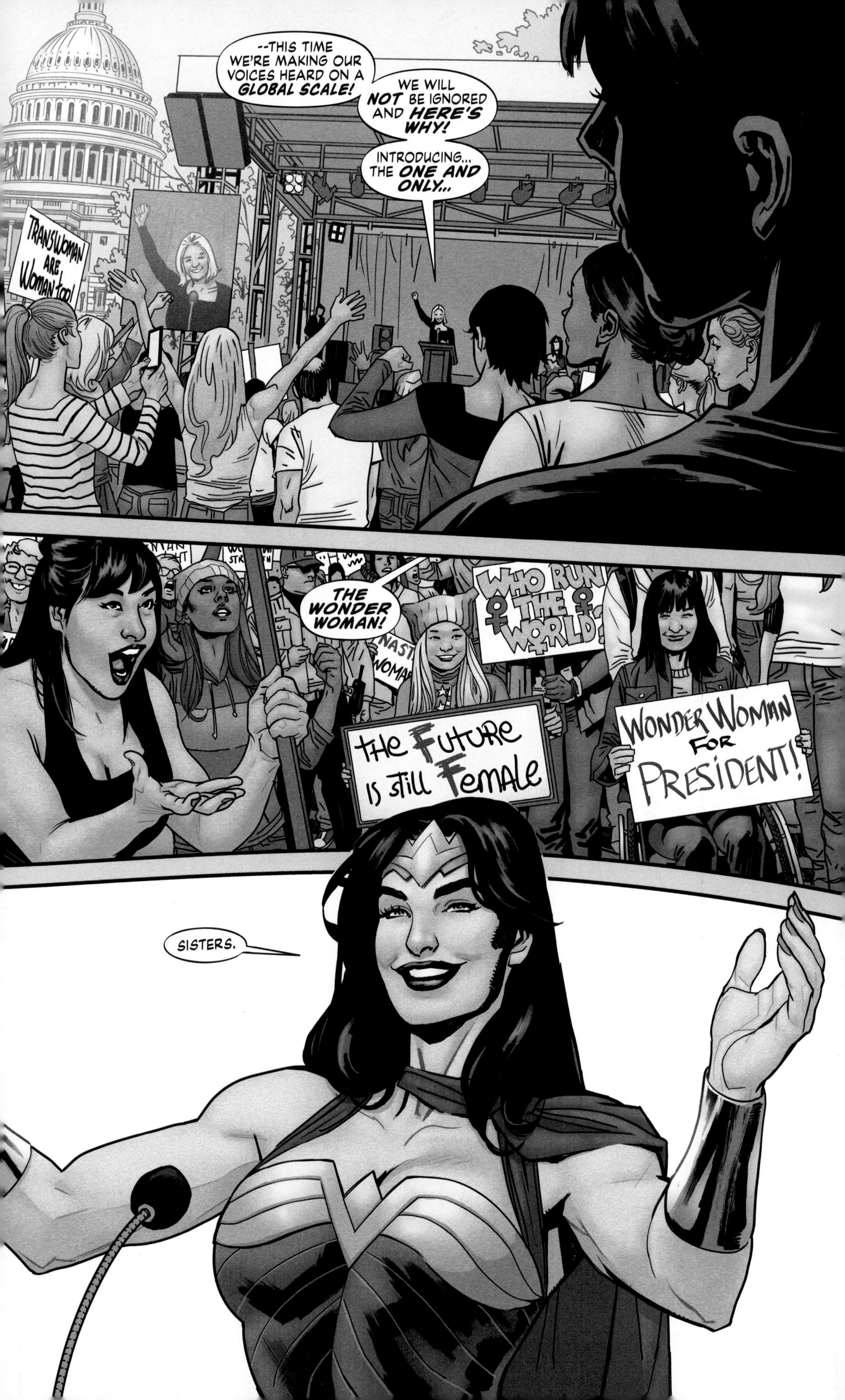
--THIS TIME WE'RE MAKING OUR VOICES HEARD ON A GLOBAL SCALE!
WE WILL NOT BE IGNORED AND HERE'S WHY!
INTRODUCING... THE ONE AND ONLY...
TRANSWOMAN ARE WOMAN too!
THE WONDER WOMAN!
WHO RUN THE WORLD?
THE FUTURE IS STILL FEMALE
WONDER WOMAN FOR PRESIDENT!
SISTERS.

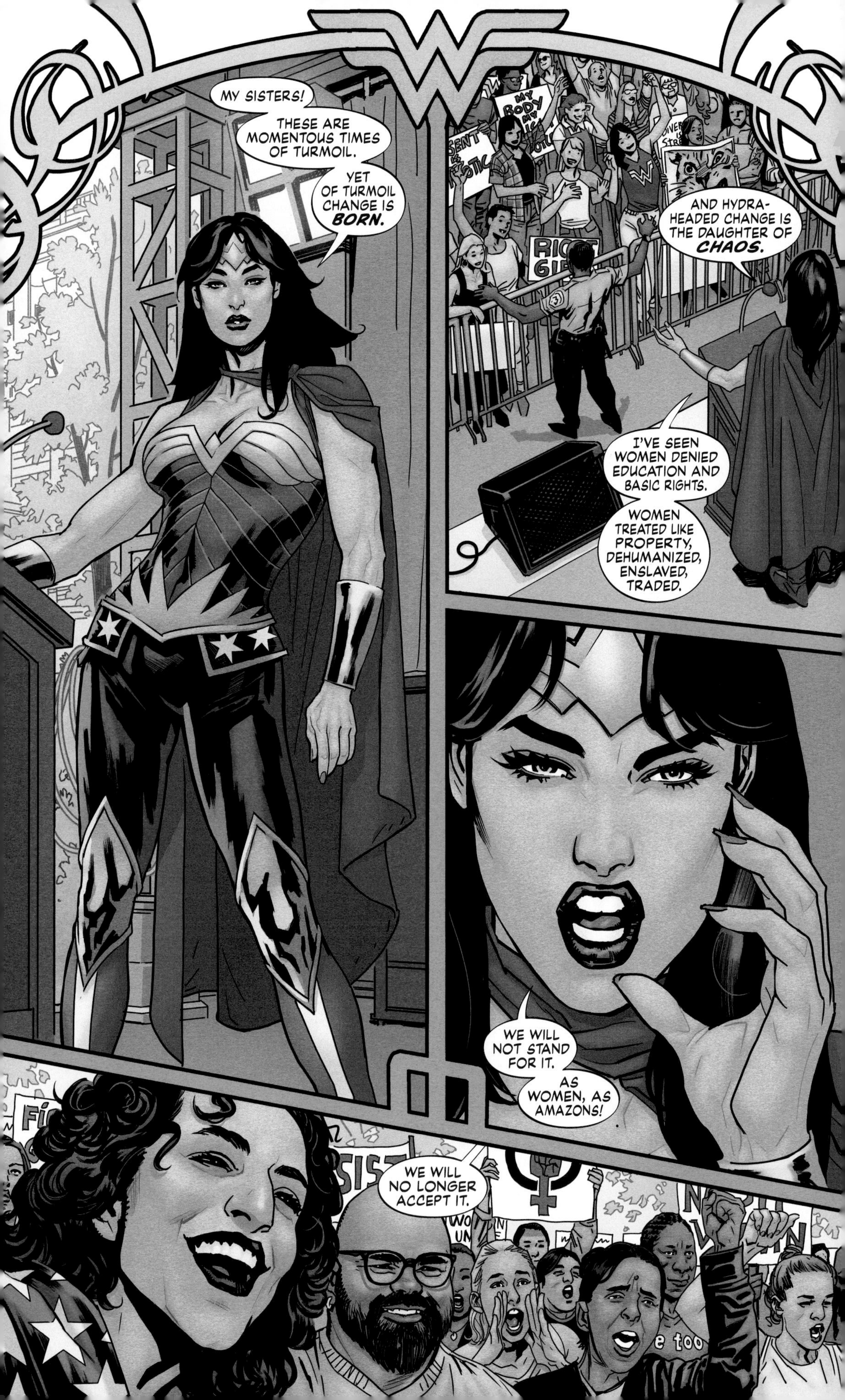
MY SISTERS!
THESE ARE MOMENTOUS TIMES OF TURMOIL.
YET OF TURMOIL CHANGE IS **BORN.**
AND HYDRA-HEADED CHANGE IS THE DAUGHTER OF **CHAOS.**
I'VE SEEN WOMEN DENIED EDUCATION AND BASIC RIGHTS.
WOMEN TREATED LIKE PROPERTY, DEHUMANIZED, ENSLAVED, TRADED.
WE WILL NOT STAND FOR IT.
AS WOMEN, AS AMAZONS!
WE WILL NO LONGER ACCEPT IT.

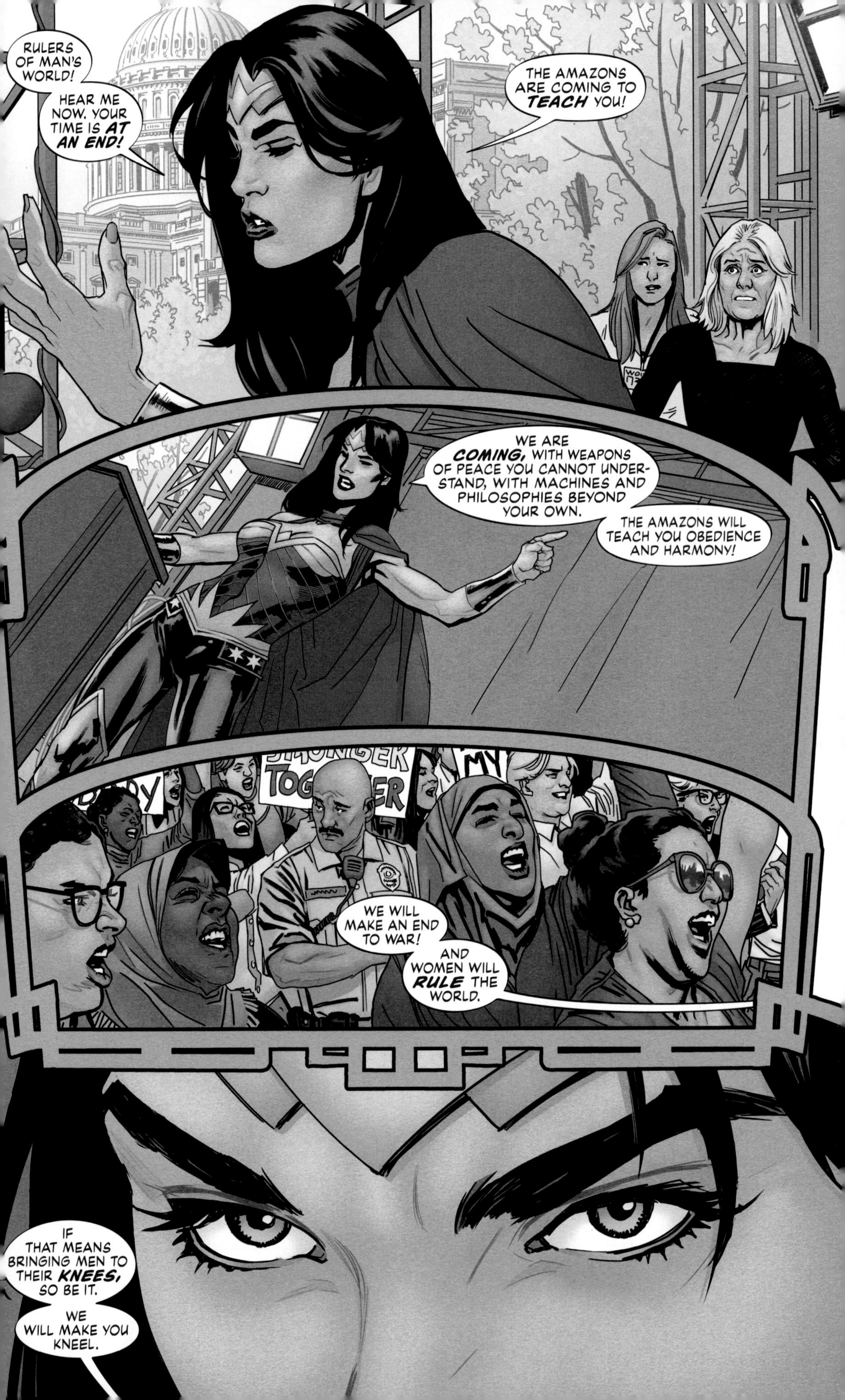
RULERS OF MAN'S WORLD!
HEAR ME NOW. YOUR TIME IS AT AN END!
THE AMAZONS ARE COMING TO TEACH YOU!
WE ARE COMING, WITH WEAPONS OF PEACE YOU CANNOT UNDER-STAND, WITH MACHINES AND PHILOSOPHIES BEYOND YOUR OWN.
THE AMAZONS WILL TEACH YOU OBEDIENCE AND HARMONY!
WE WILL MAKE AN END TO WAR!
AND WOMEN WILL RULE THE WORLD.
IF THAT MEANS BRINGING MEN TO THEIR KNEES, SO BE IT.
WE WILL MAKE YOU KNEEL.

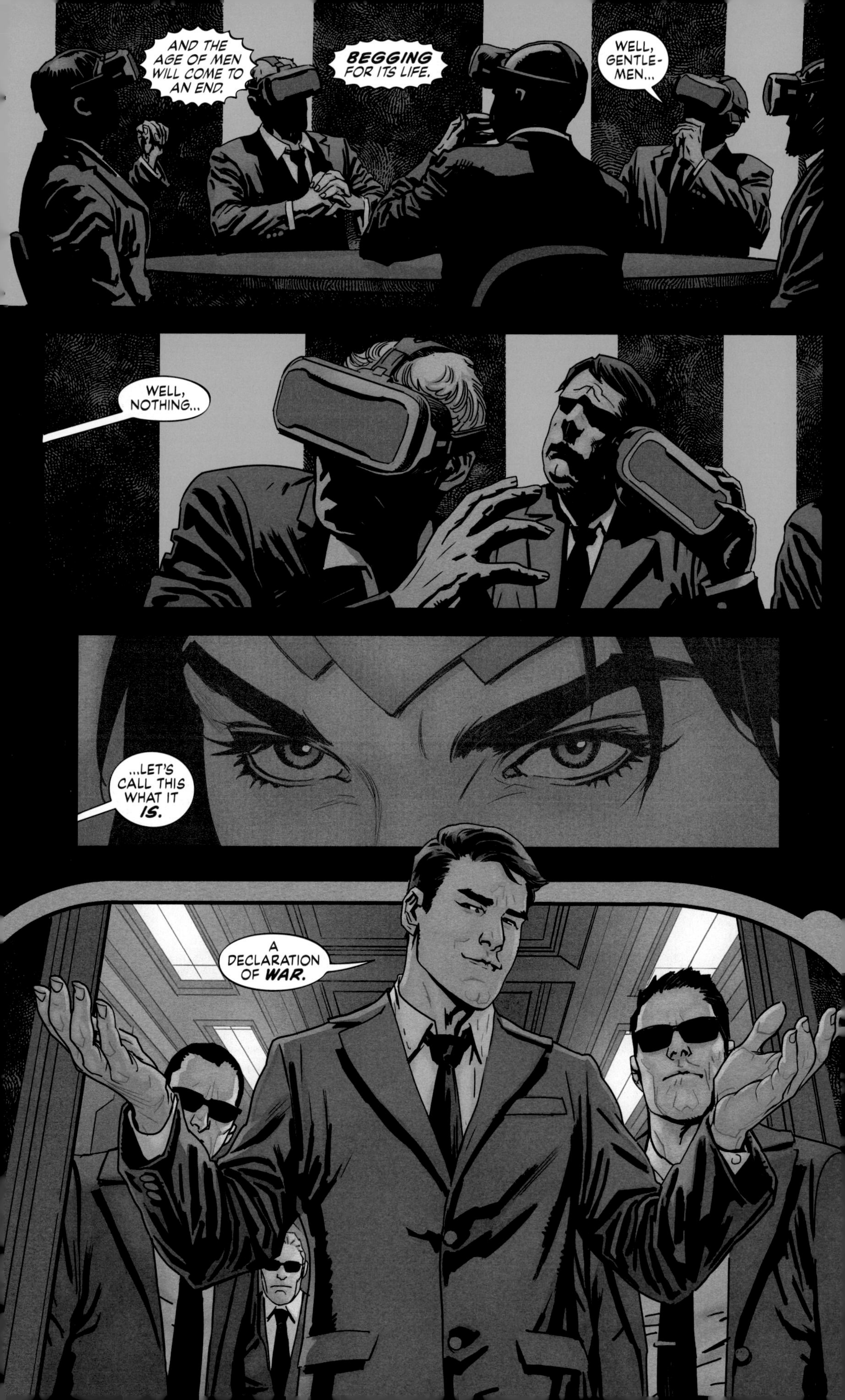
AND THE AGE OF MEN WILL COME TO AN END.
BEGGING FOR ITS LIFE.
WELL, GENTLE-MEN...
WELL, NOTHING...
...LET'S CALL THIS WHAT IT IS.
A DECLARATION OF WAR.

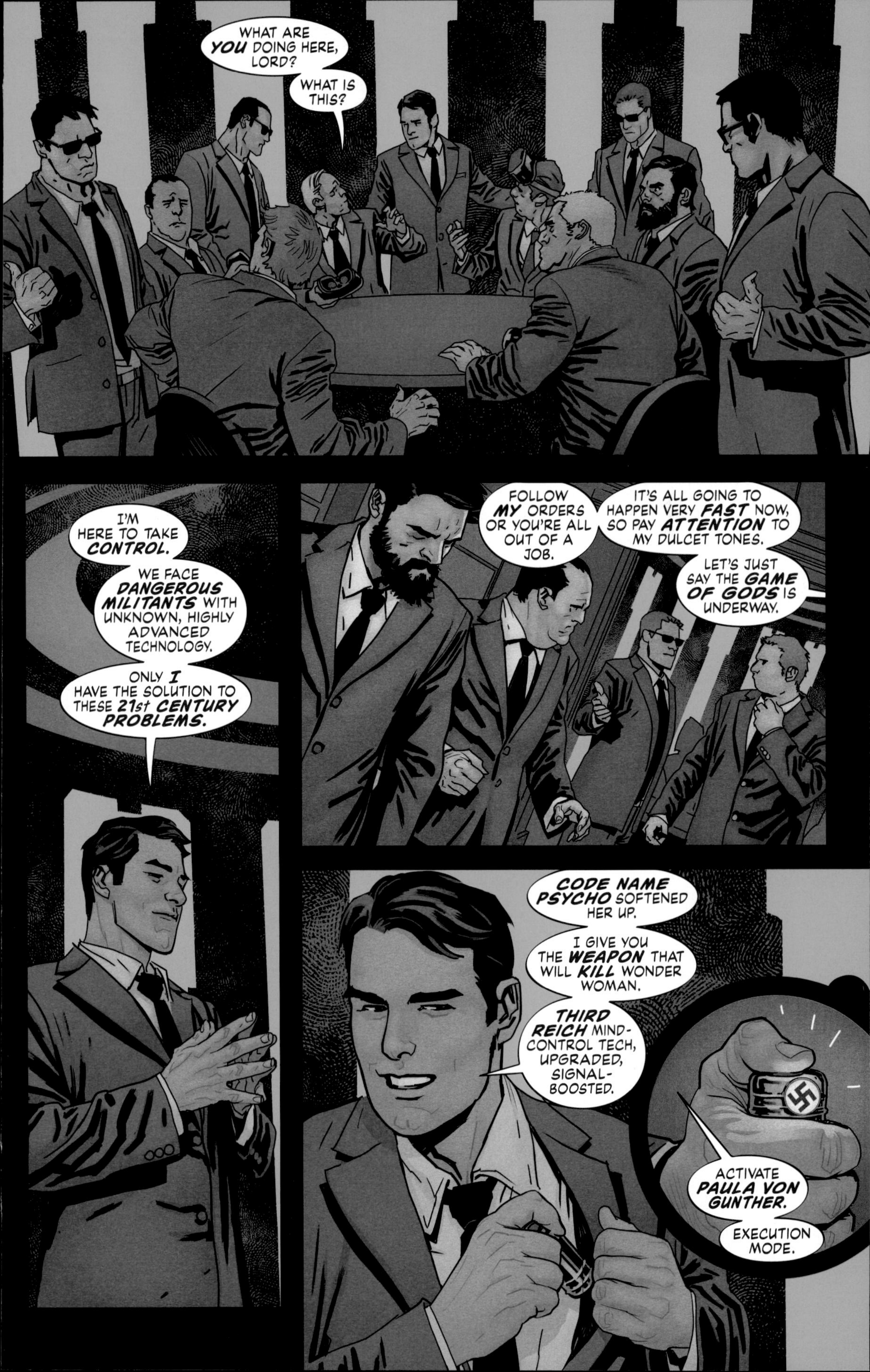
WHAT ARE YOU DOING HERE, LORD?
WHAT IS THIS?
I'M HERE TO TAKE CONTROL.
WE FACE DANGEROUS MILITANTS WITH UNKNOWN, HIGHLY ADVANCED TECHNOLOGY.
ONLY I HAVE THE SOLUTION TO THESE 21st CENTURY PROBLEMS.
FOLLOW MY ORDERS OR YOU'RE ALL OUT OF A JOB.
IT'S ALL GOING TO HAPPEN VERY FAST NOW, SO PAY ATTENTION TO MY DULCET TONES.
LET'S JUST SAY THE GAME OF GODS IS UNDERWAY.
CODE NAME PSYCHO SOFTENED HER UP.
I GIVE YOU THE WEAPON THAT WILL KILL WONDER WOMAN.
THIRD REICH MIND-CONTROL TECH, UPGRADED, SIGNAL-BOOSTED.
ACTIVATE PAULA VON GUNTHER.
EXECUTION MODE.

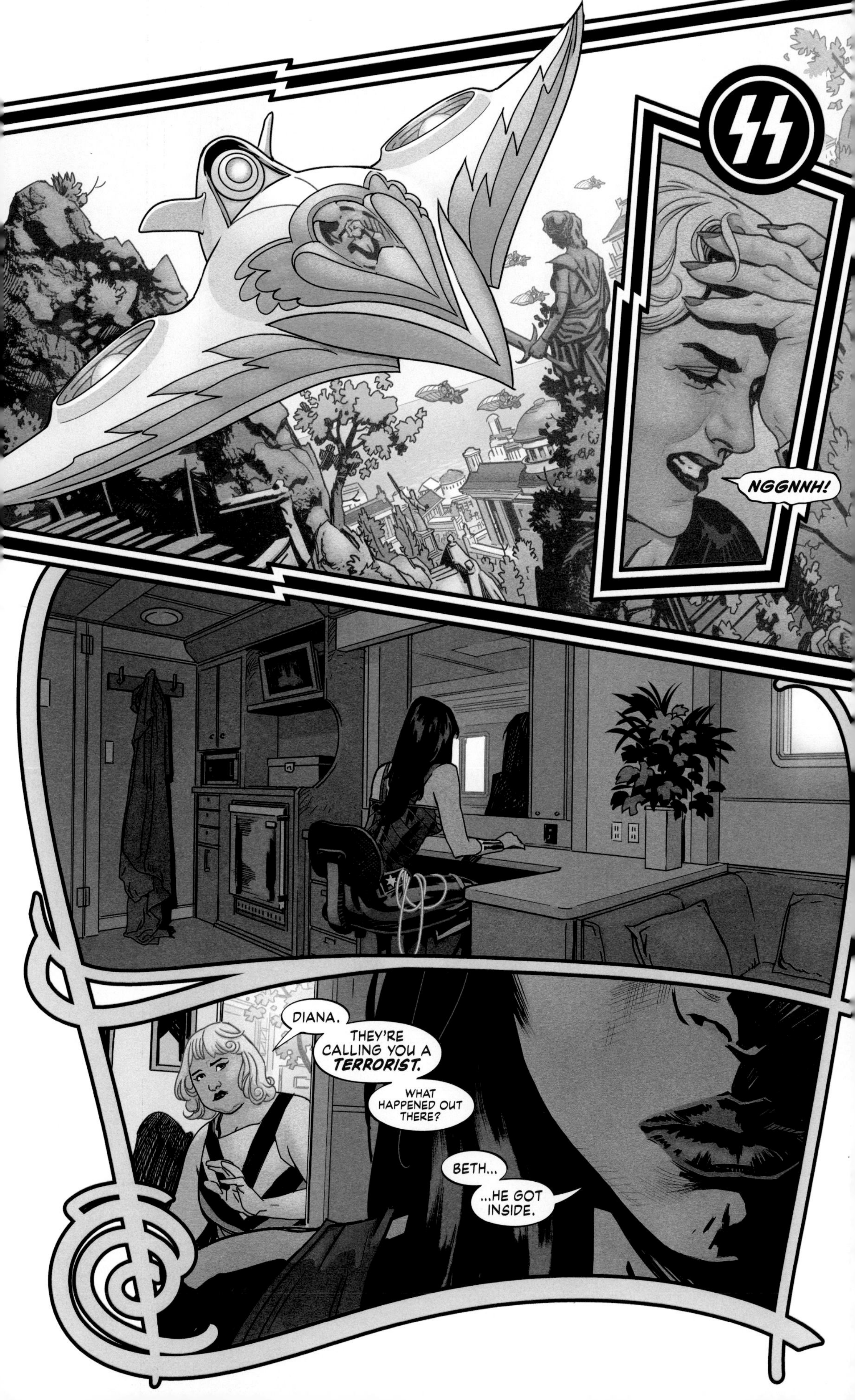
NGGNNH!
DIANA.
THEY'RE CALLING YOU A TERRORIST.
WHAT HAPPENED OUT THERE?
BETH...
...HE GOT INSIDE.

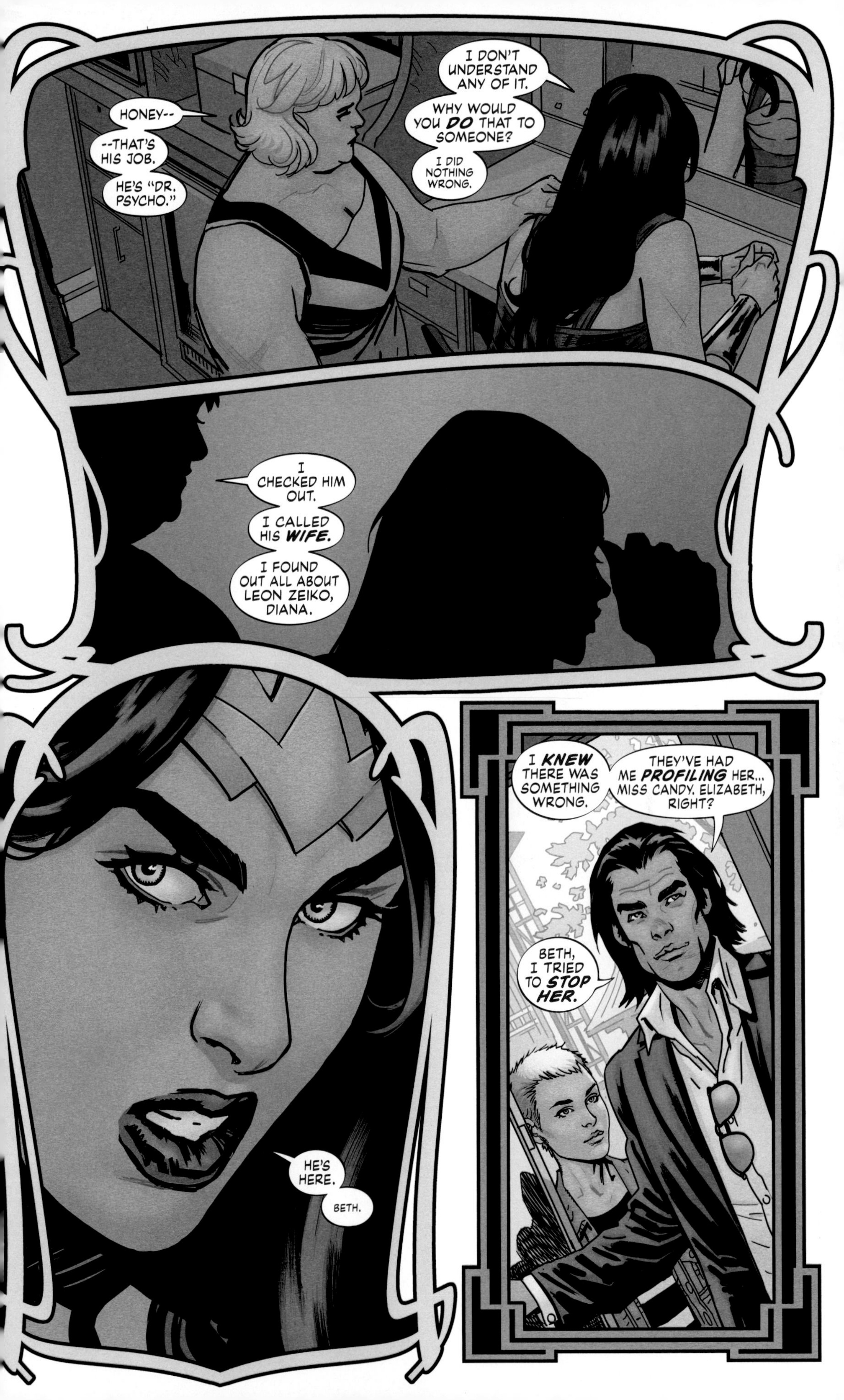
HONEY--
--THAT'S HIS JOB.
HE'S "DR. PSYCHO."
I DON'T UNDERSTAND ANY OF IT.
WHY WOULD YOU DO THAT TO SOMEONE?
I DID NOTHING WRONG.
I CHECKED HIM OUT.
I CALLED HIS WIFE.
I FOUND OUT ALL ABOUT LEON ZEIKO, DIANA.
HE'S HERE.
BETH.
I KNEW THERE WAS SOMETHING WRONG.
THEY'VE HAD ME PROFILING HER... MISS CANDY. ELIZABETH, RIGHT?
BETH, I TRIED TO STOP HER.

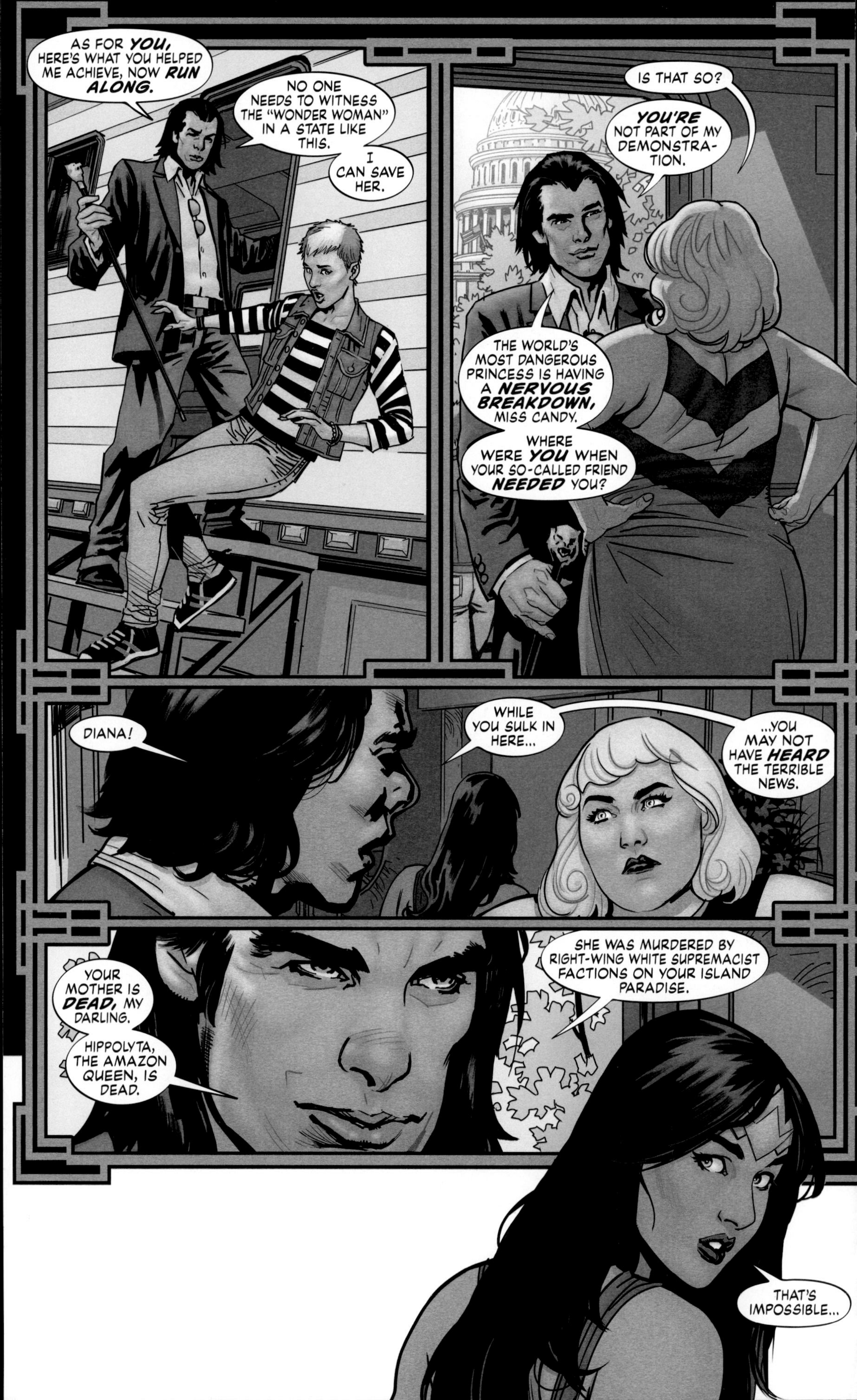
AS FOR YOU, HERE'S WHAT YOU HELPED ME ACHIEVE, NOW RUN ALONG.
NO ONE NEEDS TO WITNESS THE "WONDER WOMAN" IN A STATE LIKE THIS.
I CAN SAVE HER.
IS THAT SO?
YOU'RE NOT PART OF MY DEMONSTRA-TION.
THE WORLD'S MOST DANGEROUS PRINCESS IS HAVING A NERVOUS BREAKDOWN, MISS CANDY.
WHERE WERE YOU WHEN YOUR SO-CALLED FRIEND NEEDED YOU?
DIANA!
WHILE YOU SULK IN HERE...
...YOU MAY NOT HAVE HEARD THE TERRIBLE NEWS.
YOUR MOTHER IS DEAD, MY DARLING.
HIPPOLYTA, THE AMAZON QUEEN, IS DEAD.
SHE WAS MURDERED BY RIGHT-WING WHITE SUPREMACIST FACTIONS ON YOUR ISLAND PARADISE.
THAT'S IMPOSSIBLE...

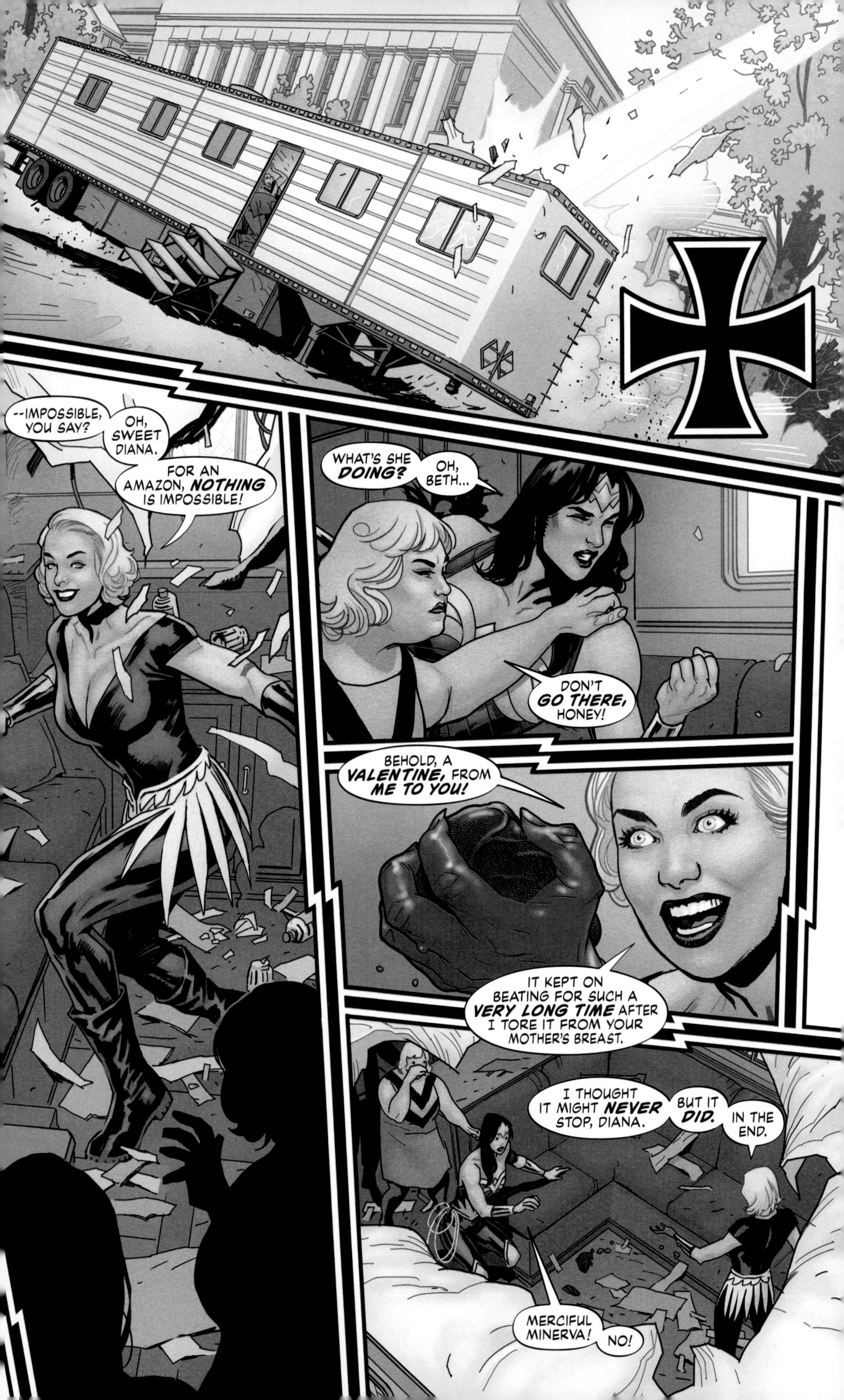

--IMPOSSIBLE, YOU SAY?
OH, SWEET DIANA.
FOR AN AMAZON, NOTHING IS IMPOSSIBLE!
WHAT'S SHE DOING?
OH, BETH...
DON'T GO THERE, HONEY!
BEHOLD, A VALENTINE, FROM ME TO YOU!
IT KEPT ON BEATING FOR SUCH A VERY LONG TIME AFTER I TORE IT FROM YOUR MOTHER'S BREAST.
I THOUGHT IT MIGHT NEVER STOP, DIANA.
BUT IT DID.
IN THE END.
MERCIFUL MINERVA!
NO!

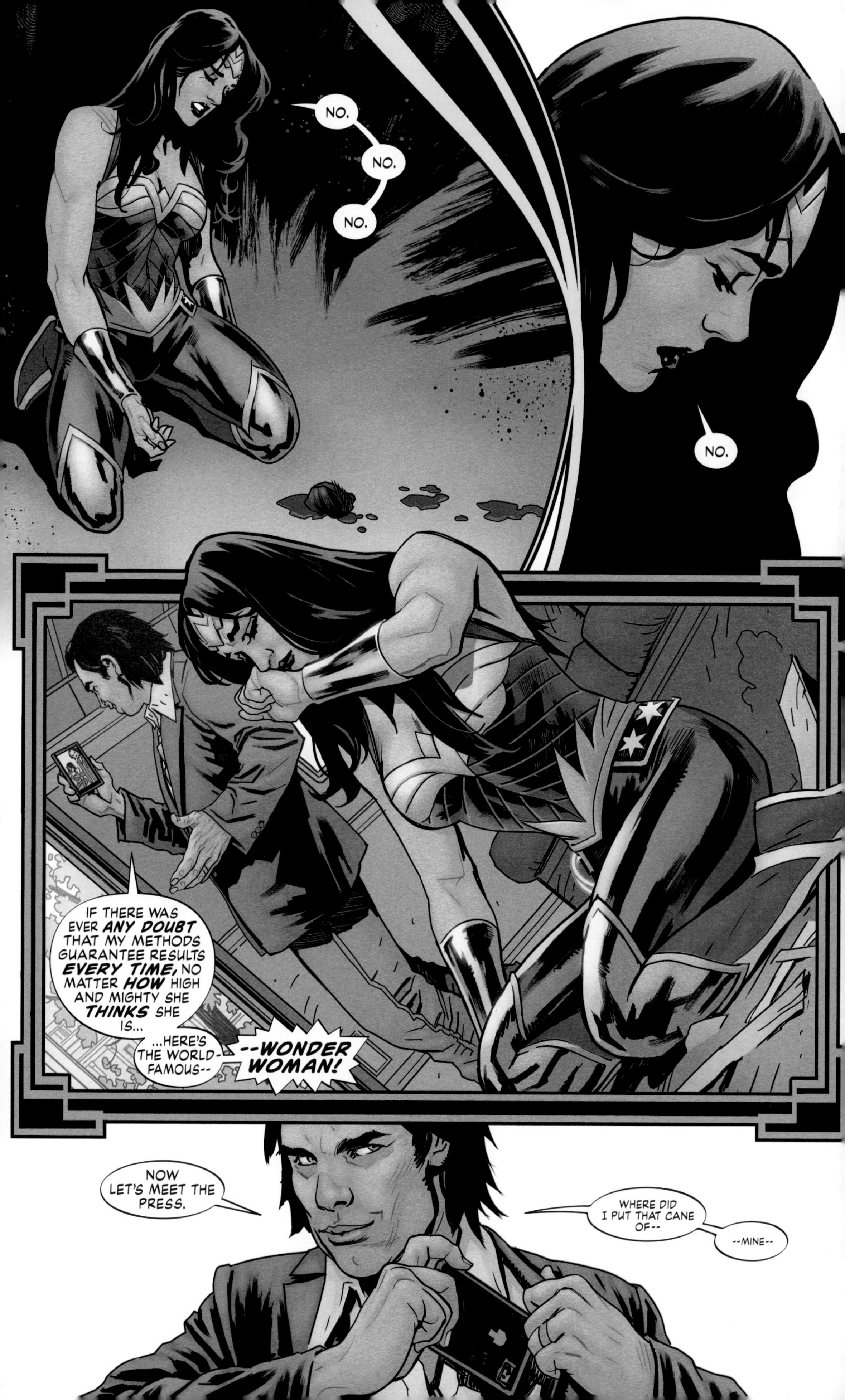
NO.
NO.
NO.
NO.
IF THERE WAS EVER ANY DOUBT THAT MY METHODS GUARANTEE RESULTS EVERY TIME, NO MATTER HOW HIGH AND MIGHTY SHE THINKS SHE IS...
...HERE'S THE WORLD-FAMOUS--
--WONDER WOMAN!
NOW LET'S MEET THE PRESS.
WHERE DID I PUT THAT CANE OF--
--MINE--

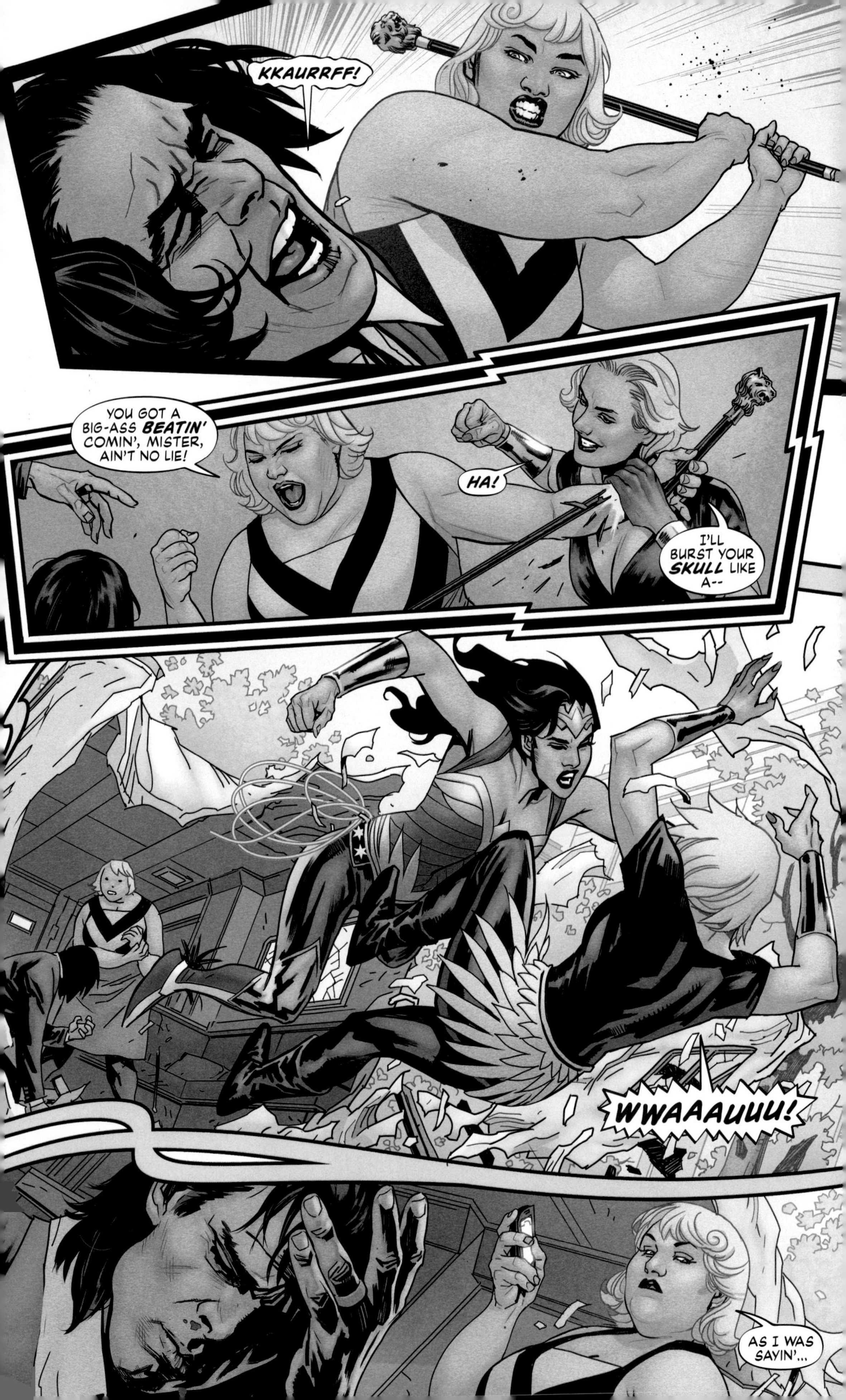
KKAURRFF!
YOU GOT A BIG-ASS BEATIN' COMIN', MISTER, AIN'T NO LIE!
HA!
I'LL BURST YOUR SKULL LIKE A--
WWAAAUUU!
AS I WAS SAYIN'...

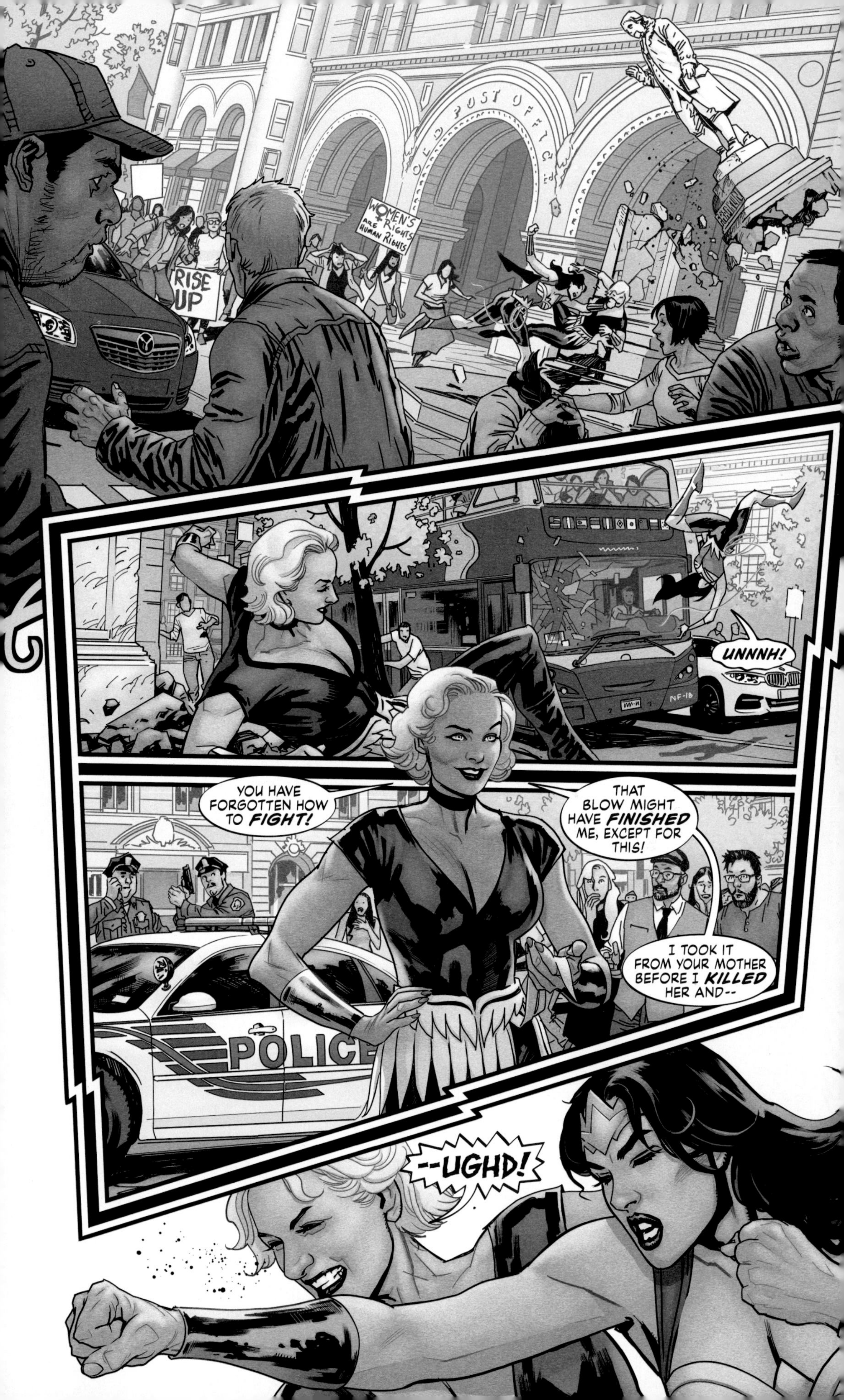
OLD POST OFFICE
WOMEN'S RIGHTS ARE HUMAN RIGHTS
RISE UP
UNNNH!
YOU HAVE FORGOTTEN HOW TO FIGHT!
THAT BLOW MIGHT HAVE FINISHED ME, EXCEPT FOR THIS!
I TOOK IT FROM YOUR MOTHER BEFORE I KILLED HER AND--
POLICE
--UGHD!

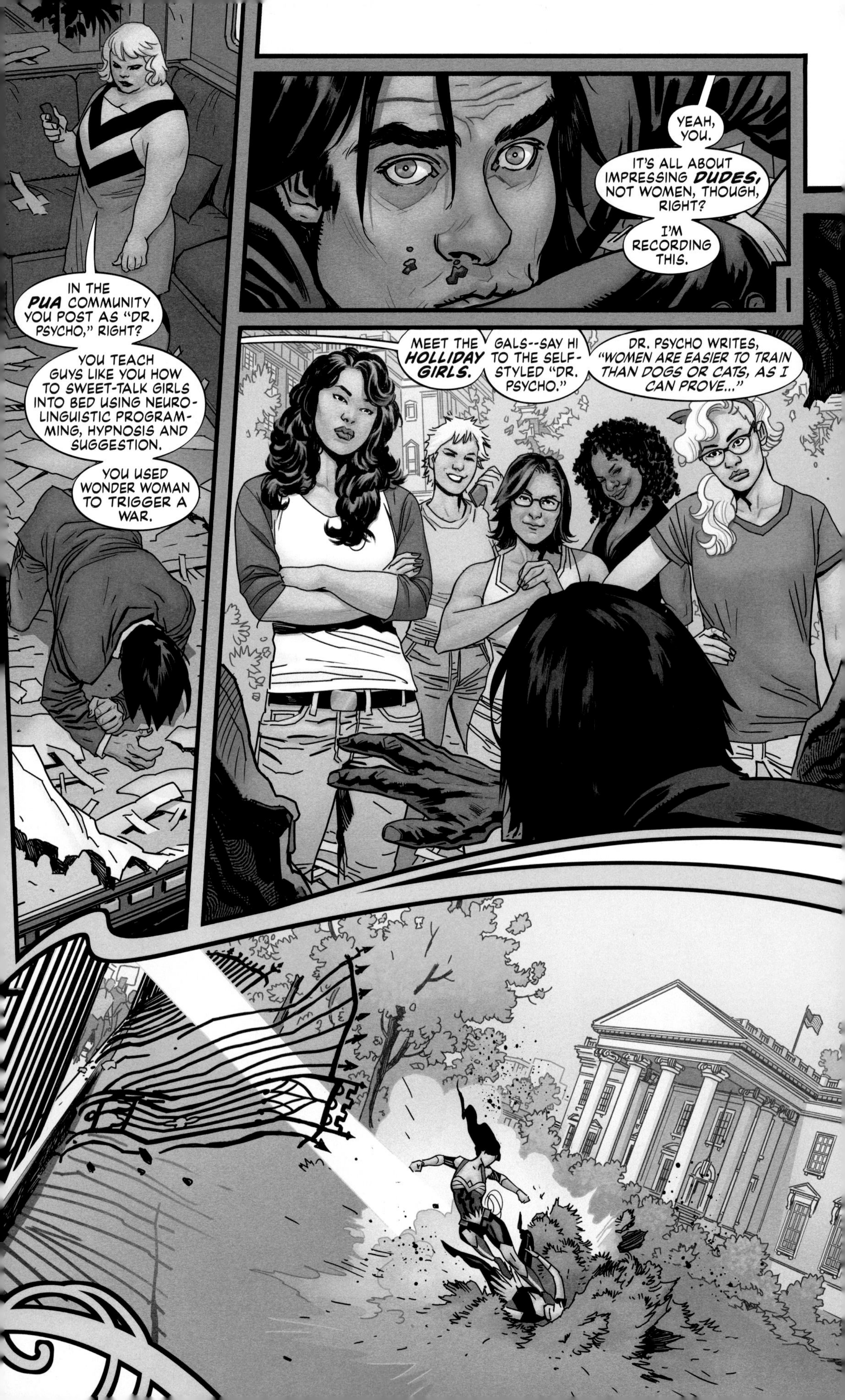

YEAH, YOU.
IT'S ALL ABOUT IMPRESSING DUDES, NOT WOMEN, THOUGH, RIGHT?
I'M RECORDING THIS.
IN THE PUA COMMUNITY YOU POST AS "DR. PSYCHO," RIGHT?
YOU TEACH GUYS LIKE YOU HOW TO SWEET-TALK GIRLS INTO BED USING NEURO-LINGUISTIC PROGRAM-MING, HYPNOSIS AND SUGGESTION.
YOU USED WONDER WOMAN TO TRIGGER A WAR.
MEET THE HOLLIDAY GIRLS.
GALS--SAY HI TO THE SELF-STYLED "DR. PSYCHO."
DR. PSYCHO WRITES, "WOMEN ARE EASIER TO TRAIN THAN DOGS OR CATS, AS I CAN PROVE..."

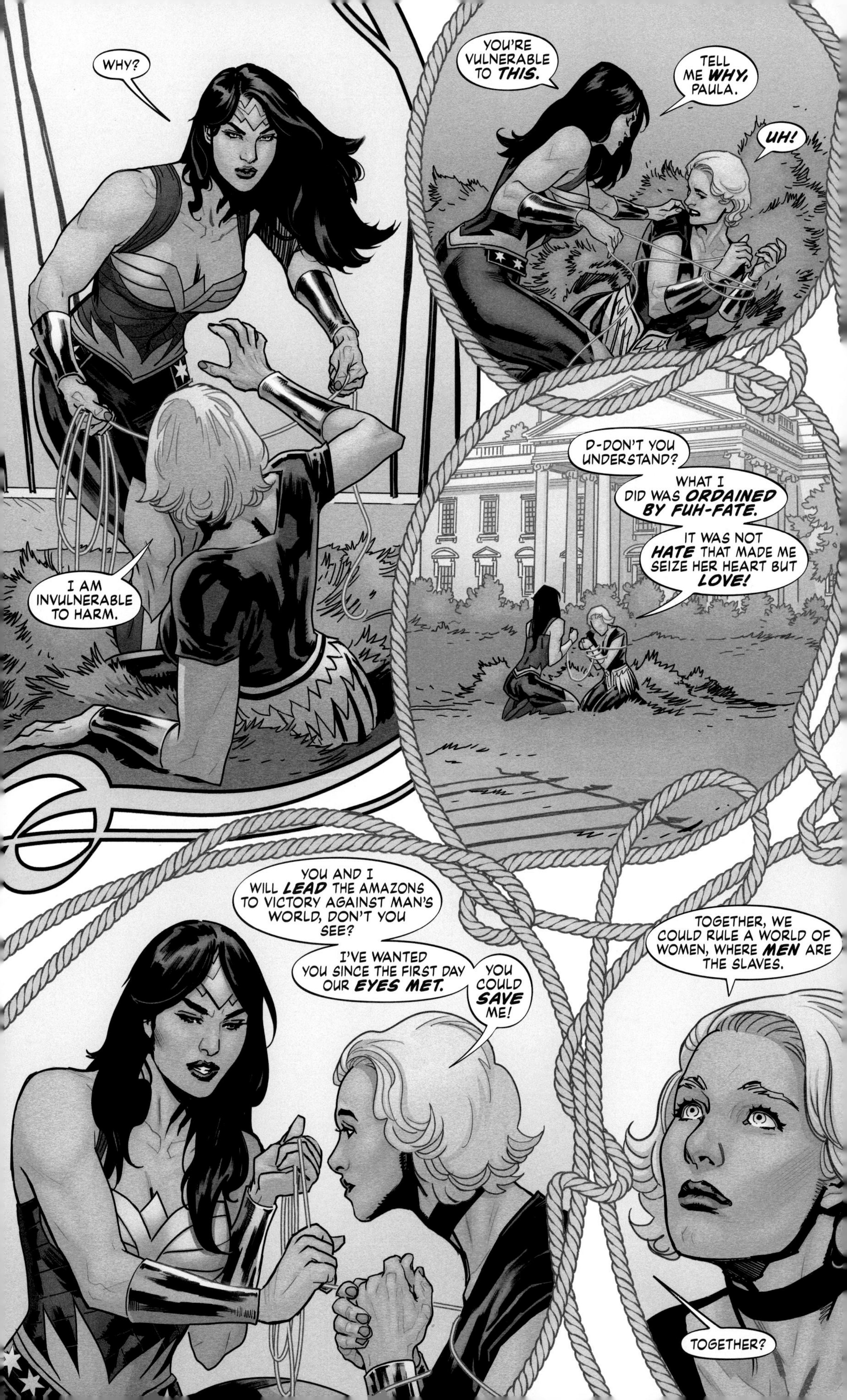
WHY?
I AM INVULNERABLE TO HARM.
YOU'RE VULNERABLE TO THIS.
TELL ME WHY, PAULA.
UH!
D-DON'T YOU UNDERSTAND?
WHAT I DID WAS ORDAINED BY FUH-FATE.
IT WAS NOT HATE THAT MADE ME SEIZE HER HEART BUT LOVE!
YOU AND I WILL LEAD THE AMAZONS TO VICTORY AGAINST MAN'S WORLD, DON'T YOU SEE?
I'VE WANTED YOU SINCE THE FIRST DAY OUR EYES MET.
YOU COULD SAVE ME!
TOGETHER, WE COULD RULE A WORLD OF WOMEN, WHERE MEN ARE THE SLAVES.
TOGETHER?

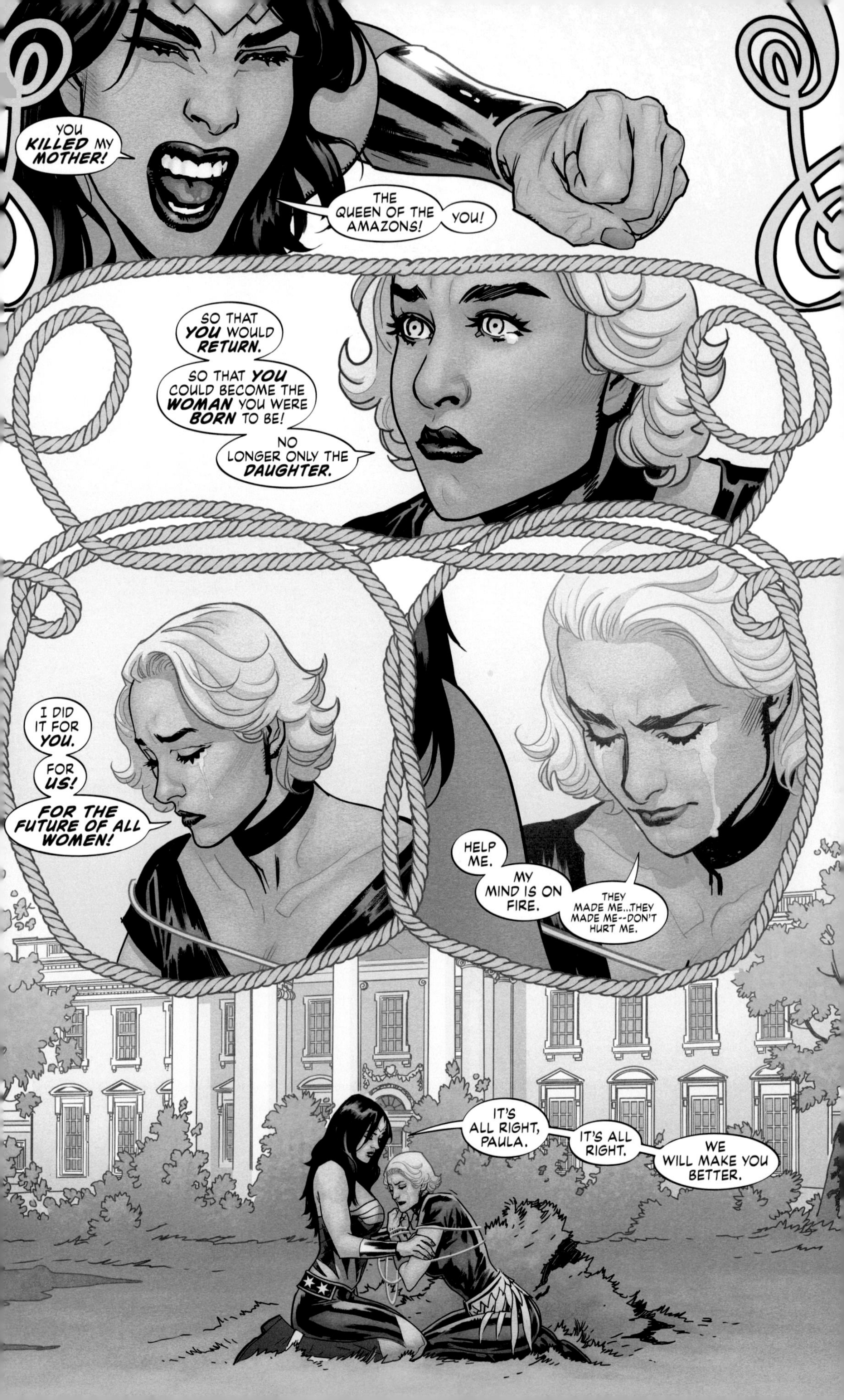
YOU KILLED MY MOTHER!
THE QUEEN OF THE AMAZONS!
YOU!
SO THAT YOU WOULD RETURN.
SO THAT YOU COULD BECOME THE WOMAN YOU WERE BORN TO BE!
NO LONGER ONLY THE DAUGHTER.
I DID IT FOR YOU.
FOR US!
FOR THE FUTURE OF ALL WOMEN!
HELP ME.
MY MIND IS ON FIRE.
THEY MADE ME...THEY MADE ME--DON'T HURT ME.
IT'S ALL RIGHT, PAULA.
IT'S ALL RIGHT.
WE WILL MAKE YOU BETTER.

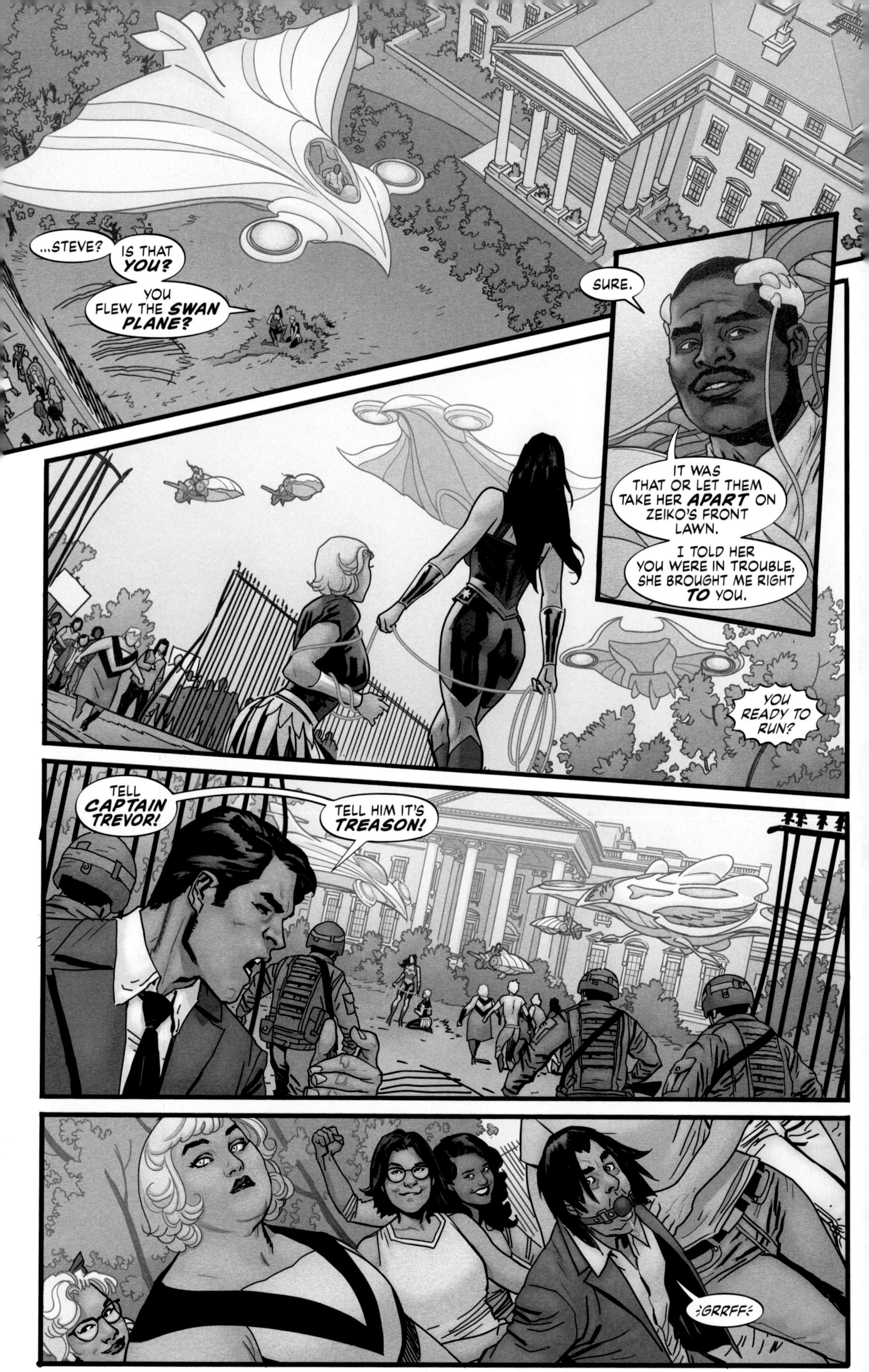
...STEVE?
IS THAT YOU?
YOU FLEW THE SWAN PLANE?
SURE.
IT WAS THAT OR LET THEM TAKE HER APART ON ZEIKO'S FRONT LAWN.
I TOLD HER YOU WERE IN TROUBLE, SHE BROUGHT ME RIGHT TO YOU.
YOU READY TO RUN?
TELL CAPTAIN TREVOR!
TELL HIM IT'S TREASON!
GRRFF

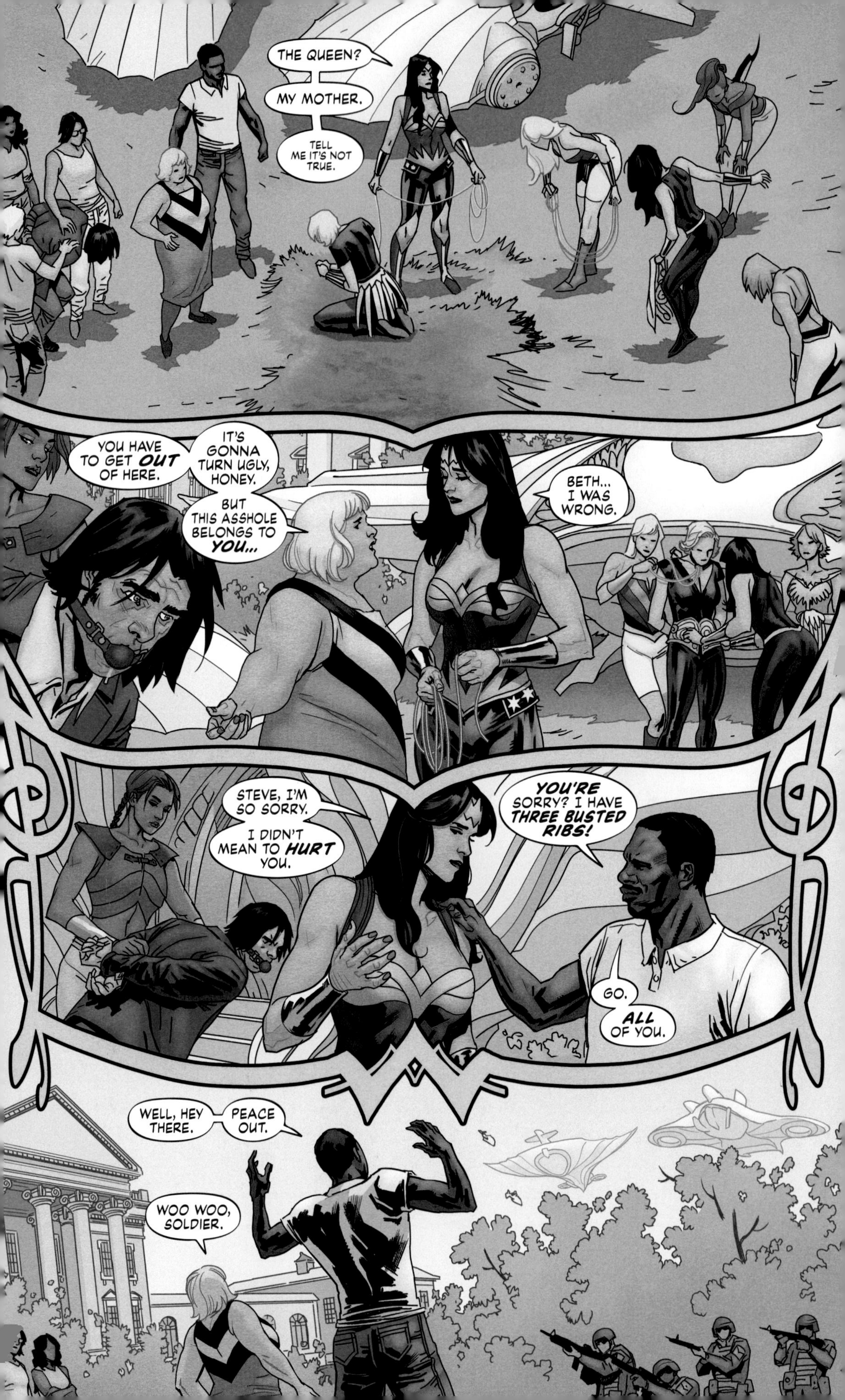
THE QUEEN?
MY MOTHER.
TELL ME IT'S NOT TRUE.
YOU HAVE TO GET OUT OF HERE.
IT'S GONNA TURN UGLY, HONEY.
BUT THIS ASSHOLE BELONGS TO YOU...
BETH... I WAS WRONG.
STEVE, I'M SO SORRY.
I DIDN'T MEAN TO HURT YOU.
YOU'RE SORRY? I HAVE THREE BUSTED RIBS!
GO.
ALL OF YOU.
WELL, HEY THERE.
PEACE OUT.
WOO WOO, SOLDIER.

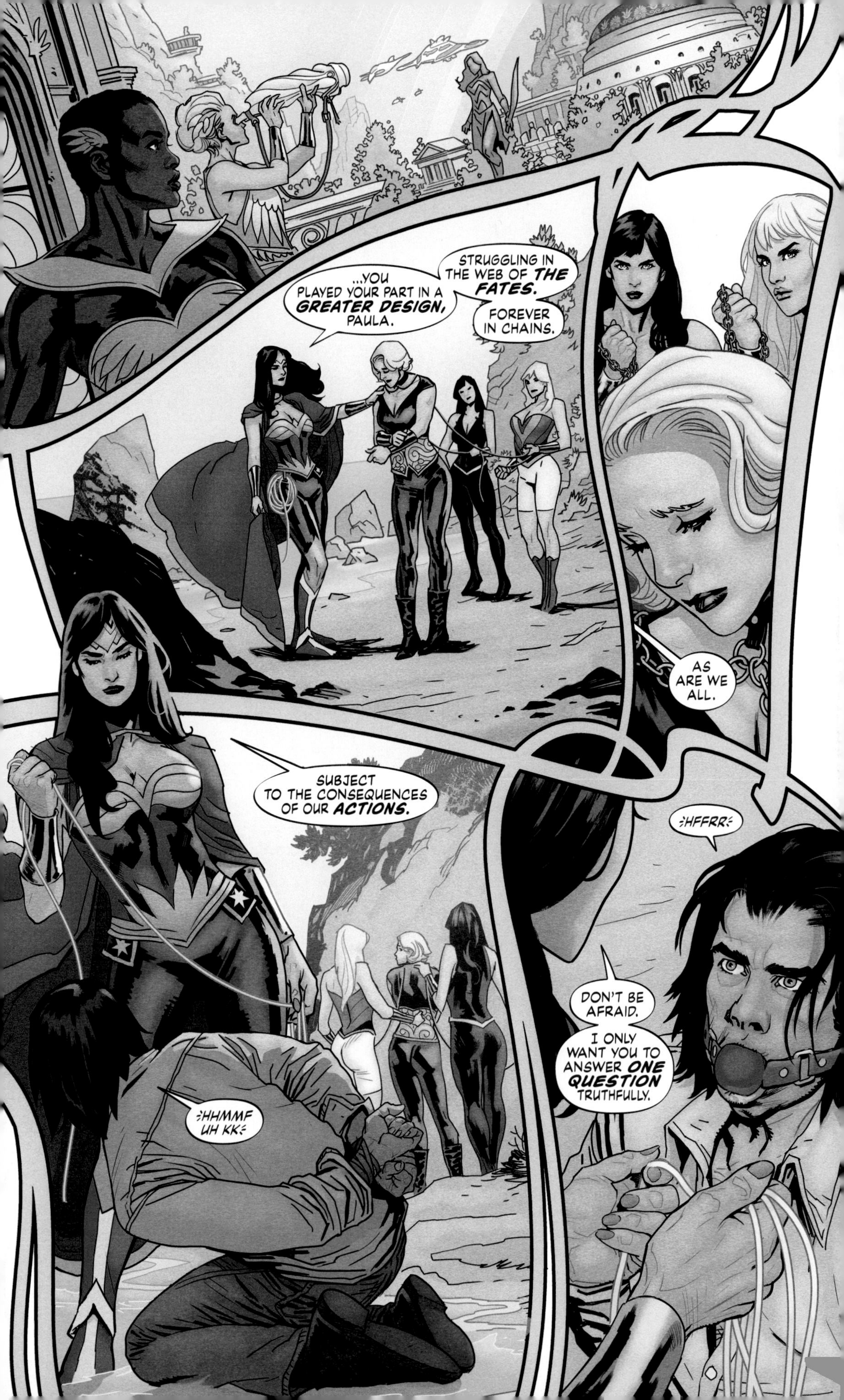

...YOU PLAYED YOUR PART IN A GREATER DESIGN, PAULA.
STRUGGLING IN THE WEB OF THE FATES.
FOREVER IN CHAINS.
AS ARE WE ALL.
SUBJECT TO THE CONSEQUENCES OF OUR ACTIONS.
HHMMF UH KK
HFFRR
DON'T BE AFRAID.
I ONLY WANT YOU TO ANSWER ONE QUESTION TRUTHFULLY.

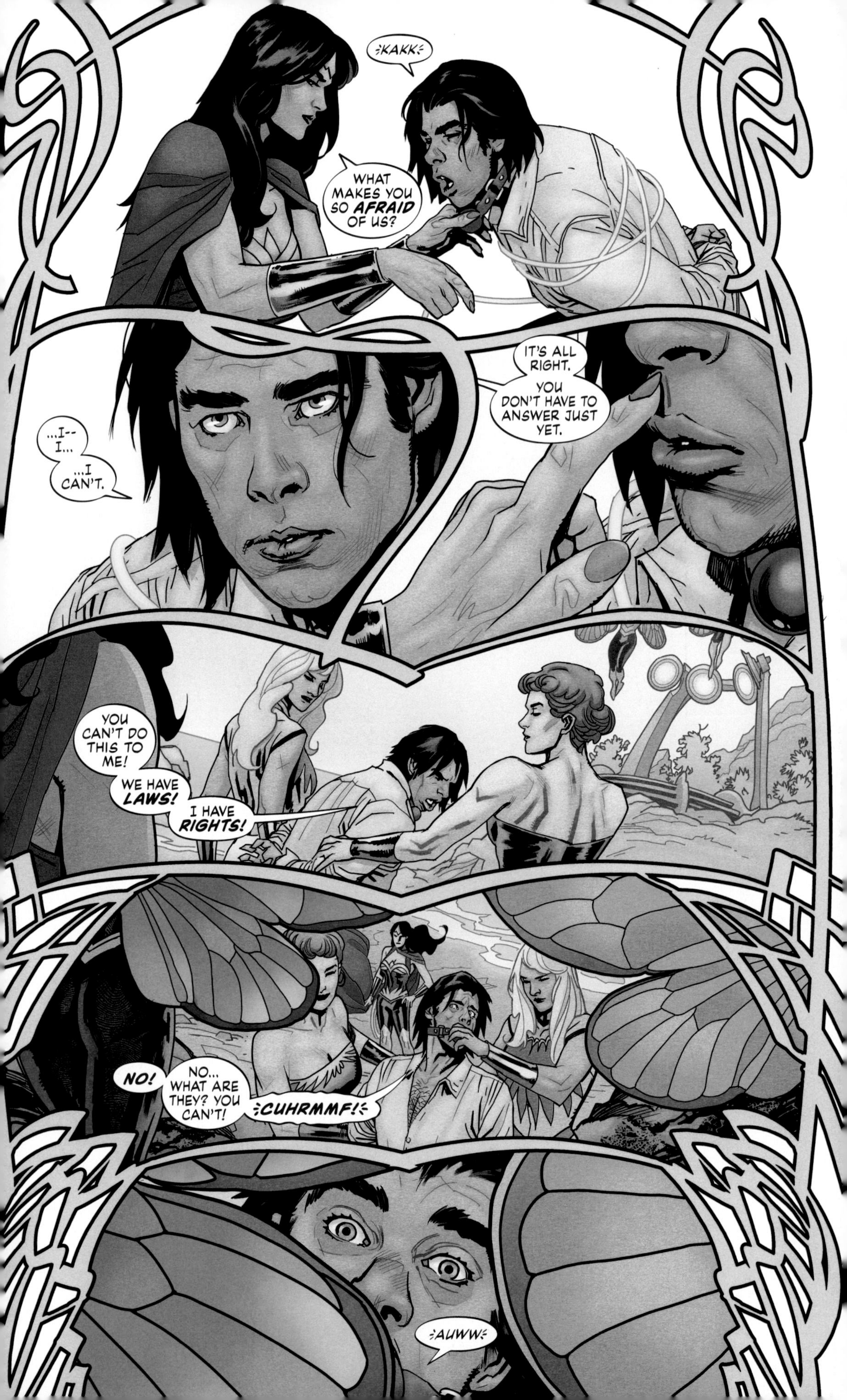
KAKK
WHAT MAKES YOU SO AFRAID OF US?
...I-- I... ...I CAN'T.
IT'S ALL RIGHT.
YOU DON'T HAVE TO ANSWER JUST YET.
YOU CAN'T DO THIS TO ME!
WE HAVE LAWS!
I HAVE RIGHTS!
NO!
NO... WHAT ARE THEY? YOU CAN'T!
CUHRMMF!
AUWW

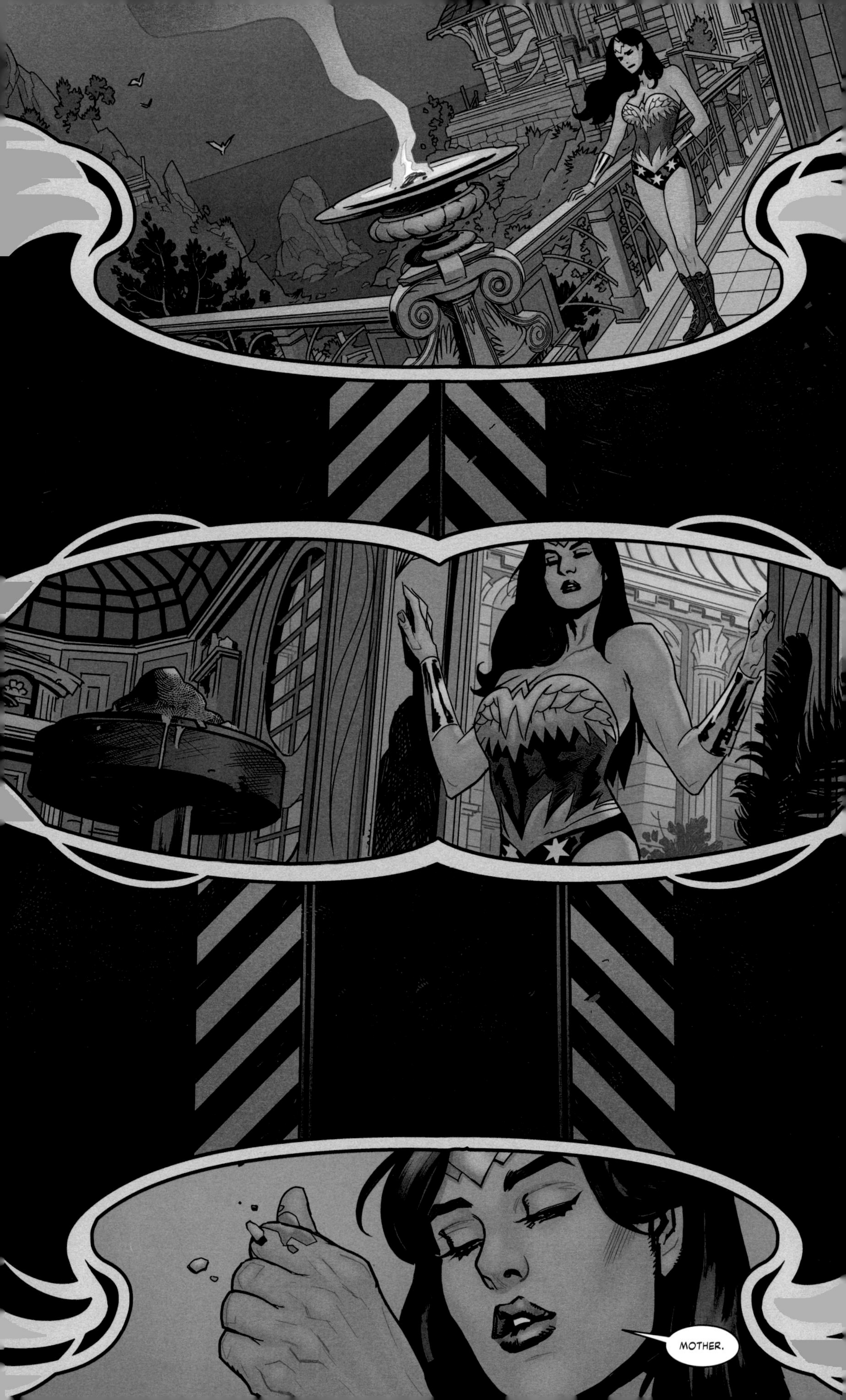
MOTHER.

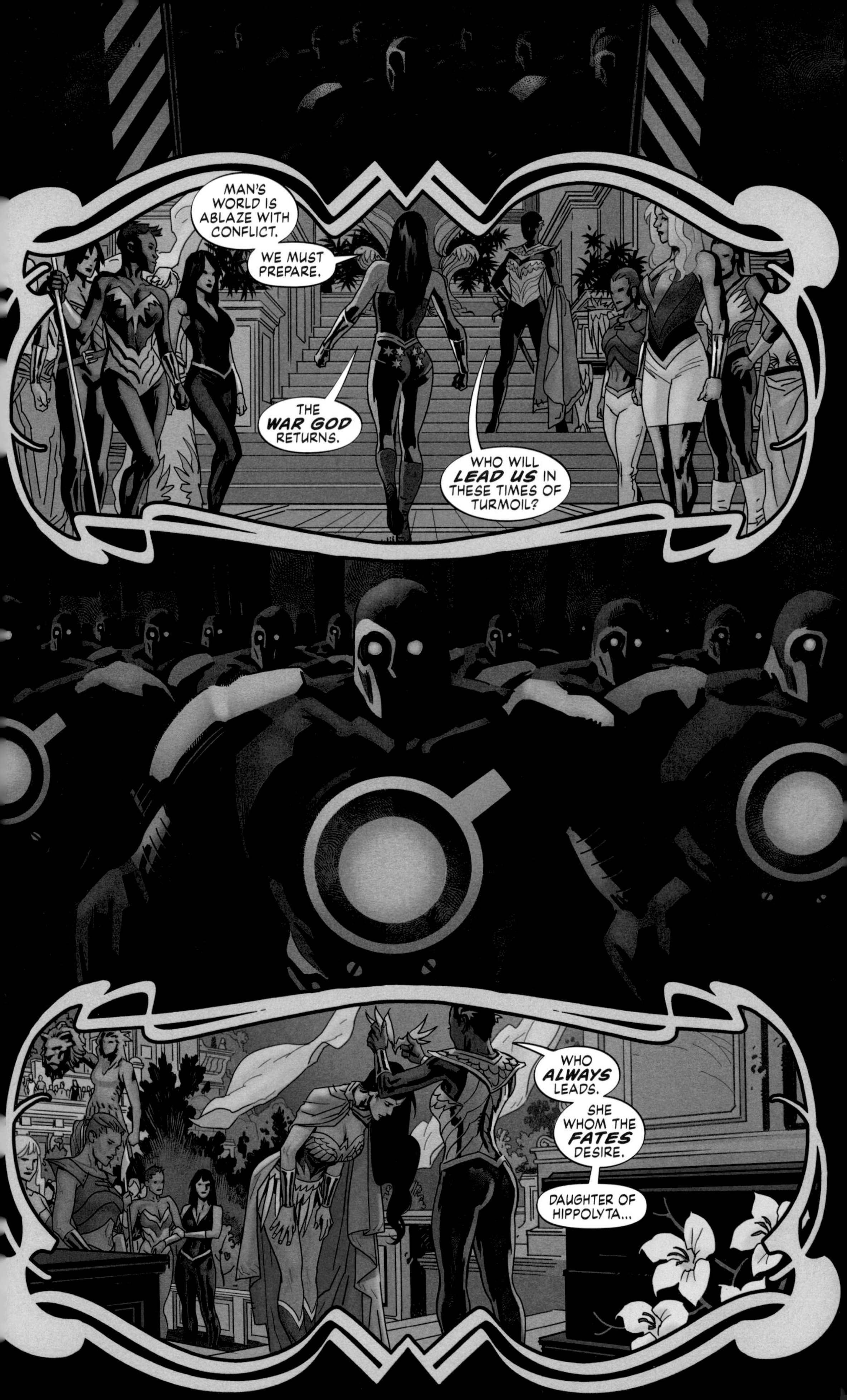
MAN'S WORLD IS ABLAZE WITH CONFLICT.
WE MUST PREPARE.
THE WAR GOD RETURNS.
WHO WILL LEAD US IN THESE TIMES OF TURMOIL?
WHO ALWAYS LEADS.
SHE WHOM THE FATES DESIRE.
DAUGHTER OF HIPPOLYTA...

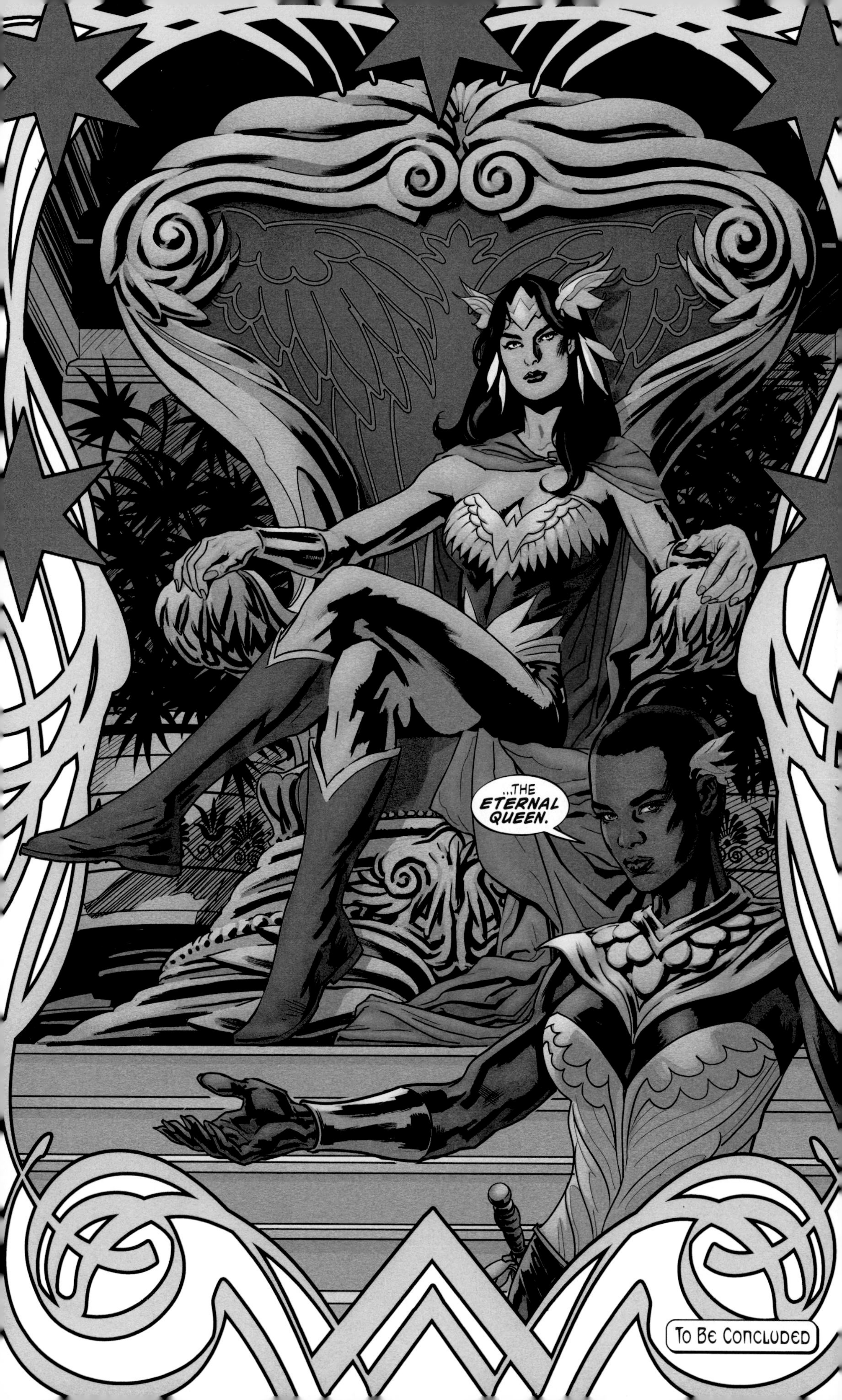
...THE ETERNAL QUEEN.
To Be Concluded

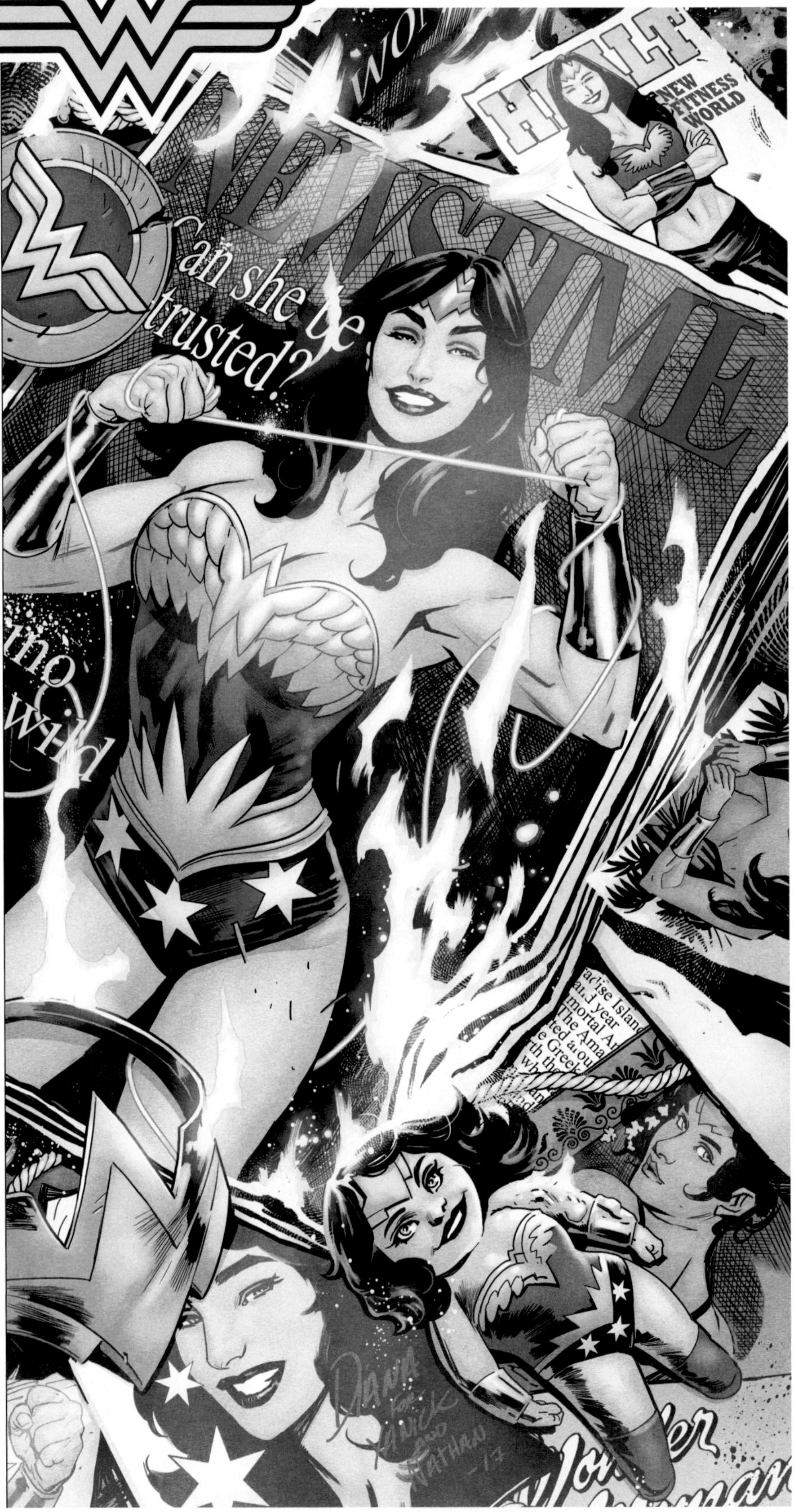
NEWSTIME
can she be trusted?
NEW FITNESS WORLD

Earth One Sketchbook

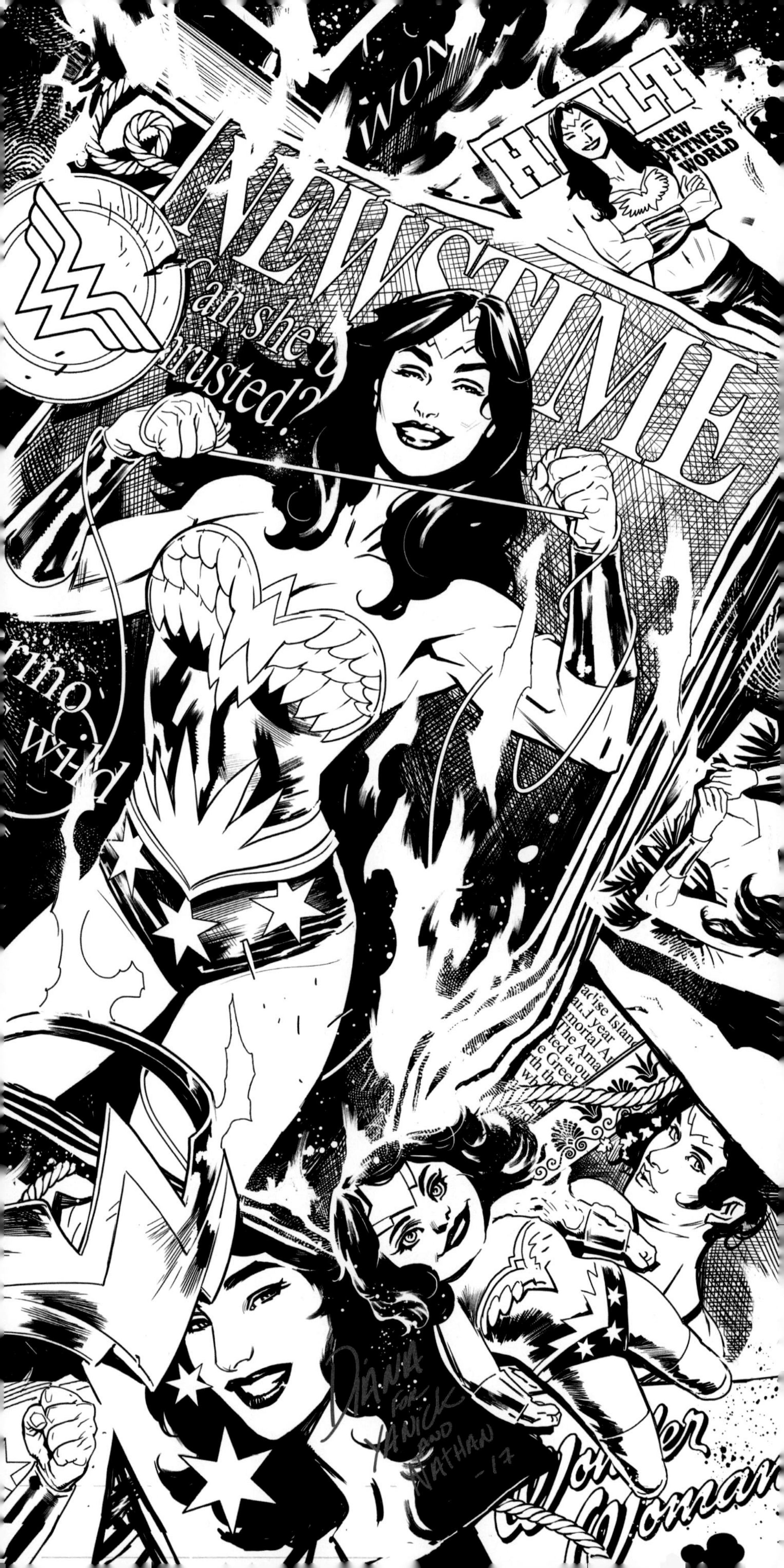

WON
NEWSTIME
an she
rusted?
NEW
FITNESS
WORLD
Paradise Island
Diana
for
Yanick
and
Nathan
-17

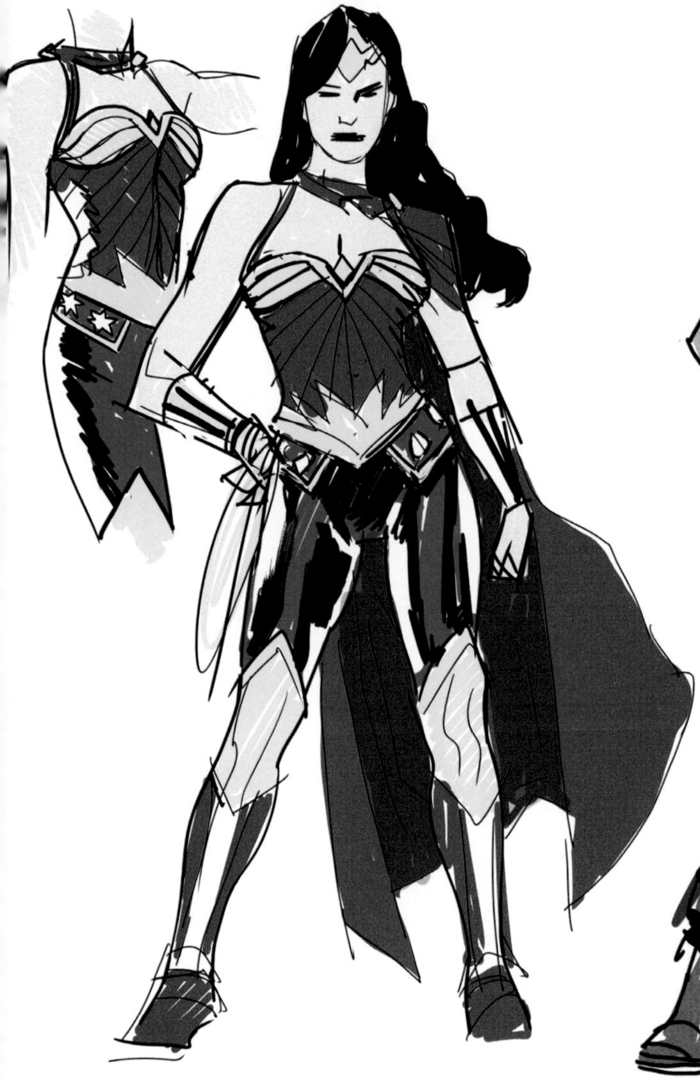

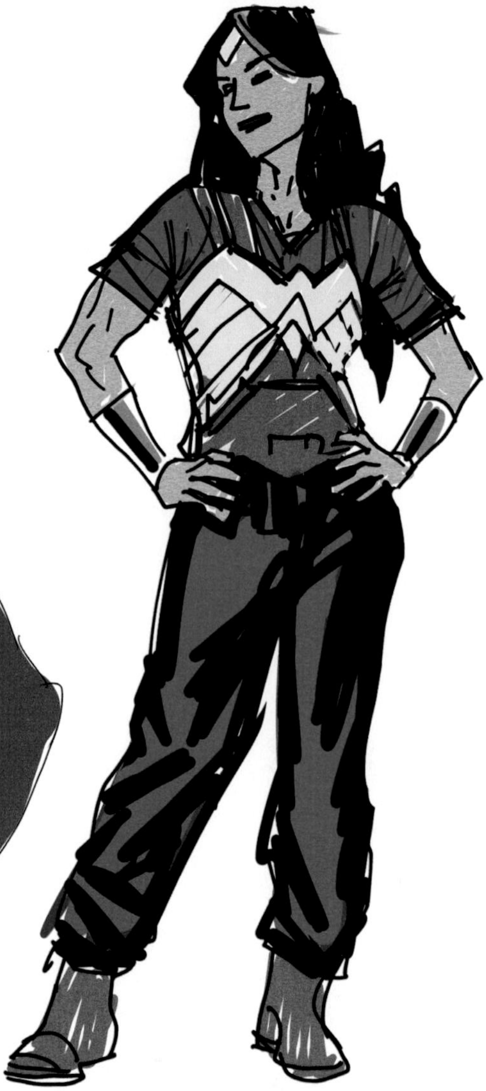

MILITARY TENT INSIDE

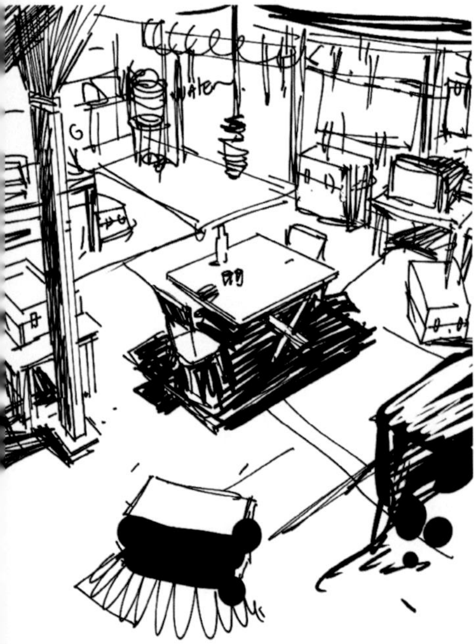

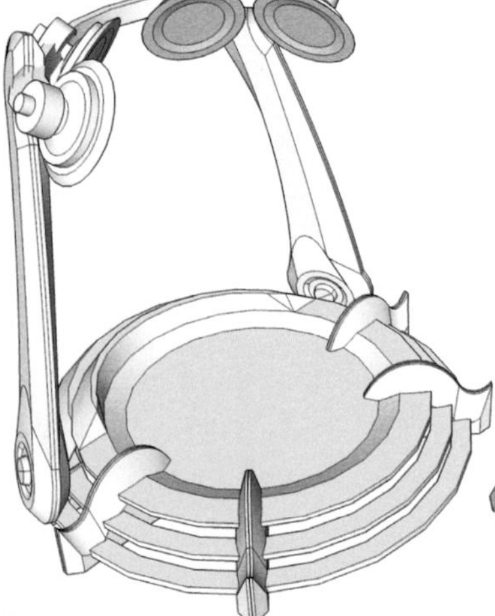

VENUSIAN TELEPORTER

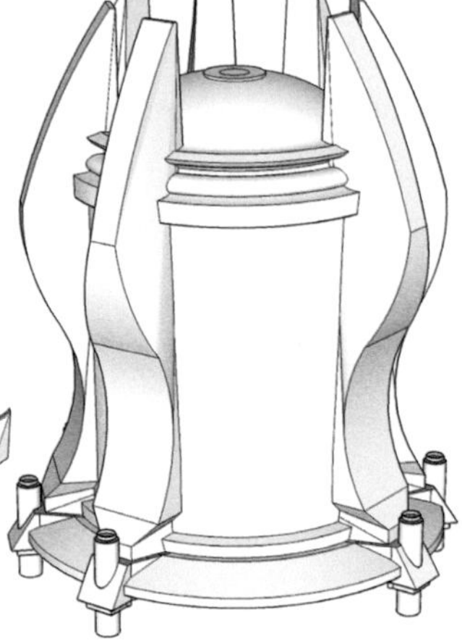

MENTAL RADIO

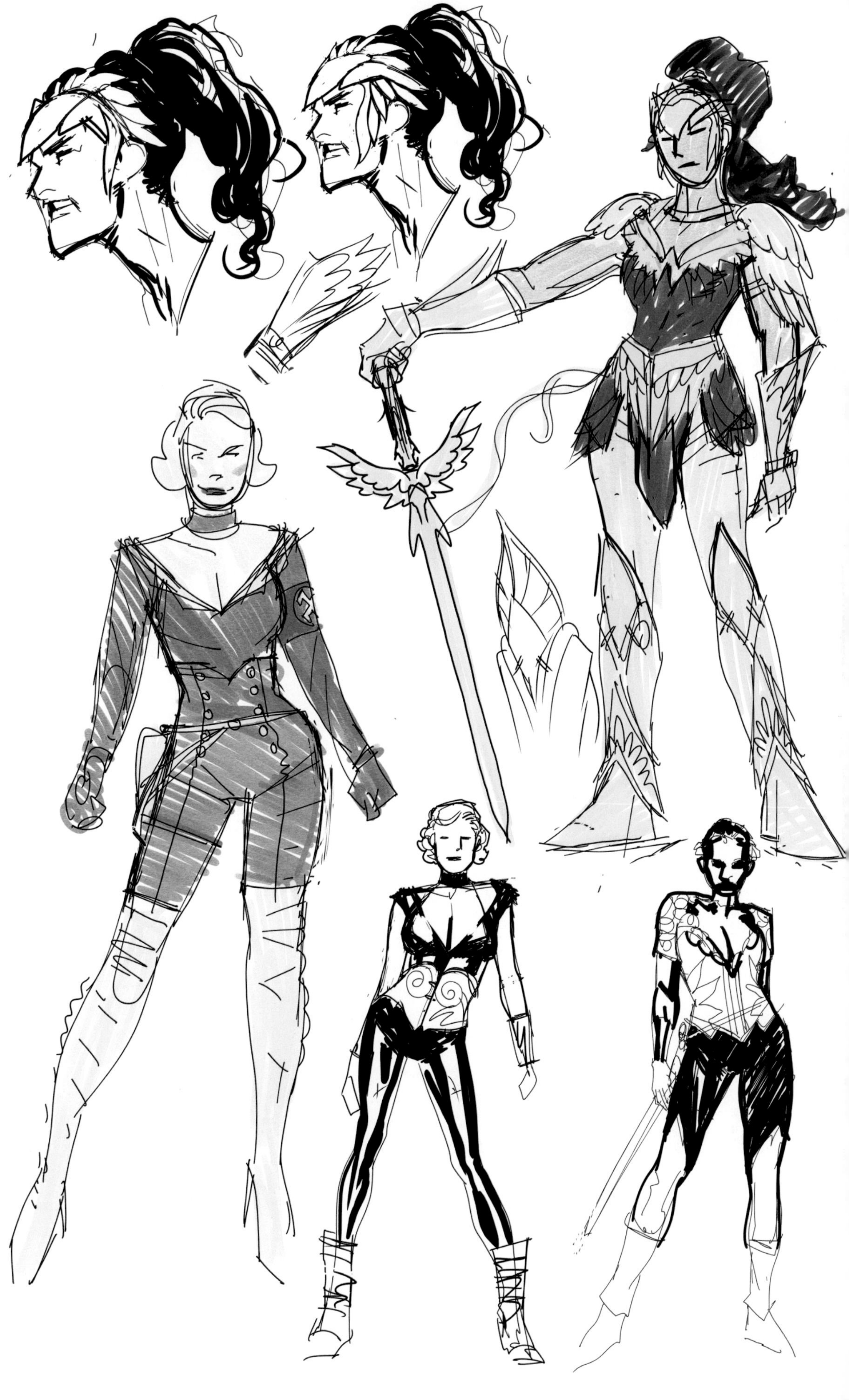

WONDER BURKA!

Grant had this bold and thought-provoking idea of having our Diana dress in a burka for her Middle Eastern adventure, thus embracing, open mindedly, diversity and other cultures! I wasn't convinced with my early burka ideas and felt this potentially slippery design needed some respectful, legit cultural grounding. My Muslim friend, ex-studio-mate and wonderful artist **Sanya Anwar** came to my rescue with these gorgeous designs. We ended up with a Wonder Niqab instead.
Thanks, Sanya!
—Yanick

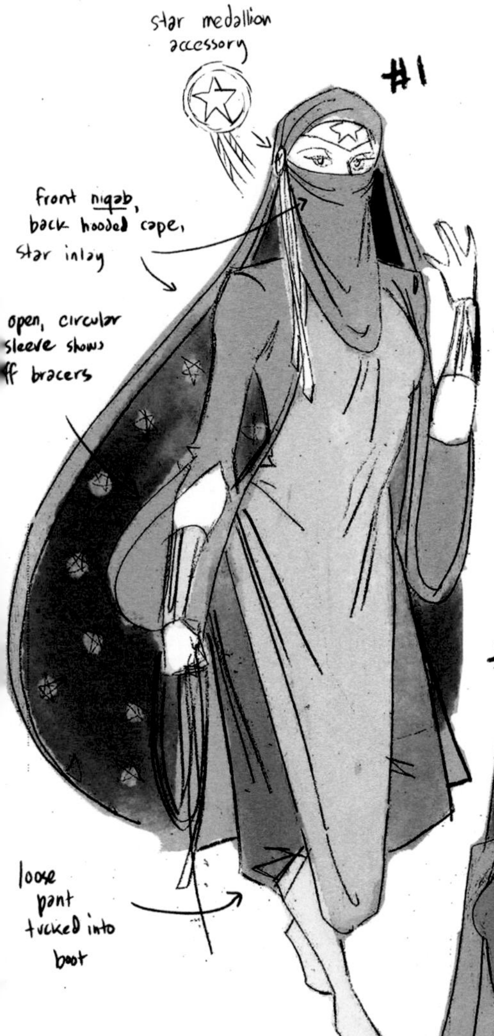

star medallion accessory
#1
front niqab, back hooded cape, star inlay
open, circular sleeve shows ff bracers
loose pant tucked into boot

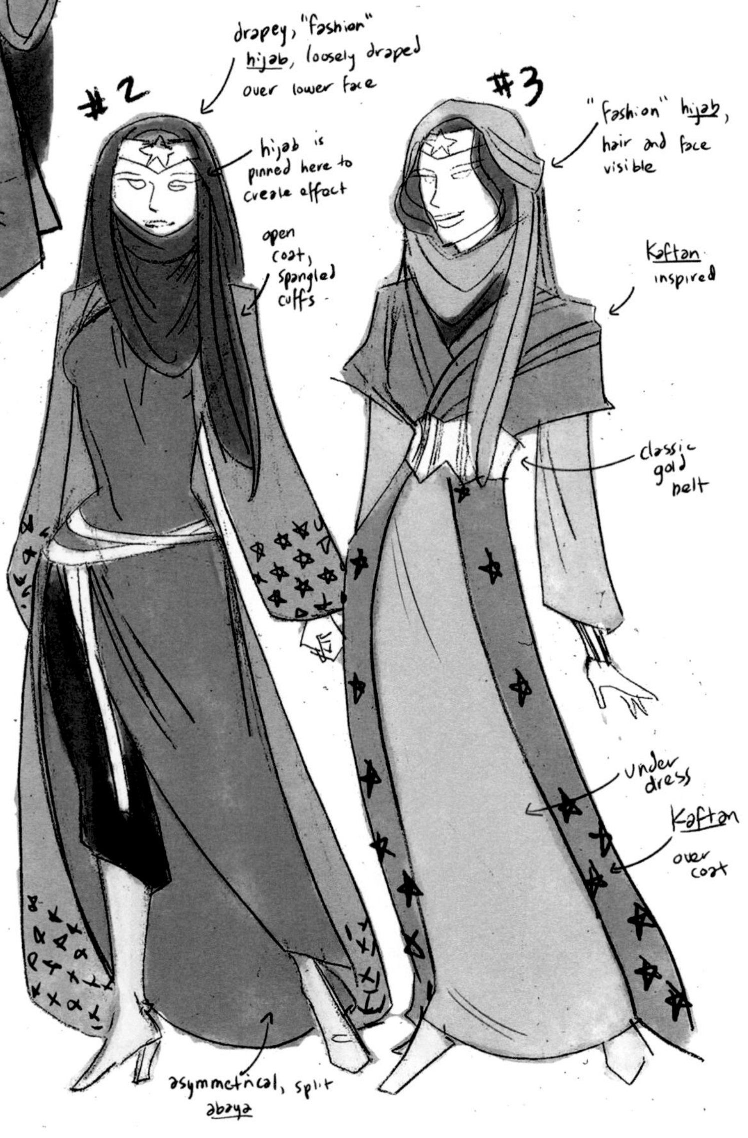

drapey, "fashion" hijab, loosely draped over lower face
#2
#3
hijab is pinned here to create effect
open coat, spangled cuffs
"fashion" hijab, hair and face visible
Kaftan inspired
classic gold belt
under dress
Kaftan over coat
asymmetrical, split abaya

Art and designs by
Sanya Anwar

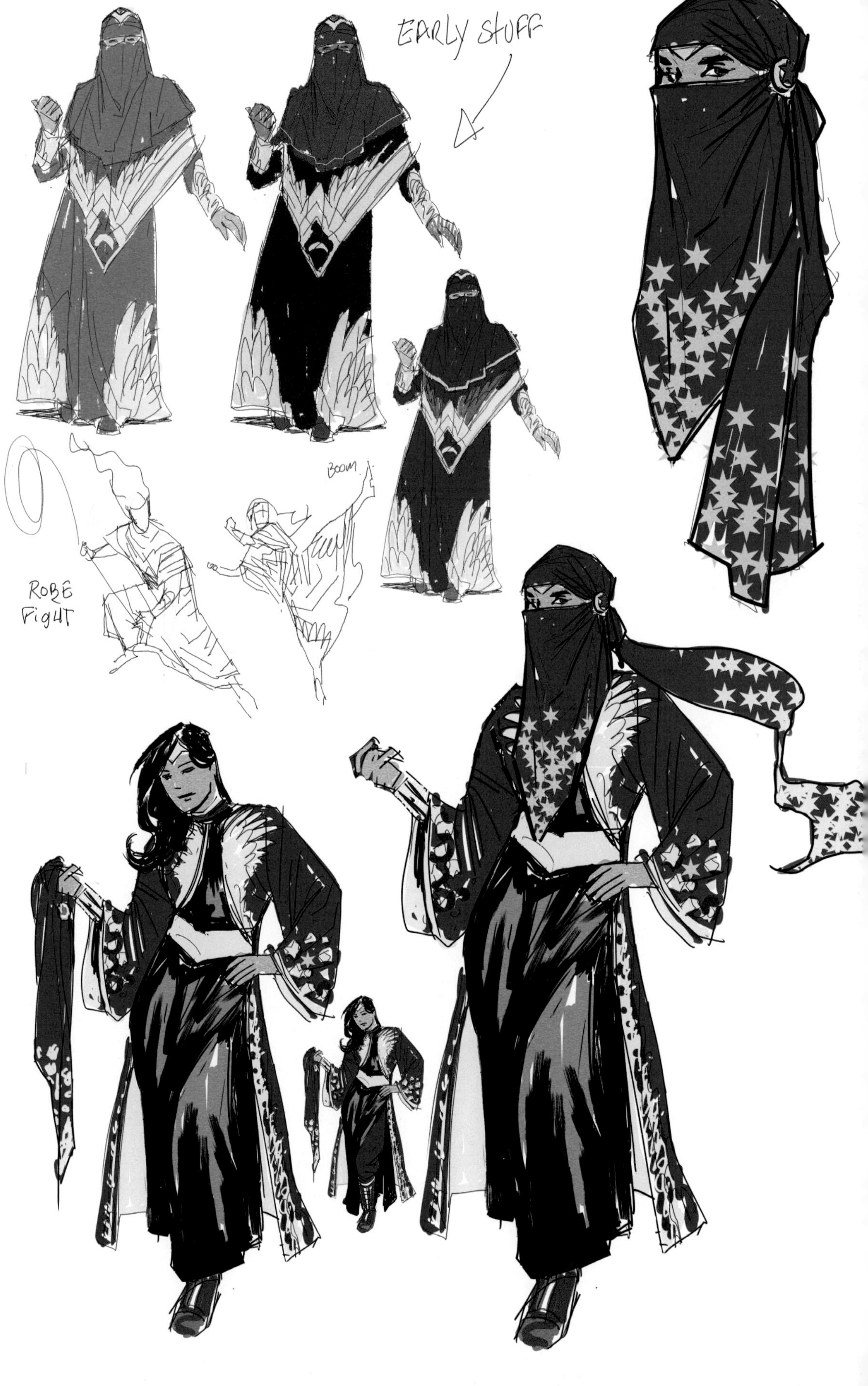

EARLY STUFF
BOOM
ROBE FIGHT

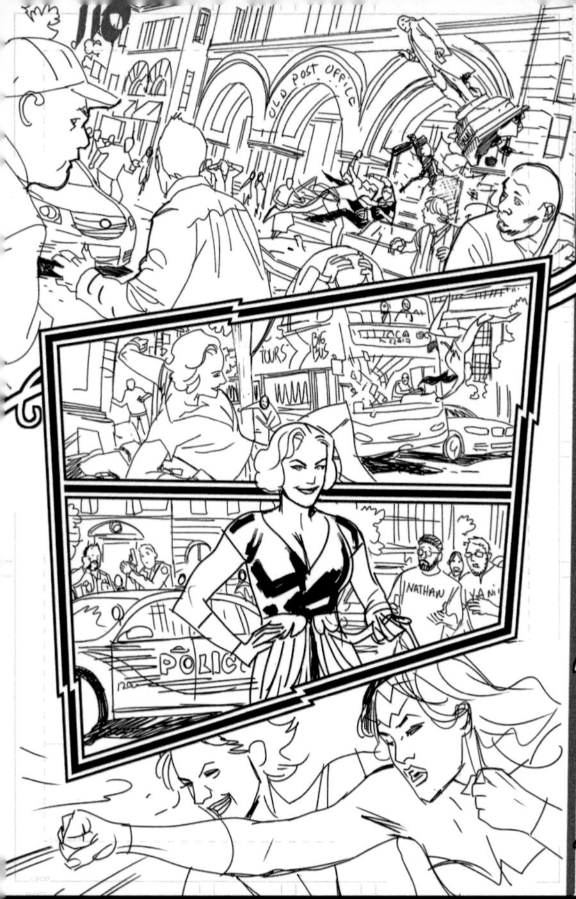
110
OLD POST OFFICE
TOURS
BIG BUS
NATHAN
POLIC

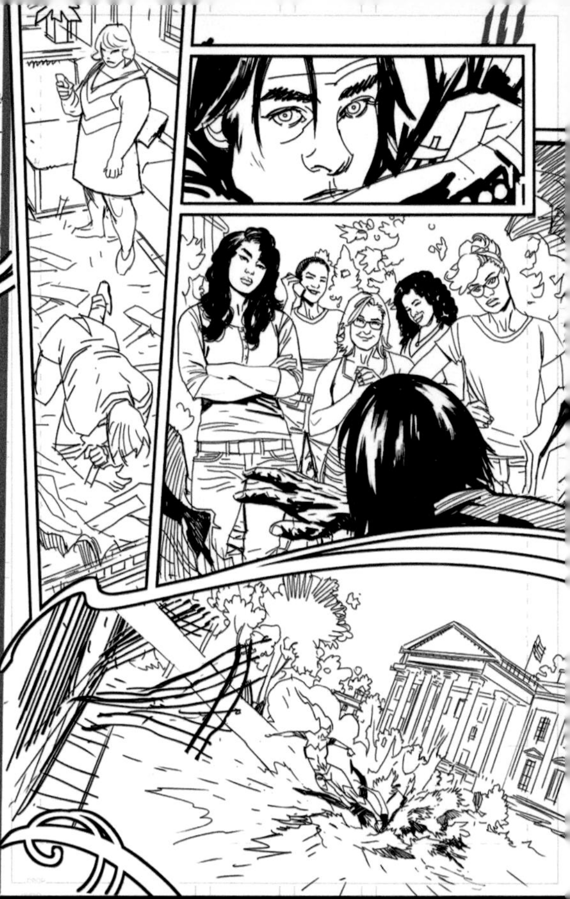
111

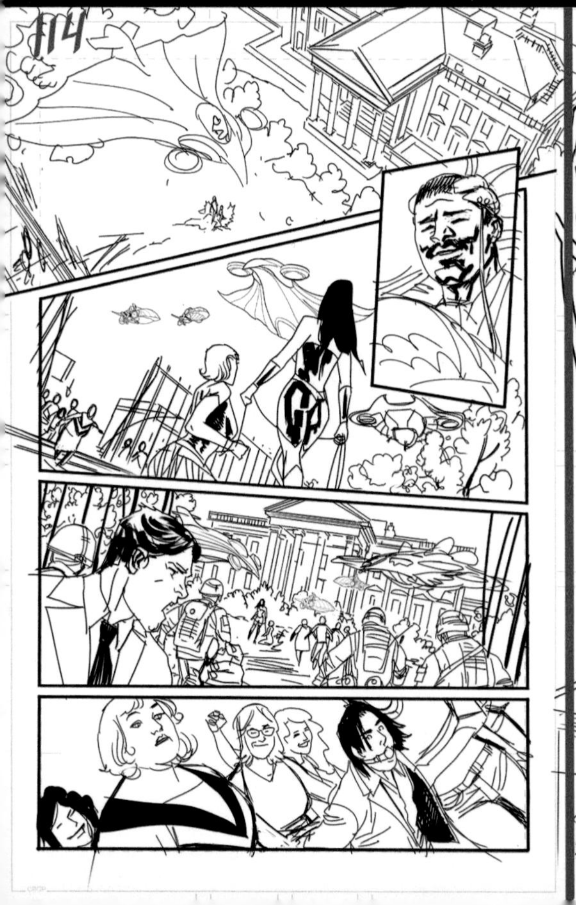
114

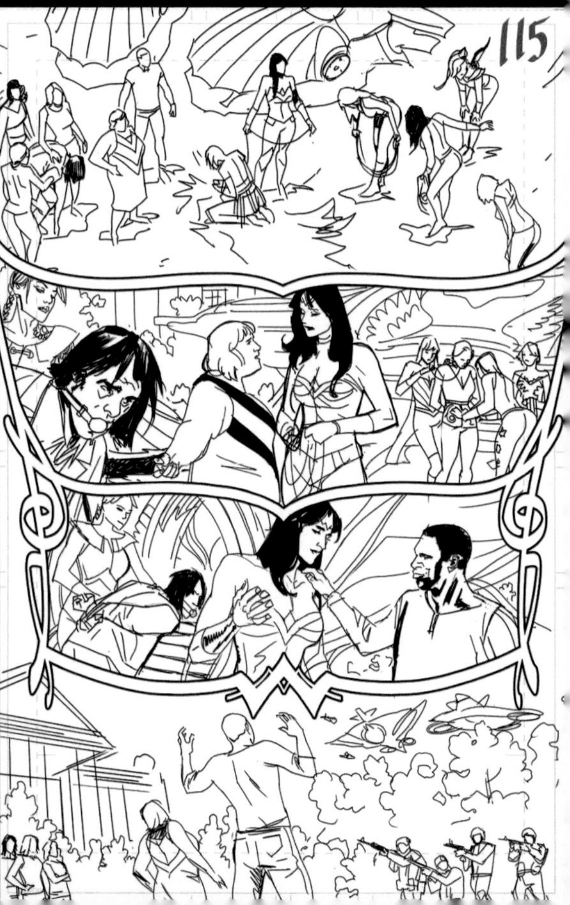
115

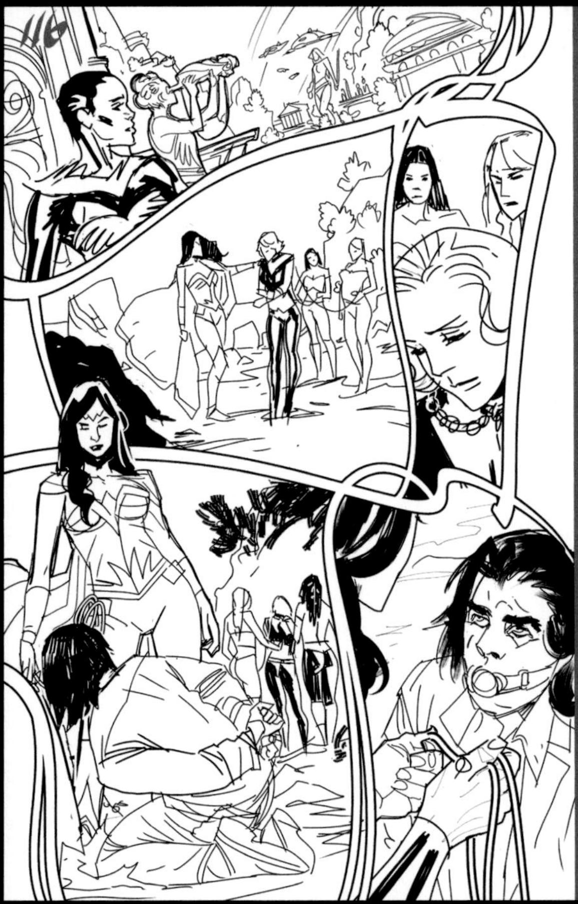
116

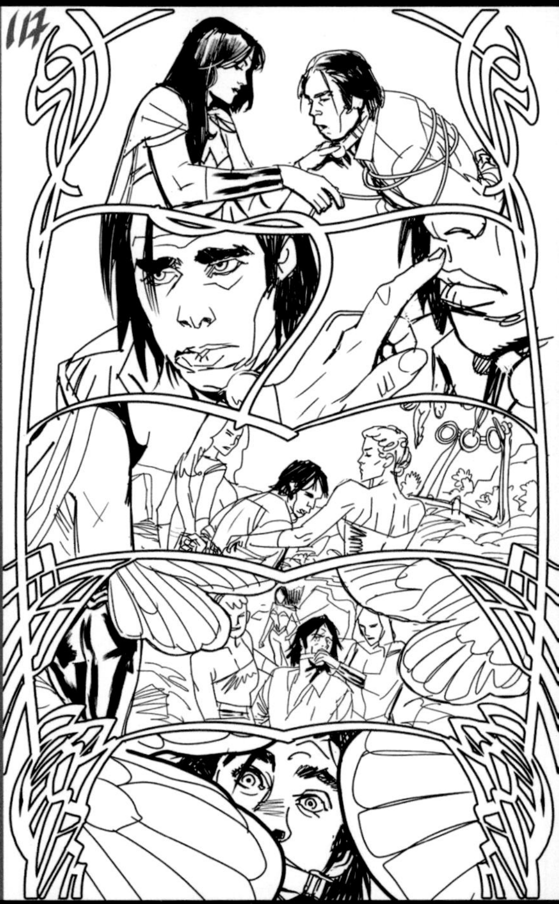
117

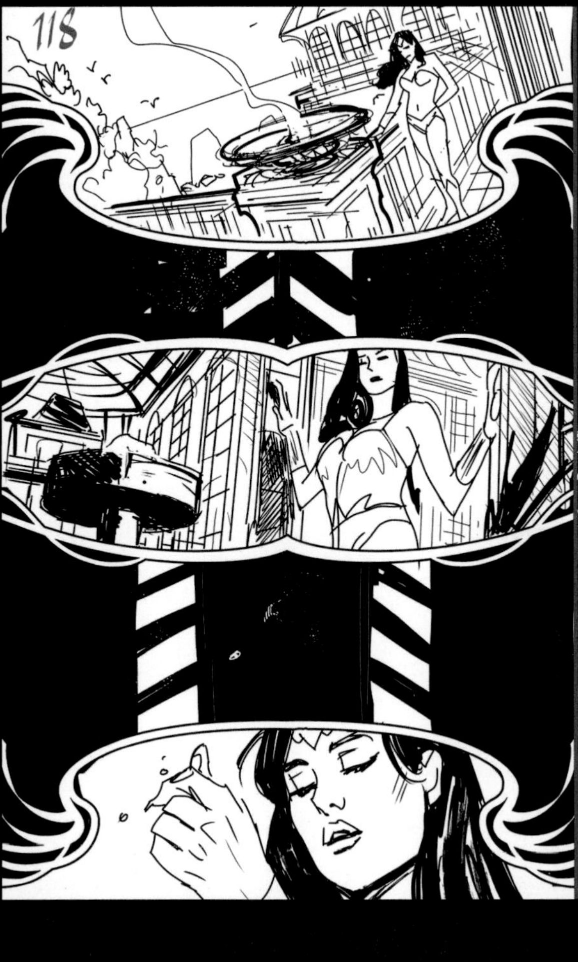
118

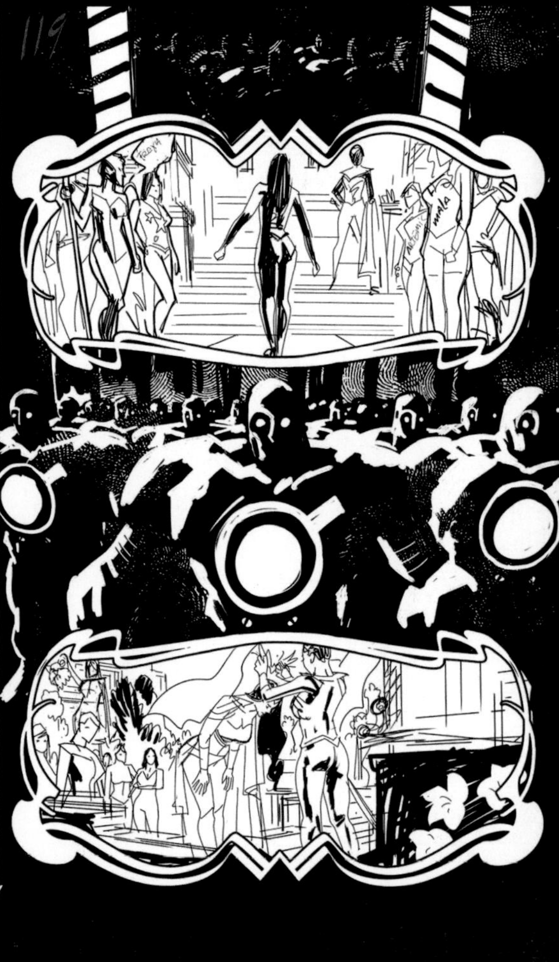
119

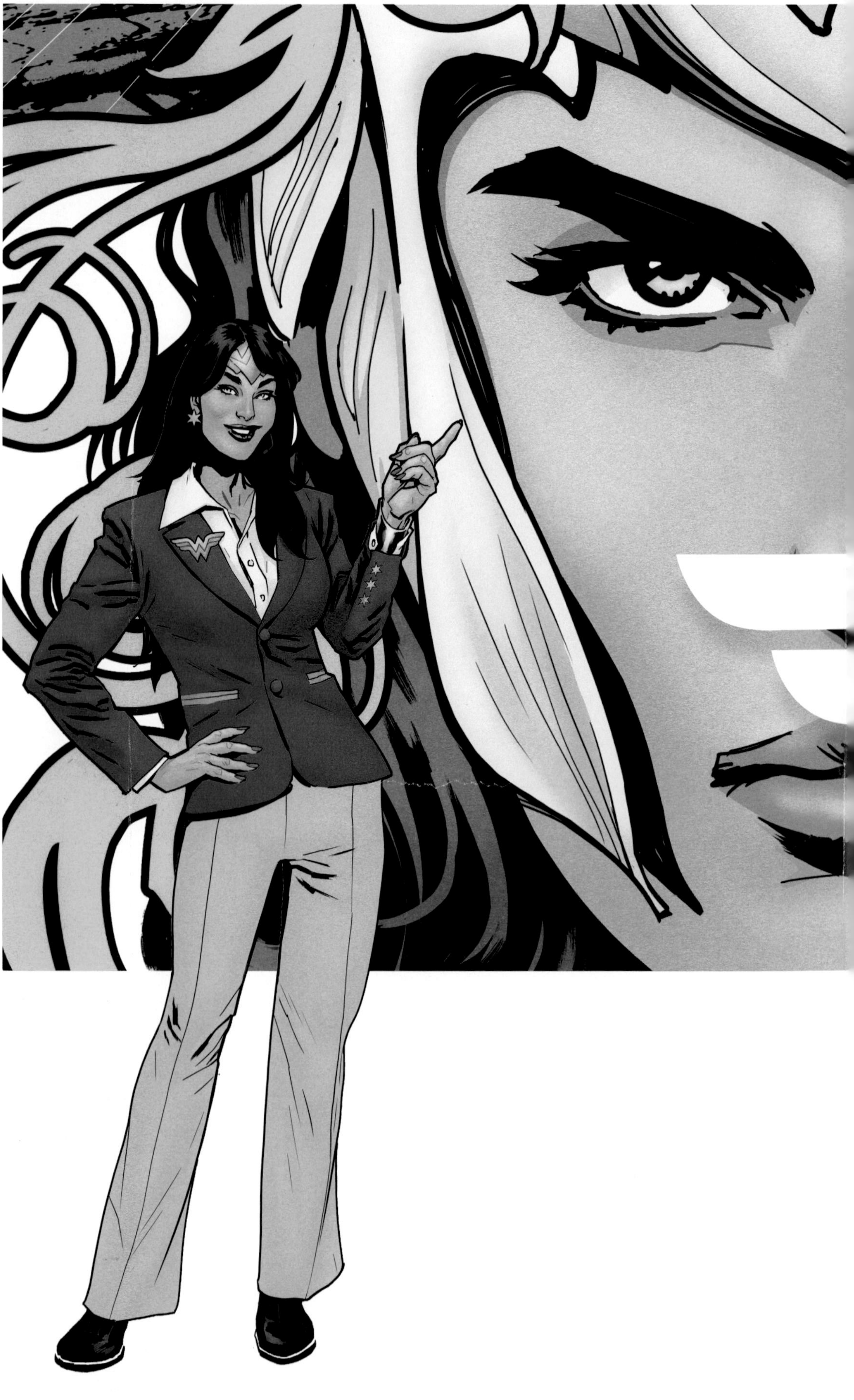

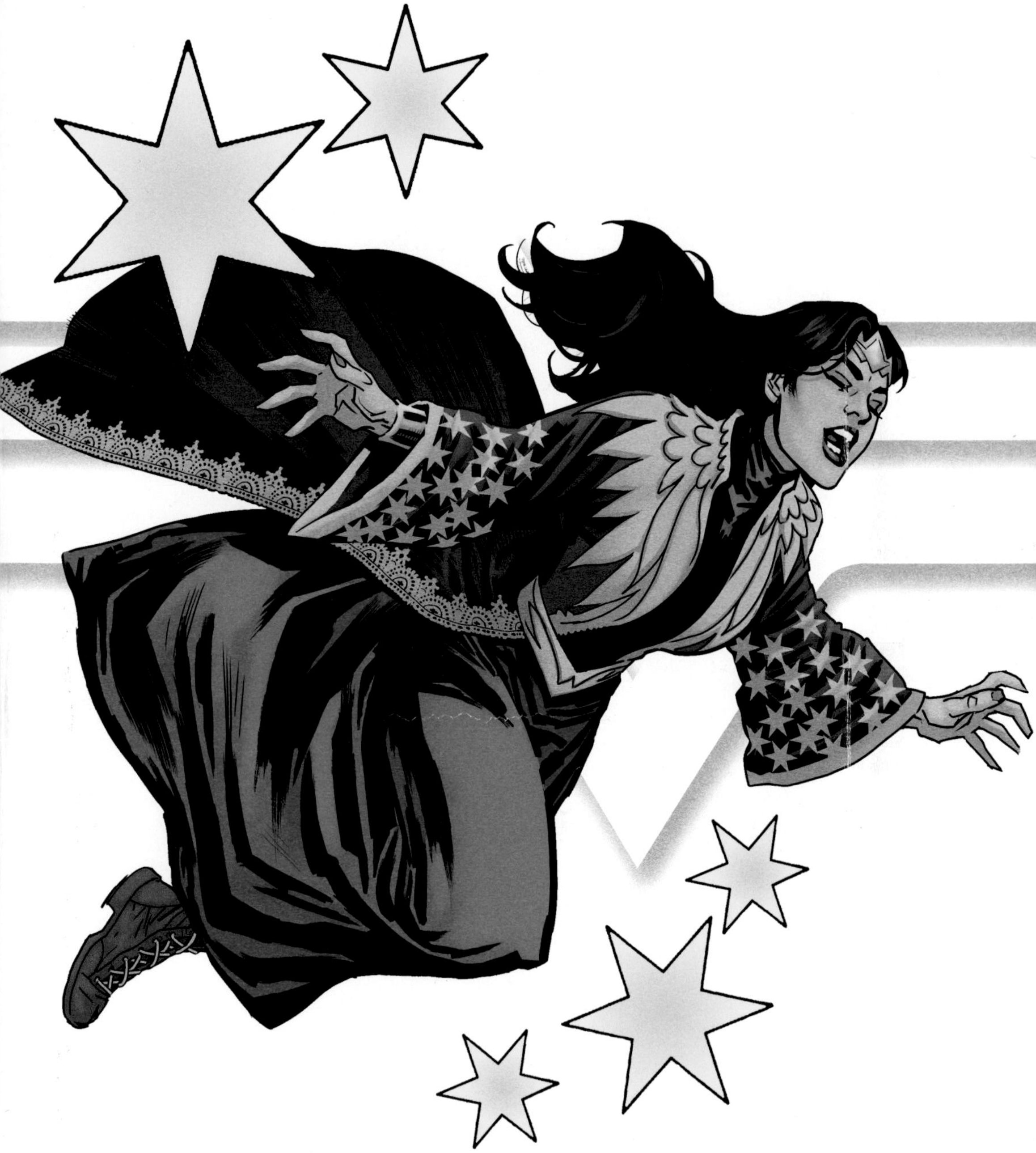